Social Linguistics and Literacies

Social
docum
studies
histori
materi
of a pa
conten
particu
state o

Thi
and lit
history
theorie
the mo
how la
edition
analyti
special

Bui
reflect
reform
cultura
book,
widely
researc

that deals with language, especially in social or cultural terms.

James Paul Gee is the Mary Lou Fulton Presidential Professor of Literacy Studies at Arizona State University, Tempe.

Also by James Paul Gee

Introduction to Discourse Analysis (1999)

Situated Language and Learning (2004)

Social Linguistics and Literacies

Ideology in discourses

Third edition

James Paul Gee

Routledge
Taylor & Francis Group

LONDON AND NEW YORK

First published 1990

This edition first published 2008
by Routledge
2 Park Square, Milton Park, Abingdon, Oxon OX14 4RN

Simultaneously published in the USA and Canada
by Routledge
270 Madison Ave, New York, NY 10016

Reprinted 2009

Routledge is an imprint of the Taylor and Francis Group, an informa business

© 1990, 1996, 2008 James Paul Gee
Typeset in TimesNewRoman and GillSans by
Keystroke, 28 High Street, Tettenhall, Wolverhampton
Printed and bound in Great Britain by
TJ International Ltd, Padstow, Cornwall

British Library Cataloguing in Publication Data
A catalogue record for this book is available from the British Library

Library of Congress Cataloging in Publication Data
A catalog record has been requested for this book

ISBN10: 0–415–42775–4 (hbk)
ISBN10: 0–415–42776–2 (pbk)
ISBN10: 0–203–94480–1 (ebk)

ISBN13: 978–0–415–42775–3 (hbk)
ISBN13: 978–0–415–42776–0 (pbk)
ISBN13: 978–0–203–94480–6 (ebk)

Contents

Acknowledgments

This book argues that what we say, think, feel, and do is always indebted to the social groups to which we have been apprenticed. Thus, to thank those who apprenticed me to their expertise is to thank them for helping me to think and write this book, however much or little they may want the credit. Since the first edition of *Social Linguistics* appeared I have met a great many people whose reactions to the book, and to my subsequent work, have contributed greatly to the new editions of this book.

Sarah Michaels, years ago, showed me some wonderful stories by African-American children, stories that were viewed as failures in school. These stories brought forcefully to my attention the need for a linguistics that could account for how these children could possess such beautiful linguistic abilities and still, nonetheless, fail in school. This experience helped transform my view of what linguistics ought to be about. Sarah's work and ideas and style have been central to mine ever since.

Years ago, also, Courtney Cazden invited me (at the time I was just making my transition from theoretical linguistics to social linguistics and education) to take part in group activities with her at the Harvard University School of Education. This book owes a huge debt to this apprenticeship, and surely would never have been written without it. Though she might very well not like to hear it, she has always been for a great many of us a unique "role model."

Colin Lankshear and Donaldo Macedo have stuck with me for the long haul, though thick and thin, not just in the world of ideas, but in the world of souls. It's been a long trip and they can't know how much I appreciate their being fellow travelers.

The list of those who have helped and influenced me is now too long to list as I tried to do in the second edition. My borrowings are everywhere clear in this book and I have contracted so many debts I can now neither list them, nor ever repay them. A great many of the people I cite in this book I know personally and so I have had ample opportunity to learn from them. Their ideas have everywhere colored mine, making me, over the years, seem better than I am, which is, given the theory in this book, much as it should be.

Partly as a result of this book, I have met a great many teachers throughout the world. It is impossible to overstate how much it means to someone like me, someone not "at home" in the conflicts and "power networks" of academics, to have a teacher or workplace literacy person— people actually working "in the trenches"—come up to me and say that the book had "made a difference." Such help and encouragement have kept me going.

As I pointed out in the first edition of this book, many of my views on society have been formed in discussions with my identical twin brother, John Gee. The fact that my father—Ernest Lefel Gee—was born in poverty in the southern United States and left school in the third grade, never to return, but ended his life fighting racism and reading German and French theologians to us over the dinner table has a lot to do with my views on literacy and Discourses. The fact that my mother—Kathleen Bonner Gee—born and raised in the working class in Derby, England, spent most of her adult life as a housewife in the United States, but towards the end of her life ended up, through no choice of her own, taking a rough-and-tumble cab company in San Jose, California, out of deep debt and successfully running it to enable her children to survive and go to college also has a lot to do with my views on Discourses. Thank God that neither my father nor my mother was "one type" of person and that they did not allow social forces to "fix" them in terms of their beginnings, however hard those forces tried.

The text analyzed in Chapter 6 is reproduced by permission from D. Schiffrin, *Discourse Markers*, copyright © 1987 Cambridge University Press. (Stanza markings are my own.) Table 1 is reproduced by permission from J. K. Chambers and P. J. Trudgill, *Dialectology*, copyright © 1980 Cambridge University Press.

J.P.G.

Introduction

As a linguist, I wrote the first edition of *Social Linguistics* with a personal sense of paradox. While the human eye sees best what is in the center of its field of vision, it had become apparent to me that the clearest way to see the workings of language and literacy was to displace them from the center of attention and to move society, culture, and values to the foreground. Paradoxically, this leads to better and deeper ways of analyzing language. It leads to a different sort of linguistics as well, one in which language-in-society is the heart of the field. So while we immerse ourselves in language in this book, language here always comes fully attached to "other stuff": to social relations, cultural models, power and politics, perspectives on experience, values and attitudes, as well as things and places in the world.

Sociocultural approaches to language and literacy have made great progress since the first (1990) and second (1996) edition of *Social Linguistics*. I hope, too, that I have myself made some progress. In 1996 I rewrote the book in its entirety. I brought it up to date and tried to make it easier to read, as well. I added and subtracted material, though the same ground was covered and the same themes were stressed. I revised old analyses and added new ones, and, I hope, further clarified my approach to language and literacy. In this third edition, I have done much the same, though less drastically than in 1996. Nonetheless, through all three editions, the book has remained at core the same book.

Social Linguistics is not a textbook, though it has, over the years, often been used in classes. It was initially an attempt to do two things: first, to argue that a new field was emerging out of work from different disciplines, a field I called "The New Literacy Studies," and, second, to develop a particular perspective within this field on language and literacy with special reference to educational issues. The New Literacy Studies is now established and the perspective has become one standard viewpoint within that field, alongside others. Thus, what started as an "intervention" is now "after the fact" and the book can now serve as an introduction to what it originally only hoped to help bring into existence.

As I point out in this edition, the term "New Literacy Studies" is probably unfortunate, since anything that was once "new" is soon "old" and the New Literacy Studies is now no longer young. The New Literacy Studies is really just a way to name work that, from a variety of different perspectives, views literacy in its full range of cognitive, social, interactional, cultural, political, institutional, economic, moral, and historical contexts. When this book was written, the traditional view of literacy was "cognitive" or "psychological," the view that literacy is a set of abilities or skills residing inside people's heads. Because the cognitive or psychological was already entrenched, I did not stress cognitive features of literacy in this book, but, rather, tried to show the limitations of a purely cognitive or psychological view. In subsequent work I have written a good bit about psychological issues and how to integrate them with a sociocultural approach to language and literacy (see Gee 1992, 2003, 2004, 2005). In this book, I retain a strong focus on the social and cultural.

The book seeks to accomplish three things: first, to give readers an overview of sociocultural approaches to language and literacy, approaches which coalesced into the New Literacy Studies; second, to introduce readers to a particular style of analyzing language-in-use-in-society (see also Gee 2005); and, third, to develop a specific perspective on language and literacy centered around the notion of "Discourses" (with a capital "D"). I will return to "Discourses" below. Chapters 2–5 engage in the first task; the sixth and seventh chapters engage directly with the second, though there are examples of analysis throughout the book; and the final two chapters engage with the last task. The first chapter starts with the meanings of words, introducing some of the basic themes of the book, and closes on a discussion of the moral viewpoint that lies behind the book as a whole.

The general argument of the book, then, is this: to appreciate language in its social context, we need to focus not on language alone, but rather on what I will call "Discourses," with a capital "D." Discourses ("big 'D' Discourses") include much more than language. To see what I mean, consider for a moment the unlikely topic of bars (pubs). Imagine I park my motorcycle, enter my neighborhood "biker bar," and say to my leather-jacketed and tattooed drinking buddy, as I sit down: "May I have a match for my cigarette, please?" What I have said is perfectly grammatical English, but it is "wrong" nonetheless, unless I have used a heavily ironic tone of voice. It is not just the content of what you say that is important, but how you say it. And in this bar, I haven't said it in the "right" way. I should have said something like "Gotta match?" or "Give me a light, wouldya?"

But now imagine I say the "right" thing ("Gotta match?" or "Give me a light, wouldya?"), but while saying it, I carefully wipe off the bar stool with a napkin to avoid getting my newly pressed designer jeans dirty. In this case, I've still got it all wrong. In this bar they just don't do that sort of thing: I have said the right thing, but my "saying–doing" combination is nonetheless all wrong. It's not just what you say or even just how you say it, it's also *who* you are and *what* you're doing while you say it. It is not enough just to say the right "lines."

Other sorts of bars cater to different "types of people." If I want to— and I am allowed to by the "insiders"—I can go to many bars, and, thereby, be many different "types of people." So, too, with schools. Children are "hailed" ("summoned") to be different sorts of students in different classrooms, even in different domains like literature or science. In one and the same classroom, different children may well be "hailed" to be different types of students, one, for example, a "gifted" student and the other a "problem" student. There are specific ways to get recognized—different in different schools and at different times—as "gifted" or "a problem." The teacher, the student, and fellow students need, however unconsciously, to know these ways for "business as usual" to go on. Conscious knowledge can, I will argue, sometimes disrupt this "business as usual." A good deal of what we do with language, throughout history, is to create and act out different "types of people" for all sorts of occasions and places.

Discourses are ways of behaving, interacting, valuing, thinking, believing, speaking, and often reading and writing, that are accepted as instantiations of particular identities (or "types of people") by specific groups, whether families of a certain sort, lawyers of a certain sort, bikers of a certain sort, business people of a certain sort, church members of a certain sort, African-Americans of a certain sort, women or men of a certain sort, and so on and so forth through a very long list. Discourses are ways of being "people like us." They are "ways of being in the world"; they are "forms of life"; they are socially situated identities. They are, thus, always and everywhere social and products of social histories.

Language makes no sense outside of Discourses, and the same is true for literacy. There are many different "social languages" (different styles of language used for different purposes and occasions) connected in complex ways with different Discourses. There are many different sorts of literacy—many literacies—connected in complex ways with different Discourses. Cyberpunks and physicists, factory workers and boardroom executives, policemen and graffiti-writing urban gang members engage in different literacies, use different "social languages," and are in different Discourses. In fact, Hispanic gangs and African-American gangs use graffiti in different ways, and engage in different Discourses. And, too, the cyberpunk and the physicist might be one and the same person, behaving differently at different times and places. In this book I will use schools and communities, rather than bars, as examples of sites where Discourses operate to integrate and sort persons, groups, and society.

Each of us is a member of many Discourses, and each Discourse represents one of our ever multiple identities. These Discourses need not, and often don't, represent consistent and compatible values. There are conflicts among them, and each of us lives and breathes these conflicts as we act out our various Discourses. For some, these conflicts are more dramatic than for others. The conflicts between the home-based Discourse of some African-American children and the Discourses of the school are many, deep, and apparent. Indeed, the values of many school-based Discourses treat African-American people as "other" and their social practices as "deviant" and "non-standard." In becoming a full member of school Discourses, African-American children run the risk of becoming complicit with values that denigrate and damage their home-based Discourse and identity. The conflicts are real and cannot simply be wished away. They are the site of very real struggle and resistance. Such conflicts also exist for many women between their ways of being in the world as women of certain types and the dominant Discourses of male-based public institutions. Similar sorts of conflicts exist for many others, as well, most certainly for many people, white, brown, or black, based on social class. They are endemic in modern plural societies.

Each Discourse incorporates a usually taken for granted and tacit set of "theories" about what counts as a "normal" person and the "right" ways to think, feel, and behave. These theories crucially involve viewpoints on the distribution of "social goods" like status, worth, and material goods in society (who should and who shouldn't have them). The biker bar "says" that "tough guys" are "real men"; some schools "say" that certain children—often minority and lower socioeconomic children—are not suited to higher education and professional careers. Such theories, which are part and parcel of each and every Discourse, and which, thus, underlie the use of language in all cases, are what I call in this book ideologies. And, thus, too, I claim that language is inextricably bound up with ideology and cannot be analyzed or understood apart from it.

I do not in this book intend to hide my claims behind linguistic or sociological jargon unless that jargon is integral to the claim being made. Real people really get hurt by the workings of language, power, ideology, and Discourse discussed in this book. I see no reason to sanitize such damage with distancing language. At the same time, the fact that the issues discussed in this book relate to the workings of power and hurt does not mean that these are not also theoretical issues. In fact, the book constitutes an overt theory both of literacy and a socially based linguistics, a theory that claims that all practice (human social action) is inherently caught up with usually tacit theories that empower or disempower people and groups of people. I will claim that it is a moral obligation to render one's tacit, taken-for-granted theories overt when they have the potential to hurt people. This book makes some of my theories about language and society overt and invites you, not to agree with me, but to make your theories in this area overt also.

I do not believe there is any one uniquely "right" way to describe and explicate the workings of language in society. Thus, I do not see myself as in competition in a "winner take all" game with other social and critical theorists, many of whom I greatly admire. Certain ways of describing and explicating language and society are better and worse for different purposes. And any way of doing so is worthwhile only for the light it shines on complex problems and the possibilities it holds out for imagining better and more socially just futures.

Furthermore, I believe that a great many of us, coming from different disciplinary backgrounds, are using different words to say very similar things, at least where the important matters are concerned. Thus, too, I believe we have made a good deal of progress, more than our different terminologies might at first suggest. It is for these reasons that I attempt to sketch out a sociocultural approach to language and literacies in Chapters 1–5 without using my own favored terms. Rather, I develop what I hope is a rather consensus-like overview using the work and words of many different people.

Chapter 1

Meaning and ideology

Words and their meanings

A great many people believe that words have fixed and settled meanings, the sorts of things we can find in a dictionary. So, for example, a word like "bachelor" means "unmarried male" and that's the end of the matter. Furthermore, they believe that the meaning of a word is something that resides in people's heads, perhaps in terms of what some people call a "concept." When people hear or see a word they can consult this concept or definition in their heads to know what the word means. Of course, since other people also understand words, we must then assume, for communication to work, that everyone (rather mysteriously) has the same concepts or definitions in their heads. However, thanks to the fact that the insides of people's heads are private, we can never really check this.

These ideas about words and their meanings are quite common, so common they are, for many people, a form of common sense. These ideas are, in fact, a "theory" that many people believe, though they may not be all that conscious of the fact that they hold this theory; they may not have ever tried to put it into words; and they may just pretty much take it for granted. In that case, it is what we can call a "tacit theory." Or, perhaps, they are more consciously aware that that this is their theory of how words and meaning work. Then the theory is overt. Either way, tacit or overt, this is a theory that many "everyday" people—that is, people who are not linguists or specialists of any other sort—believe. But, of course, it is also a theory that some (but not all) professional linguists and psychologists believe and argue for, as well (see Clark 1989 and Gee 2004 for further discussion). In that case, the theory is certainly overt and is usually more formal, explicit, and elaborated. In such a situation, we have a professional theory that also reflects a commonsense, taken-for-granted and often tacit everyday theory.

We can see how this theory might influence educational practice. Vocabulary is important for success in school. This theory that words have fixed meanings would imply we can teach word meaning by giving young people lists and definitions and having them write sentences containing the new words. We can tell them to memorize the meaning of the word, presumably by memorizing its definition. And, indeed, this is how vocabulary was traditionally taught in schools, and still is in some cases.

We don't often think about everyday people—non-specialists—having theories, especially tacit ones. We tend to say that such people —all of us when we are not doing our specialist jobs, if we have one— have beliefs, viewpoints, or perspectives on things, even prejudices. Nonetheless, I will say that people hold theories about all sorts of things, because in many cases—like this one—people's beliefs (and even prejudices) hang together and cohere in ways that are certainly like theories. Sometimes these theories contradict professional theories, sometimes they don't. In some cases, everyday people have picked up their theories from having heard about professional theories from other people, the media, or from their own studies. On the other hand, in some cases, though not all, the professionals' more formal theories are simply reflections of their commonsense everyday theories.

Some people are uncomfortable using the word "theory" both for people's everyday beliefs and for the perspectives of professionals like linguists. And it is true that logical consistency may sometimes be less common in everyday theories than in professional ones (diSessa 2006). For this reason, some people have used the phrase "cultural model" for what I have just been calling people's everyday theories (D'Andrade and Strauss 1992; Gee 2005; Holland and Quinn 1987). They retain the word "theory" just for professional theories. And this is fine with me. In this case, then, we can say that the cultural model that words have fixed meanings in terms of concepts or definitions stored in people's heads (an everyday theory) is similar to a theory (professional theory) held by and elaborated much further by professional linguists and psychologists.

Even when cultural models match a professional theory to a certain extent—and they often don't—this does not mean that either of them are right or useful. Both everyday people and professionals can be wrong, of course. In fact, I will argue in this book, along with some other linguists (though, of course, not all), that the cultural model that words have fixed meanings in terms of concepts or definitions stored in people's heads is misguided. So, too, is the professional theory version of this cultural model. Thus, in this regard, both "common sense" and some professionals are wrong.

Most words don't have fixed meanings. Take even so simple a word as "coffee" (Clark 1989). If I say, "The coffee spilled, go get a mop," the word betokens a liquid. If I say, "The coffee spilled, go get a broom," the word betokens beans or grains. If I say, "The coffee spilled, stack it again," the word betokens tins or cans. If I say, "Coffee growers exploit their workers," the word betokens coffee berries and the trees they grow on.

You can see that the word "coffee" is really related not to a definite concept so much as a little "story" (using the word loosely) about how coffee products are produced and used. (Berries grow on trees, get picked, their husks are removed and they are made into beans, then ground up, used as a flavoring or made into a liquid which is drunk or used for other purposes, for instance, to stain things.) And, indeed, you can fail to know parts of the story (as I most surely do) and still be quite happy using the word. You trust other people know the full story or, at least, that such a full story could be discovered if the need arose (which it rarely does). And, of course, new meanings can arise in new contexts. For example, though you have never heard it, you would probably know what I meant if I said, "Big coffee is opposed to the new legislation" (which you might take to mean something like "Powerful coffee growers, producers, and other businesses connected to coffee opposed the new legislation").

We can also call the little "story" connected to "coffee" a "cultural model." Cultural models are "models." Think about what a model is, for example a toy plane or a blueprint for a house. A model is just a scaled-down and simplified way of thinking about something that is more complicated and complex. Children can use toy planes to fantasize about real flight and scientists can use model planes to test ideas about real planes. Architects can use cardboard models of houses or blueprints (just quite abstract models) to think about designing real houses. So, too, theories and stories, whether used by everyday people or professionals, are, in this sense, models, tools used to simplify complex matters somewhat so they can be better understood and dealt with.

We will have a lot more to say about cultural models in Chapter 5. For now, we take them to be everyday theories, stories, images, metaphors, or any other device through which people try to simplify a complex reality in order to better understand it and deal with it. Such models help people to go about their lives efficiently without having to think through everything thoroughly at all times. We pick up our cultural models through interactions in society and often don't think all that much about them, using them as we go about our business on "automatic pilot," so to speak.

Of course, a word like "coffee" seems to mean something pretty simple, at least compared to words like "honor," "love," or "democracy." But even the "coffee" example shows that the meanings of words are more like encyclopedia entries—even Wiki entries, as we will see below, since people can negotiate, contest, and change meaning—than they are like formal dictionary definitions. Words are connected more to knowledge and beliefs, encapsulated into the stories or theories that constitute cultural models, than they are to definitions. Lots of information based on history and what people do in the world is connected to each word, even a word like "coffee." Lots of this information is picked up in conversation and in our dealings with texts and the media; not all or even most of it is attained in school. Some people know more or less of this information than do others. And, since history and what people do change, meanings change, as well.

Take another simple word, the word "bachelor" (Fillmore 1975). If any word has a definite definition, this word would seem to be it: "unmarried male." However, now let me ask you, Is the Pope a bachelor? Is an older man who has lived with his homosexual lover for thirty years a bachelor? Is a young man in a permanent coma a bachelor? We are not really comfortable saying "yes" in each of these cases, even though in each case these people are unmarried males. Why? Because we really use the word "bachelor," like the word "coffee," in relation to a little "story," a story like this: People usually get married to a member of the opposite sex by a certain age, men who stay unmarried, but available to members of the opposite sex, past a certain age are bachelors. In fact, this little story is our everyday theory of how the world usually goes or even, for some people, how it should go. It is, in that sense, a cultural model (an everyday theory), just like the cultural model that words have fixed meanings in terms of concepts or definitions in people's heads. We humans, as we will see, have lots and lots of cultural models about all sorts of things.

The Pope, the committed gay, and the young man in the coma just don't fit well in this story. For different reasons they aren't really available to members of the opposite sex. So we are uncomfortable calling them "bachelors." We go with the story and not the definition. Furthermore, people have for some time now actually challenged the story connected to the word "bachelor." They have made a tacit cultural model overt by saying the story is sexist, especially since "bachelor" seemed once to carry a positive connotation while its twin, "spinster," did not. Some of these people started calling available unmarried women "bachelors," others starting using the word "spinster" as a term of praise.

We could even imagine the day when the Catholic Church both ordains women and allows priests to marry and where we are willing, then, to call the Pope a bachelor and the Pope happens to be a woman! Words and their meanings can travel far as their stories change and as our knowledge about the world changes.

So here is where we have gotten so far. The meanings of words are not fixed and settled once and for all in terms of definitions. They vary across contexts (remember "The coffee spilled, go get a mop" versus "The coffee spilled, go get a broom"). And they are tied to cultural models (stories and theories that are meant to simplify and help us deal with complexity). In fact, it is the cultural models that allow people to understand words differently in different contexts and even to understand new uses of a word for new contexts (e.g., remember "Big Coffee opposed the new legislation"). Now we will add a third point: that the meanings of words is also tied to negotiation and social interactions.

To see this point, let's take yet another simple word—again, nothing fancy like "love" or "honor"—the word "sausage" and consider what the African-American activist and lawyer Patricia Williams (1991) had to say in court once about this seemingly simple word. Williams was prosecuting a sausage manufacturer for selling impure products. The manufacturer insisted that the word "sausage" meant "pig meat and lots of impurities." Williams, in her summation, told the jury the following:

> You have this thing called a sausage-making machine. You put pork and spices in at the top and crank it up, and because it is a sausage-making machine, what comes out the other end is a sausage. Over time, everyone knows that anything that comes out of the sausage-making machine is known as a sausage. In fact, there is a law passed that says it is indisputably sausage.
>
> One day, we throw in a few small rodents of questionable pedigree and a teddy bear and a chicken We crank the machine up and wait to see what comes out the other end. (1) Do we prove the validity of the machine if we call the product sausage? (2) Or do we enlarge and enhance the meaning of "sausage" if we call the product sausage? (3) Or do we have any success in breaking out of the bind if we call it something different from "sausage"?
>
> In fact, I'm not sure it makes any difference whether we call it sausage or if we scramble the letters of the alphabet over this thing that comes out, full of sawdust and tiny claws. What will make a difference, however, is a recognition of our shifting relation to the word 'sausage,' by:

(1) enlarging the authority of sausage makers and enhancing the awesome, cruel inevitability of the workings of sausage machines—that is, everything they touch turns to sausage or else it doesn't exist; or by

(2) expanding the definition of sausage itself to encompass a wealth of variation: chicken, rodent, or teddy-bear sausage; or, finally, by

(3) challenging our own comprehension of what it is we really mean by sausage—that is, by making clear the consensual limits of sausage and reacquainting ourselves with the sources of its authority and legitimation.

Realizing that there are at least three different ways to relate to the facts of this case, to this product, this thing, is to define and acknowledge your role as jury and as trier of fact; is to acknowledge your own participation in the creation of reality.

(pp. 107–108)

It's pretty clear that Williams approves of option 3. But, exactly what are the consensual limits of a word's meaning? When does sausage cease to be sausage? How far can a company stretch the meaning of the word? What are the sources that authorize and legitimate the meaning of a word? These are not the sorts of questions we are used to thinking about in regard to words and meaning when we are tempted to just open a dictionary to settle what the meaning of a word is.

So let's look at the sausage issue—the sausage story, knowledge about sausage in the world—a bit more deeply. The sausage company engages in a social practice that involves making sausage in a certain way and selling it. Its social practice is fully caught up with a vested interest: making a profit. Consumers of sausage have another social practice, one involving buying and eating sausage. Their practice too is fully caught up with vested interests, namely, buying sausage for a low price and feeling well after eating it.

These two social practices exist only in relation to each other. Furthermore, the two practices happen to share some common interests. For example, it is not in the interest of either party to get too fussy about what gets labeled "sausage," otherwise it will cost too much to buy or sell. But, the producers and consumers may conflict in exactly where they want to draw the boundary between what is and what is not sausage. This conflict opens up a negotiation about what the word "sausage" will mean. The negotiation can take place in court or in the supermarket where people buy or refuse to buy what the sausage company labels "sausage."

In this negotiation, power plays a role—the power of the producers is pitted against the power of the consumers.

But, can this negotiation come out just any old way? Are there no limits to it? Williams says there are consensual limits. The producers and consumers are, though engaged in different practices, members of a larger community that has a consensus around certain values. One of these values is the health and well-being of its members, if only so that they can buy and sell more sausage. If one side of the negotiation violates these values, they can lose the negotiation, provided the community has the power to exclude them if they refuse to concede. Law is one way to try to do this. Boycotting the company is another. Systematically failing to apply the word "sausage" to the company's products is still another.

Meanings are ultimately rooted in negotiation between different social practices with different interests by people who share or seek to share some common ground. Power plays an important role in these negotiations. The negotiations can be settled for the time, in which case meaning becomes conventional and routine. But the settlement can be reopened, perhaps when a particular company introduces a new element into its social practice and into its sausage. The negotiations which constitute meaning are limited by values emanating from "communities"—though we need to realize it can be contentious what constitutes a "community"—or from attempts by people to establish and stabilize, perhaps only for here and now, enough common ground to agree on meaning.

But how can we characterize what constitutes such a community, for example, the community of people that authorizes and legitimates, for a given time and place, the meaning of the word "sausage"? Following the lead of Amy Shuman, in her paper "Literacy: Local Uses and Global Perspectives" (1992), I will characterize these communities as persons whose paths through life have for a given time and place fallen together. I do not want to characterize them as people "united by mutual interest in achieving a common end," since groups may negotiate a consensus around meaning when they share few substantive interests and have no common goals, or at least, when they have many conflicting interests and goals.

The word "community" here is probably not a good one. (See, I am negotiating meaning with you.) We might hope for—and, of course, often get—a more robust sense of community supporting the meanings of words and the shared communication of people. But, in the end, we often get more tenuous connections among people, ones in terms of which even foes can communicate, though there may always come a point where "words run out," agreement (on words, or facts, or actions) can't be reached, and there is the risk of violence. (How well we know this in our current world.) In the end, one and the same person can be a "terrorist" to some and a "freedom fighter" to others, and communication is on the verge of failure and with it, perhaps, understanding, common ground, and peace.

So this is a different way to look at meaning. Meaning is not something locked away in heads, rendering communication possible by the mysterious fact that everyone has the same thing in their heads, though we don't know how that happened. Meaning is something we negotiate and contest over socially. It is something that has its roots in "culture" in the very deep and extended sense that it resides in an attempt to find common ground. That common ground is very often rooted in the sorts of things we think of us "cultures," whether something like "American culture" or "African-American culture," though we will see the notion of "culture" (like "sausage") is itself problematic.

But meaning, as I have argued above, can be rooted in relationships that are less stable, long-term, enduring, or encompassing as "cultures" in the traditional sense. Two people don't need to "share a culture" to communicate. They need to negotiate and seek common ground on the spot of the here and now of social interaction and communication. In fact, we see such a thing every day in our current world in chat rooms and massive multiplayer worlds (like *World of WarCraft* or *Second Life*) where people of sometimes quite different ages, races, ethnicities, countries, genders, and social and political orientations of all sorts group together to engage in joint action and communication. Here very often the processes of negotiation, contestation, and the seeking or forestalling of common ground are obvious and foregrounded. Such processes are, I suggest, always part and parcel of language and communication, but they are often more hidden and taken for granted in our everyday lives in the "real" world, though they became obvious in Patricia Williams's trial, as well.

Take, for example, a married couple. They each think that the meaning of the word "work" is clear and definite. Further, they each think they mean the same things by the word. Then, one day one of them says to the other, "I don't think this relationship is working, because relationships shouldn't take work." The other partner, stunned, says, "But I have worked hard on this relationship and I think relationships require work." They realize that they don't really know, once and for all, what "work" means, that the word is being used in several different ways in these very utterances, and that here and now, in a quite consequential way, they have to negotiate the matter. (Perhaps, they should have done so earlier.) They realize as well that they may hold different cultural models about work and relationships or that there are competing models available in society.

Notice, too, that there is no good way to clearly distinguish fighting over words and fighting over things and actions in the world. One partner doesn't like what he or she is being required to do, but if he or she didn't see—didn't feel—this was "work" or if he or she saw such "work" as good for relationships, then there wouldn't be a problem. Words, meanings, and the world are married and will stay together even if this couple doesn't. They are married because the primary way we humans deal with the world is by getting words to attach to the world in certain ways—like "sausage" above—and this is a matter we have to negotiate over and contest with in the face of other people, their practices and their interests.

Now I have made it seem like we are always fighting over words and their meanings. But, of course, we are not. Most of the time there is peace. But the question is why and how there is peace. There is peace because in many cases and for many parts of their lives people have come to agreements about what words will mean in different situations. These are "conventions." We take them for granted until someone proposes to break them or we find areas or situations they don't really cover. We become party to these conventions by leading our lives with other people, by being parts of shared histories, groups, and institutions.

Indeed, we can see these histories, groups, and institutions as, in part, existing in order to stabilize and conventionalize meanings so that people can get on with their lives and their interests (unfortunately, sometimes at the cost of other people's interests). Looking at things this way shows us another side of the claim that meaning is social and cultural and not really just a matter of what is inside your head. It takes massive amounts of social work on the parts of groups and institutions to "police" meaning, to settle negotiations in terms of more or less stabilized conventions that everyone will abide by, often without giving the matter too much thought.

At one time in U.S. history, our government and military encouraged right-wing forces in some South American countries to harm civilians in order to encourage these civilians to oppose left-wing governments or left-wing revolutionary forces (Sikkink 2004). Some members of our government called such people "freedom fighters." When Islamic fighters did the same thing to us and our allies, they, however, were called "terrorists." Such a distinction takes work to uphold in terms of policies, media treatments, and political arguments, and is, in turn, contested by some people.

To see another example of the same sort of thing, consider a video game made in Syria called *Under Ash* (Gee 2003), a game whose hero is a young Palestinian who throws stones to fight Israeli soldiers and settlers. The game operates by a cultural model that holds that while "civilians" should not be harmed, Israeli settlers don't count as civilians, but rather as the "advance" troops of an occupation army. Of course, Israeli settlers don't in reality count as anything until they are "modeled" in terms of their relationships to other things and people. If we see them as "civilians" (not combatants), then people who harm them are "terrorists." If we see them as combatants and not civilians, then people who harm them are, at worst, fighting a war and, at best, are "freedom fighters." Needless to say, lots of political works needs to go on to "enforce" the meanings we give words like "civilian" or "terrorist" in the face of people who wish to contest these meanings.

All this does *not* mean that "anything goes," that it doesn't matter whether we call someone a "civilian" or a "terrorist," that "it's all just words." Nor is the matter "merely political" in the sense that it just all amounts to political rhetoric to advance one party over another. What it means is that what meanings we give to words is based on knowledge we acquire and choices we make, as well as values and beliefs—and, yes, even interests—we have. Words are consequential. They matter. Words and the world are married.

So we have developed a viewpoint (a theory) that the meanings of words:

1 Can vary across contexts of use.
2 Are composed of changing stories, knowledge, beliefs, and values that are encapsulated in cultural models, not definitions.
3 Are a matter, as well, of social negotiations rooted in culture if only in the broad sense of a search for common ground.
4 For many words at many points in their histories meaning is relatively stabilized thanks to the fact that many people accept and share a convention about what they mean in different contexts of use.
5 These conventions can be undone, contested, and changed.
6 Finally, it takes social work to enforce and police the meanings of words, work that never in the end can ensure their meanings will not change or be contested.

Combining words

So the theory of words and their meanings we have developed so far makes learning word meanings via lists and definitions—the sort of thing that sometimes goes on in school—pretty implausible. But the situation is actually worse for lists and definitions. First, there really is no definitive list of the words one needs to know. Partly this is so because new words arise all the time and old ones die. Furthermore, each specialty area in society—from video gamers to gangster and lawyers—has its own words, some of which eventually filter into more general use (as have Freud's terms like "ego" and "subconscious," for example). But, worse, it is also so because we don't always use single words, but often combine words into combinations that have their own meanings, that function, more or less, like single words. We saw this above with "Big Coffee." You probably have never heard this combination before, but you can give it a meaning because you have heard things like "Big Oil" and "Big Business" and can, by analogy, guess a meaning for "Big Coffee."

Our daily communication is filled with word combinations that take on their own life and meaning. And I am not now referring to idioms like "kick the bucket." I am referring to compounds and phrases that take on their own non-idiomatic meanings in terms of stories, knowledge, beliefs, and values encapsulated in cultural models. No list could ever suffice. For example, consider the word combination "correct English" or "good English" or even "to speak English correctly." These combinations—just like single words like "sausage" or "democracy"—have their own connections to cultural models in terms of which people can give them specific meanings in specific contexts, negotiate over such meanings, or contest them.

To see how matters work here—the sorts of trouble we can get ourselves into with words, words in this case that are not listed in any dictionary—consider the following sentence, uttered by a seven-year African-American child in the course of telling a story at "sharing time" ("show and tell") at school (Gee 1985: 32–35; see also Gee 2005 and Chapter 7 in this book):

1   My puppy, he always be followin' me.

Let's consider a possible reaction to this sentence. From my years of teaching introductory linguistics, I know that many people on hearing a sentence like this one will say (or think) something like the following:

> This child does not know how to speak correct English. This is probably because she attends a poor and neglected school and comes from an impoverished home with few or no books in it, a home which gives little support for and encouragement to education.

Note our word combination "correct English" and the work it is doing. This word combination (and related ones like "good English" or "to speak English correctly") is connected to a cultural model something like this: There are right ways and wrong ways to speak English. How educated people speak and write determines which ways are right. If there is dispute about the matter, there are experts (grammarians) who can settle the matter, because they know how educated people do speak or, at least, how they should speak (because, of course, even educated people have lapses). This cultural model is often associated with another one (Finegan 1980) that holds that languages are always deteriorating over time because uneducated people and other debilitating social forces change them and that historically earlier forms of language are, thus, often more correct than later ones, something that can be put right, if it all, by experts telling us how we ought to speak (and write).

The "correct English" cultural model tells us the little girl is "wrong" (alas, then, she doesn't even really know her native language) and the "language is deteriorating" model tells us she is part of a larger problem. There are two things in this little girl's sentence that contribute to these claims. First is the juxtaposition of the subject "my puppy" to the front of the sentence, followed by the pronoun "he." People who hold the above cultural models may well feel that this is simply "sloppy" or "colloquial," much as is, they will say, using "followin'" instead of "following," rather like slurping one's soup. We all are prone in moments of carelessness to do things like this, but this little girl, they may feel, probably does it more than she ought to.

People with the above cultural models are likely to be more seriously disturbed by the "bare" helping verb "be," rather than "is." Why can't the child say, "My puppy is always following me"? Can it be that hard? The problem will get worse when we add the fact that this child can be heard to say such things as "My puppy followin' me" on other occasions. The child will now be said to be inconsistent, simply varying between different forms because she doesn't really know the right form, doesn't really know the language in this regard, despite the fact that it is her first and only language.

Let's now juxtapose to the above cultural models what a linguist who has actually studied the matter might say about the little girl's sentence. This is a case where cultural models and professional theories differ. So what is the linguist's theory about sentence 1? We will start with the most striking feature, the bare "be."

To understand how this "bare be" form is used, and to grasp its significance, we must first explicate a part of the English aspect system

(Comrie 1976). "Aspect" is a term that stands for how a language signals the viewpoint it takes on the way in which an action is situated in time. Almost all languages in the world make a primary distinction between the perfective aspect and the imperfective aspect.

The imperfective aspect is used when the action is viewed as on-going or repeated. English uses the progressive (the verb "to be" plus the ending -ing on the following verb) to mark the imperfective, as in "John is working/John was working" or "Mary is jumping/Mary was jumping." In the first of these cases, John's working is viewed as on-going, still in progress in the present ("is") or the past ("was"); in the second, Mary's jumping is viewed as having being repeated over and over again in the present ("is") or past ("was").

The perfective is used when an action is viewed as a discrete whole, treated as if it is a point in time (whether or not, in reality, the act took a significant amount of time or not). English uses the simple present or past for the perfective, as in "Smith dives for the ball!" (sportscast), in the present, or "Smith dived for the ball," in the past. The imperfective of these sentences would be: "Smith is diving for the ball" and "Smith was diving for the ball."

Linguists refer to the distinctive English dialect that many, but by no means all, African-American speakers speak as "Black Vernacular English"—"BVE" for short—or African-American English—"AAE" for short (Baugh 1983, 1999; Green 2002; Labov 1972a, b; Mufwene *et al.* 1998; Rickford and Rickford 2000). Some people prefer the term "Ebonics" (see Baugh 2000 for discussion) here, but, for better or worse, terms like "BVE" or "AAE" are in wider currency in linguistics (and, in general, linguists don't name languages or dialects after the color of their speakers). Of course, there is, just as we would expect, negotiation and contestation to be had over "AAE" versus "Ebonics" (and, thus, we see that what we said about words above applies to specialist "jargon" as well). We will refer to the English that elites in society are perceived as speaking and that many others accept and do their best to emulate as "Standard English." (There are actually different varieties of Standard English, see Bex 1999; Finegan and Rickford 2004; Milroy and Milroy 1985.)

AAE and Standard English do not differ in the perfective, though an older form of AAE used to distinguish between a simple perfective ("John drank the milk") and a completive that stressed that the action was finished, complete and done with ("John done drank the milk up"). Like all languages, AAE (a dialect of English) has changed and is changing through time.

AAE and standard English do differ in the imperfective. Young African-American-speakers make a distinction between on-going or repeated (thus, imperfective) events which are of limited duration and on-going or repeated events which are of extended duration. For limited duration events they use the absent copula, as in "My puppy following me," and for extended events they use the "bare be" as in "My puppy be following me." Thus, the following sorts of contrast are regular in the variety of English spoken by many young African-American speakers in the United States (Bailey and Maynor 1987):

Limited duration events

2a   In health class, we talking about the eye.
     [Standard English: "In health class, we are talking about the eye"]

 b   He trying to scare us.
     [Standard English: "He is trying to scare us"]

Extended duration events

3a   He always be fighting.
     [Standard English: "He is always fighting"]

 b   Sometimes them big boys be throwing the ball, and . . .
     [Standard English: "Sometimes those big boys are throwing the ball, and . . ."]

In 2a, the talk about the eye in health class will go on only for a short while compared to the duration of the whole class. Thus, the speaker uses the absent copula form ("we talking"). In 2b, "he" is trying to scare us now, but this doesn't always happen or happen repeatedly and often, so once again the speaker uses the absent be ("he trying"). On the other hand, in 3a, the fighting is always taking place, is something that "he" characteristically does, thus the speaker uses the bare be form ("he be fighting"). And in 3b, the speaker is talking about a situation that has happened often and will in all likelihood continue to happen. Thus, she uses the bare be ("big boys be throwing"). Standard English makes no such contrast, having to rely on the context of the utterance, or the addition of extra words, to make the meaning apparent.

Two things are particularly interesting about this contrast in AAE. First, it is one that is made in many other languages. It is one linguists expect to find in languages, though it is not always found—for instance, it is not found in Standard English (Comrie 1976). That Standard English fails to overtly draw this contrast is then somewhat odd, but, then, all languages fail to make some contrasts that others make.

Second, older African-American speakers did not use "bare be" in this way, but somewhat differently. Young African-American people redrew their dialect to make this distinction, using forms that already existed in AAE (the absent "be" and the bare "be"), but with somewhat different uses (Bailey and Maynor 1987). That is, they are changing their language, as all children have done through all the time language has been around. It is as if they have (unconsciously) seen a gap or hole in the English system—the failure to clearly signal in the imperfective a distinction between limited and extended duration—and filled it in. All languages have gaps or holes, and children are always attempting to fill them in (Slobin 1985). Indeed, AAE has changed in certain respects since the first edition of this book (1990)—as, of course, has Standard English, though dialects less tied to writing than Standard English change more rapidly.

This is one of the major ways languages change through time. Children invent distinctions that they think (unconsciously) should be in the language. Some linguists believe this invention is based on a biologically specified view of what the optimal design of a human language ought to be (Chomsky 1986: 1–50; Pinker 1994). Other linguists believe this sort of invention is based on children's social and cognitive development, their ways of thinking about the world that they gain through their early interactions with the world and people in it (see Hoff 2004 for general discussion).

Linguists disagree about exactly how to phrase the matter, though they do not disagree about the creativity of children as language acquirers or on the important role of children in language change. Languages are changing all the time, losing and gaining various contrasts. If a language loses the ability to draw a certain contrast, and the contrast seems to be an important one from the perspective humans take on the world, children may well replace it.

But, one might ask, why has the non-standard dialect introduced this distinction, and not also the standard dialect? One price speakers pay for standard dialects is that they change more slowly, since the fact that a standard dialect is used in writing and public media puts something of a brake on change. This is good in that the dialect remains relatively constant across time, thus serving the purposes of standardization (Milroy and Milroy 1985).

However, since non-standard dialects are freer to change on the basis of the human child's linguistic and cognitive systems, non-standard dialects are, in a sense, often "more logical" or "more elegant" from a linguistic point of view. That is, they are "more logical" or "more elegant" from the viewpoint of what is typical across languages or from the viewpoint of what seems to be the basic design of the human linguistic system.

Non-standard dialects and standard ones often serve different purposes: the former signal identification with a local, often non-mainstream community, and the latter with a wider, plural and technological society, and its views of who are elite and worth emulating (Bex 1999; Chambers 1995; Finegan and Rickford 2004; Milroy 1987a, b; Milroy and Milroy 1985). In fact, a change in a non-standard dialect, since it makes the non-standard dialect different from the standard, may enhance its ability to signal identification with a "local" community as over against the wider "mainstream" society.

However, we should keep in mind that in today's complex, global world, where people can communicate with each other nearly endlessly via a wide variety of media, "local varieties" can spread and be used for political activism and as a badge of identity in contesting what is and what is not "mainstream." In turn, what is or was "mainstream" in a given context can change as people adopt "local varieties" for the purposes of creating new consumer niches in a global market place. Both things have happened with AAE as it plays a role in rap and hip hop, for instance.

But both standard and non-standard dialects are marvels of human mastery. Neither is better or worse. Furthermore, it is an accident of history as to which dialect gets to be taken to be the standard—a reversal of power and prestige in the history of the United States could have led to a form of AAE being the standard, and the concomitant need here to save from negative judgments dialects that are closer to what is currently viewed as Standard English.

The other features of our sentence are also quite common across languages. The juxtaposition of the subject "my puppy" to the front of the sentence is a way to signal that a speaker is switching topics or returning to an old one. It is actually common in many dialects of spoken English and in many other languages (Ochs and Schieffelin 1983).

The variation between "followin'" in informal contexts and "following" in more formal contexts occurs in all dialects of English, including dialects closer to the standard. It turns out that people aren't very good at actually hearing what they and others are really saying—though they think they are good at it—so you can't trust your ears in this regard, you have to make tape-recordings and listen repeatedly and carefully.

The two forms ("followin'" and "following"), in all dialects of English, actually have different social implications (Milroy and Milroy 1985: 95). The form "followin'" means that the speaker is signaling more solidarity with and less deference toward the hearer, treating the hearer more as a peer, friend, or comrade. The "following" form signals that the speaker is signaling less solidarity with and more deference towards the hearer, treating the hearer less as a peer and intimate and more as one higher in status than the speaker. Of course, these matters are matters of degree, and so one can (unconsciously) mix and match various degrees of "-in'" and "-ing" in a stretch of language to achieve just the right level of solidarity and deference (Labov 1972a, b; Chambers 1995; Gee 1993a, Gee 2005; Milroy 1987a).

So we have a conflict between a theory in linguistics—one that says that this little girl speaks "correct English" in terms of her own dialect—and an everyday, often taken-for-granted tacit cultural model (theory) that says the little girl doesn't speak English correctly—indeed, claims that she speaks "bad English." Of course, this doesn't settle the matter. Common sense can be wrong, but so can experts.

Many readers are probably saying at this point, "Look, the issue is not what to mean by a combination of words like 'correct English', rather it's a matter of what is true, a matter of whether the linguist's facts are correct or everyday people's facts." Alas, you already know I don't think language and the world can be separated that cleanly. What is at issue between the linguist's theory and the everyday cultural model is not solely or only a disagreement over whose generalizations or facts are "true" or accurate or whatever. People who hold the everyday cultural model—even after they have heard the linguist's views—can still choose to use the words "correct English" to mean "the dialect people speak (and write) whom we (or elites in society) view as intelligent and educated." In this case they have conceded the linguist's point about dialects, but have shored up their cultural model to claim that only Standard English is correct and other dialects are not, or some are not, namely ones like the one this little girl speaks. Such people can also, of course, just ignore linguists (probably the more common course).

Meaning is a matter of negotiation and contestation, and people by no means just give into experts. In fact, this point was made clear during the Oakland "Ebonics controversy." The Oakland School Board had sought federal funds to aid African-American students who spoke AAE. The controversy had many aspects. But when newspapers and other media claimed that AAE was "bad English" or "slang," linguists sought to correct them. The claim that these children were not speaking "bad

English" or "slang" was one that linguists had taken as proven for several decades by the point of the controversy. Nonetheless, many people in the media and many everyday people refused to change their cultural model and agree with the linguists, though, of course, they became more consciously aware of their model.

The final and ultimately the real issue for those who hold the everyday cultural model associated with "correct English," once their tacit theory has been made explicit by being juxtaposed to the linguist's theory, is this: Do they really want to define "correct English" in the way their cultural model does? Or, do they want, rather, to adopt the linguist's framework? This choice is, of course, partly based on how people assess the linguist's factual claims. But, in the end, the choice can only be based, for the most part, on a value judgment about the current social world and about what one takes to be both possible and desired changes in this world.

Such judgments are ultimately ethical or moral decisions. It is clear, also, that I personally believe that, exposed to the linguist's theory and the everyday cultural model, the only ethical choice is to use "correct English" the way linguists use it. This is so because the linguists' theory, I believe, will lead to a more just, humane, and happier world. I haven't spelled this argument out here in full, but I believe that it is fairly obvious. In any case, the following chapters will make clear why I hold this belief.

A further moral we can draw here is this: Arguing about what words (ought to) mean is not a trivial business—it is not "quibbling over mere words," "hair splitting," "just semantics." Such arguments are what lead to the adoption of social beliefs and values and, in turn, these beliefs and values lead to social action and the maintenance and creation of social worlds. Such arguments are, in this sense, often a species of moral argumentation.

Before going on, let me hasten to add that it is simply a piece of inaccurate "folk wisdom," encouraged by the popular press and other media, that linguists claim that people never say anything wrong or can't make mistakes in language. The sentence "Whom should I say is calling?" exists in the grammar of no variety (dialect) of English. It fails to fit any pattern of generalizations that characterizes any dialect of English. Some speakers do not use the "who/whom" contrast in their dialects; this is, in fact, true of the informal, colloquial speech of many speakers of dialects close to Standard English. Such speakers will sometimes say such a thing as "Whom should I say is calling?" when they are trying to sound very formal and sound as if they know where Standard (in this case, for the most part, written) English calls for the placement of "whom" and "who." This is called "hypercorrection" and it is indeed a mistake. People do such things, and linguists know they do.

Linguists do not claim that "anything goes." They do, however, perfectly well know that the sentence uttered by our seven-year-old is grammatical ("correct") in her dialect. And they know it is grammatical because it fits the "rules" of her variety of English, the pattern of generalizations that characterize her speech and that of her fellow community members sharing her dialect. These rules or generalizations are acquired through exposure to the language as a child, and not through overt instruction at home or school. Children come to school already well along in the acquisition of their dialect of English. To me—as well as to other linguists—it would seem important for teachers to realize this if they wish this little girl to acquire Standard English (another dialect) in school and affiliate with school as an institution that respects her, her family, and her culture.

What we have seen is that when we interrogate the cultural models associated with some words and word combinations we get to moral decisions. Attributing certain meanings to such words and word combinations leads to value-laden moral decisions about how the world is and should be and how we could make it better or worse. It leads to claims and beliefs about who and what is "good," "right," "normal," "acceptable," and who and what are not, judgments that have consequences in the world. When people negotiate over such words and word combinations they are also negotiating over social issues of moral import. I will call such words and word combinations "socially contested terms." "Correct English" is one such term, but so, we will see in this book, is "literacy."

Socially contested terms are words and word combinations whose cultural models hold implications about "right" and "wrong," "good" and "bad," "acceptable" and "not acceptable," "appropriate" and "not appropriate," and other such value-laden distinctions. When these distinctions are applied to people they have implications for how "social goods" are or should be distributed in the world, and this is, for me, ultimately a moral matter. Saying a child does not know how to speak her own native language correctly has implications about that child, her abilities and her deficits—and these carry over into how she is treated in school and society.

Morality and communication

We have seen that people hold cultural models and that these are theories. Such theories—like the one about "correct" English—are often tacit in the sense that people have not thought about them much and take them for granted. They seem "obvious," even commonsense. If people have thought about them more explicitly, then they are overt and now, at least, people who hold them can engage in overt argument with people who don't.

We can always ask where a person got his or her cultural models. In most cases, they picked them up from talk, interaction, and engagement with texts and media in society and within their own cultural spheres. In some cases, the cultural models may have come from that person's thought and research into the matter, carried out in discussion and debate with others, especially if their models have been challenged by others or they have become, for whatever reason, aware they hold them and have become wary of them. Such thought and research, I will call "primary research."

Even if the person has not engaged in primary research, he or she may have thoughtfully consulted, through discussion, listening or reading, a variety of such original thought and research, and discussed it with others. In either of these cases—where the person has actually carried out primary research or, at least, thoughtfully considered it—I will say that the person is operating now with "a primary theory," something on the way from a cultural model to a more explicit theory. The issue here is not whether the person is "right," rather it is this: Have people allowed their viewpoints to be formed through serious reflection on multiple competing viewpoints (Bakhtin 1981, 1986; Billig 1987)?

Primary theories are not the possession solely of academics. My twenty-seven-year-old son was ten when I first wrote this book (1990). When he was ten, his theories about *Iron Man*, a comic book super-hero, were quite assuredly primary theories. He had read the books and discussed them with others, as well as, in fact, looked into something of the history of *Iron Man*. My theories of *Iron Man* were and are, however, not primary theories, as all I know about the matter I have heard in snippets from him and picked up in informal conversations with others about their children's reading of "super-hero" comics. I have never studied the matter or confronted alternative viewpoints and opinions.

Basil Bernstein (1971, 1975) pointed out that the theories presented to teachers in training are very often "third-hand" knowledge. The teachers do not themselves read primary literature in linguistics, for example.

Nor do they read secondary sources written by linguists summarizing and discussing that literature. Nor do they do any research themselves. Rather, they are presented, orally and in their reading, with third-hand reports presented by people, not themselves trained in linguistics, summarizing and discussing secondary sources at best. Thus, the teachers hold their theories about language at some remove from being a primary theory.

In our daily lives, the beliefs we have and the claims we make on the basis of these beliefs have effects on other people, sometimes harmful, sometimes beneficial, sometimes a bit of both, and sometimes neither. There are, I believe, two conceptual principles that serve as the basis of ethical human communication and interaction. These principles are grounded in no further ones, save that the second relies on the first, and, if someone fails to accept them, then argument has "run out." They are absolutely basic. The first principle (Wheatley 1970: 115–134) is:

> *First principle*. That something would harm someone else (deprive them of what they or the society they are in view as "goods") is always a good reason (though perhaps not a sufficient reason) not to do it.

What this principle says is that when we consider whether to believe, claim, or do anything, then it is always a good reason not to do it if we believe that our believing, claiming, or doing it would harm someone else. This does not mean that there may not be other reasons that override this one, reasons that lead us to do the harmful thing nonetheless.

I have, and can have, I believe, no argument for this principle, and, in particular, for well known reasons, utilitarian arguments for it won't work (Smith 1988: ch. 6). The principle is simply a basic part of what it means to be a moral human being. All I, or anyone, can say is that if people do not accept it, or if they act as though they do not accept it, then I and most others are simply not going to interact with them. We have come to a point at which one must simply offer resistance, not argument.

The second conceptual principle is yet more specific, and is couched in terms of our distinctions about different types of theories:

> *Second principle*. One always has the moral obligation to change a cultural model into a primary theory when there is reason to believe that the cultural model advantages oneself or one's group over other people or other groups.

What this principle says is that if I have good reason to believe, or others argue convincingly that I ought to have good reason to believe, that a cultural model or theory I hold gives me or people like me (however this is defined) an advantage over other people or other groups of people, then my continuing to hold this theory in a tacit way or on the basis of little thought and study is unethical. I have an ethical obligation to explicate my theory, make it overt, and to engage in the sort of thought, discussion, and research that would render it a primary theory for me. It is not enough just to be able to put it into words (to be able to argue): it is necessary, as well, to confront evidence and alternative viewpoints and to be open to change. I have to have engaged in dialogue with alternatives (so consulting only sources that I already agree with is not enough).

By "advantage" in this second principle I simply mean "bring oneself or one's group more of what counts, in the society one is in, as a good, whether this be status, wealth, power, control, or whatever." Once again, I do not argue that there is any "transcendental" argument for this principle, only that if one fails to accept it, argument has "run out" and all that one can do is fail to interact with such people and offer them resistance if one must interact with them. At some point we have to cease to argue with people who will not open themselves to learning when their viewpoints have the potential to harm people. Such opening up does not mean, in the end, they will change their viewpoints, but it does mean they have seriously confronted other viewpoints. This second principle is, I would claim, also the ethical basis and main rationale for schools and schooling. An unexamined life isn't moral because it has the potential to hurt other people needlessly.

Ideology

When I wrote the first edition of this book (1990), the term "ideology" was a matter of considerable interest and debate in education and the social sciences more generally (see, e.g., Giddens 1984, 1987; Jameson 1981; Thompson 1984, Voloshinov 1986; in reference to ideology and education, see Freire and Macedo 1987; Giroux 1988; Lankshear with Lawler 1987; Luke 1988; McLaren 1989). This was partly due to the deep influence of Marxist approaches to education and society that were prevalent in U.S. universities from the 1960s until well in the 1980s. People are somewhat less directly concerned with the term today, but the debates about ideology and the notion itself are still crucial.

Marx believed that human knowledge, beliefs, and behavior reflected and were shaped by the economic relationships that existed in society

(Williams 1985; Marx and Engels 1970; Marx 1977). By "economic relationships" he meant something fairly broad, something like the relationships people contracted with each other in society in order to produce and consume "wealth." ("Wealth" originally meant "well-being" and in the economic sense is still connected to the resources in terms of which people and institutions can sustain their well being, at least materially.)

In a society where power, wealth, and status are quite unequally distributed (like ours), Marx claimed that the social and political ideas of those groups with the most power, status, and wealth "are nothing more than the ideal expression of the dominant material relationships" (Williams 1985: 155–156; Marx and Engels 1970; Marx 1977). That is, what people in power believe is simply an expression of their controlling and powerful positions in the social hierarchy, and their desire, whether conscious or not, to retain and enhance their power. Elites in a society believe what they do because it helps them keep control of power and status and to feel validated in doing so.

It is the failure of the elite and powerful in a society to realize that their views of reality follow from, and support, their positions of power that, in Marx's view, creates ideology. "Ideology" is an "upside-down" version of reality. Things are not really the way the elite and powerful believe them to be, rather their beliefs invert reality to make it appear the way they would like it to be, the way it "needs" to be if their power is to be enhanced and sustained.

Marx also believed that the elite and powerful could get others with less power and status to accept their "inverted" view of reality in two ways. They could accomplish this through "intellectuals" who actively promote the views of the rich and powerful and who "make the perfecting of the illusion of the [ruling class] about itself their chief source of livelihood" (Williams 1985: 155–156; Marx and Engels 1970). And, they accomplish it, as well, through organizing society and its institutions so as to encourage ways of thinking and behaving which enhance their interests, even if these ways are, in reality, at variance with the "true" interests of many people engaged in such thinking and acting (Fiske 1993; Gramsci 1971).

There is still great power in this viewpoint. In this book we are going to be talking about language and literacy, including how language and literacy are used at school and in institutions of power. Marx warns us to reflect on the fact that people with power have a vested interest to use language and literacy in their own favor, to express views of the world that support and validated their power. He warns us not to facilely assume highly educated people see reality as it is and less educated people don't.

In fact, he suggests that to the extent that extended education and high literacy skills ally people with the rich and powerful in society, they may invest people in believing and arguing for viewpoints—and seeing the world in ways—that better reflect the interests of the rich and powerful than the way things actually are or should be.

Unfortunately, Marx seems to assume that some people see reality only through a warped ideological lens, coloring reality in their own favor, while others see reality as it is. But none of us can see or deal with reality without words or other symbols. To discuss and debate—even to think about—reality we have to attach words to it. These words are, as we have seen, always connected to negotiable, changeable, and sometimes contested stories, histories, knowledge, beliefs, and values encapsulated into cultural models (theories) about the world. Nobody looks at the world other than through lenses supplied by language or some other symbol system. (This applies even to our senses—vision, for example, must be interpreted before it is meaningful, and such interpretation is done in language or some other symbol system.)

Of course, we can always ask whether the stories, histories, knowledge, beliefs, and values about the world that someone—even someone in some specific social group or class—uses are "correct" or "useful" or "moral." But we can't settle this by assuming members of one group or class are always wrong and members of some other group or class are always right. We all use words in ways that are colored by our lives, interests, values, and desires. We all have ample opportunity to be wrong. We all have ample opportunity—even a moral obligation—sometimes to change and do better. We all live and communicate with and through "ideology." We cannot do otherwise, but we can seek to interrogate our ideology when we come to believe that aspects of it are wrong or hurtful to others.

The cultural models that are connected to words are indispensable. We cannot go about our lives and contest every cultural model we use. They exist to help us cope with complexity and get on with our businesses. Cultural models are not all wrong or all right. In fact, like all models, they are simplifications of reality. They are the ideology through which we all see our worlds. In that sense, we are all both "beneficiaries" and "victims" of ideology, thanks to the fact that we speak a language and live in culture. But we can—or at times are morally obligated to—interrogate our cultural models and replace them with others, sometimes even with explicit and well developed theories. Ultimately, these new theories are models too, but, we hope, better ones. This ability is what education owes us and why we need education, though not necessarily education just in schools.

This book is about using some tools from linguistics (e.g., discourse analysis) to reflect on and interrogate some of our cultural models germane to language, literacy, learning, and people in society. In the end, you do not need to agree with me, but I hope to have suggested here that to reflect on these matters is in the end a moral matter. We will throughout be on socially contested terrain.

Chapter 2

Literacy crises and the significance of literacy

Literacy as a socially contested term

Literacy is what I called a "socially contested term" in the last chapter. We can choose to use this word in several different ways and such choices, in the end, have social and moral consequences, as we will see. The traditional meaning of the word "literacy"—the "ability to read and write"—appears "innocent" and "obvious." But, it is no such thing. Literacy as "the ability to write and read" situates literacy in the individual person, rather than in society. As such it obscures the multiple ways in which literacy interrelates with the workings of power. To make this clear, I will first discuss historical "literacy crises," showing that they are as much about social and political dilemmas as they are about who has the ability to read and write. Then I will turn to an argument as to why we might want to define "literacy" in social and cultural terms, not just in terms of an ability that resides inside people's heads. Then in the next chapter I will pursue these matters further by looking at literacy in its historical contexts.

Massive claims have been made for the ability that literacy is supposed to name. The next chapter will examine these claims. The history of literacy leads us to reject the traditional view of literacy and to replace it with a socially and culturally situated perspective, a perspective which will be developed throughout this book. I will argue that any view of literacy is inherently political, in the sense of involving relations of power among people. The next chapter will take us from Plato, one of the originators of modern Western discursive writing and ironically literacy's first great critic, through Harvey Graff, a contemporary social historian of literacy, to Paulo Freire, the chief proponent of "emancipatory literacy" within a revolutionary political context.

But first, I want to consider, in this chapter, how talk about "literacy" and "literacy crises" is often a displacement of deeper social fears, an evasion of more significant social problems. When I first wrote this book (1990), the United States was in the midst of a widely proclaimed "literacy crisis," perhaps best encapsulated in the now famous or infamous report *A Nation at Risk* (National Commission on Excellence in Education 1983; see also Hirsch 1987; Kozol 1985). The proclaiming of "literacy crises" is a historically recurrent feature of Western "developed" capitalist societies (Graff 1987a, b), the "crisis" often masking deeper and more complex social problems. The next section will look at the literacy crisis of the 1980s and early 1990s. The section after that will look at the new literacy crisis that we are living in at the present moment.

Literacy crises: 1990

In the 1990 book I used the 1986 NAEP study *Literacy: Profiles of America's Young Adults* (Kirsch *et al.*, 1986) to study the ways in which the literacy crisis masked deeper social fears and problems. Based on data collected in 1985, the study appeared at the height of the then current "literacy crisis." Yet it found that, if one excludes people who do not speak English, the vast majority of young adults were literate: 95 percent could write a simple description of the type of job they would like, accurately locate a single piece of information from a newspaper article of moderate length, match grocery store coupons to a shopping list, enter personal information on a job application, and fill in information on a phone message form.

However, when we asked about more difficult tasks, the picture changed substantially. Consider tasks like the following: locating and matching information from a page of text on the basis of three features, producing a letter stating that an error has been made in a department store bill, interpreting the instructions from an appliance warranty in order to select the most appropriate description of a malfunction, or generating a theme from the text of a poem containing numerous allusions to a familiar theme (e.g., war). Now only 72 percent of these young adults could do these tasks, and, furthermore, there was a very sharp dropoff on the part of some minority populations. 78 percent of the whites could successfully perform these somewhat harder tasks, but only 39.9 percent of the African-Americans, 57.4 percent of the Hispanics, 41.4 percent of the young adults who had not finished high school, and 23.4 percent of those who did not go to high school. As we consider yet harder tasks the general decline and the dropoff of the minority groups become acute. For example, only about 10 percent of the whites, 3 percent of the Hispanics, and 1 percent of the African-Americans could generate an unfamiliar theme from a short poem or orally interpret distinctions between two types of employee benefits.

Thus, we see that, based on this report, young adults did not have an "illiteracy" problem (80 percent of them could read as well as or better than the average eighth-grade student): rather, they had a "schooling" problem. As tasks became more complex and "school-like," less and less of the population could do them, with failure being most prominent among those less influenced by, and most poorly served by, the schools. The NAEP study, like nearly all such studies (U.S. Department of Education 1986; Walberg 1985), found that "home support" variables, such as parents' education and access to literacy materials, were significantly related to both the type and the amount of education a young adult was liable to have received and to the young adult's "literacy skills." The failure of schools to make up for these home-based differences has been a paramount feature of both the U.S. and the British educational systems throughout their histories.

For example, the Bristol Language Project in Great Britain (the most impressive longitudinal study of its type yet done) has been studying the language development of a representative sample of 129 children born in the Bristol area in the years 1969–70 and 1971–72 (Wells 1981, 1985, 1986). The school success of these children at age ten was found to relate most strongly to the children's preparedness for literacy upon entry to school, which in turn related to the children's social class. Far from removing differences these children brought with them from home, school was found to consolidate the social class differences. If the children's early home-based preparedness for literacy is still strongly predicting their success in school at age ten, then school itself is not having much of an impact, save "to make the rich richer and the poor poorer." Later research from the project showed that the success of these children at age fourteen in foreign-language classes correlated quite highly with their family backgrounds, e.g., social class and parental education (Skehan 1989: 31–34). There is absolutely no reason, from the current research, to believe that a comparable study in the United States, done today, would not result in similar findings.

So why was all this a crisis then, when the situation was, in fact, an historical one in our schools? And why is it a *literacy* crisis? On the face of the matter, it would seem to be a crisis of social justice rooted in the fact that we supply less good schools to poorer and more disadvantaged people, and better ones to more mainstream and advantaged people. The NAEP study itself points to the answer. By the second page of the text of the report, it says:

NAEP's decision to focus its attention on our country's approximately 21 million young adults aged 21 to 25 years recognizes the importance of this population—they are among the most recent entrants into the labor force and yet represent (after teenagers) the largest proportion of unemployed people in this country. Perhaps more important, projections indicate that the composition of this young-adult population will change in significant ways over the next decade. The total number of individuals aged 21 to 25 is expected to decrease from around 21 million to 17 million, but the total group will include a larger proportion of minority group members.

(p. xiv)

The passage moves, in a rather illogical way, from the unemployment rate of young adults to the changing demographic composition of the young adult population. Since the report predicts the young adult population, given the aging of our society, will decline in both real terms and in their percentage of the population, their unemployment rate would seem to take care of itself. However, the passage ends with the information that the young adult population, though smaller, will be composed overall of a greater percentage of minority-group members. So what? No more is said. Obviously, we are supposed to make some significant inference about the increase in minority members, an inference that the report is reluctant to spell out explicitly.

Since the reader of this passage must draw his or her own inferences, here are the ones I draw. Schools have historically failed with non-elite populations and have thereby replicated the social hierarchy. This has ensured that large numbers of lower socioeconomic and minority people engage in the lowest-level and least satisfying jobs in society, while being in a position to make few serious political or economic demands on the elites.

But the report predicts the future will hold a significant demographic change in the population: there will be more elderly people and fewer young ones, but among the young there will be a greater percentage of minority-group members than ever before, especially of those minorities who have traditionally been least well served by the schools. What will ensure that these minorities will not, as they take on a more significant social and political role in society, threaten the *status quo*—a *status quo* that will increasingly involve power, status, and wealth concentrated in the hands of older elites? What if they should demand, as their social and political significance in the society increases, real social change and real social justice? The answer lies in schools socializing these minorities, not to literacy *per se*, but to school-based literacy practices that carry within them values of quiescence and placidity, values that will ensure no real demands for significant social change, nor any serious questions about the power and status of the aging elites, such as embarrassing historical questions about how they obtained that power and status (Donald 1983; Macedo 2006).

It is fascinating now to look back at this discussion—composed in the late 1980s for a book that appeared in 1990. As I write this current edition (third), massive debates about immigration are raging across the United States, Great Britain, and Australia. On both the east and west coasts of the United States, non-Anglo populations are becoming the majority and they are fast catching up in the Midwest. The situation that I argued underlie the "literacy crisis" of the 1980s has come home to roost full-blown. The future the report predicted is here, save for the fact that, thanks in part to immigration, the number of young adults, especially non-white young adults, is higher than had been predicted.

Literacy crises: now

Alas—just as we would predict—I write now from the midst of yet another "literacy crisis." Report after report has been issued by govern-mental and other official organizations bemoaning the crisis and calling for solutions. And once again there is no real "literacy crisis," but deeper social and moral problems are at stake.

In 1998, the National Academy of Sciences' report *Preventing Reading Difficulties in Young Children* (Snow *et al.* 1998) appeared amidst much applause and approval from the public, politicians, and educational orga-nizations like AERA, IRA, and NCTE, organizations which, by and large, with some dissenting voices, celebrated the report in newsletters and sessions. The report served as the intellectual basis of the highly influen-tial *National Reading Report* (National Institute of Child Health and Development 2000), a report commissioned by the government and whose results have become a legal basis for what constitutes, for federal funding, "evidence-based" research in reading.

Let's look briefly at *Preventing Reading Difficulties in Young Children*. The report seems paradoxical and, at times, nearly contradictory. While it discusses a wide range of issues relevant to reading and classroom instruction, it devotes the lion's share of its focus to the importance of early phonemic awareness (children's conscious awareness that oral words are composed of individual sounds, or "phonemes") and sustained overt instruction on "phonics" (matching letters and sounds) for learning what the report calls "real reading." In a quick survey of the report's index, categories concerned with sound, decoding, and word recognition take up nearly as many headings and subheadings as all categories concerned with society, culture, families, poverty, race, comprehension, reading stories, narrative, language, learning, development, and related terms, combined. By my count, three are 244 headings and subheadings for the former and 275 for the latter.

The Academy's report is part of a long line of reports written in the now familiar "we have a crisis in our schools" genre. Unfortunately, the report has a hard time naming the crisis to which it is directed. Its authors are well aware there is, in fact, no "reading crisis" in the United States:

> average reading achievement has not changed markedly over the last 20 years (NAEP, 1997). And following a gain by black children from 1970 to 1980, the white–black gap has remained roughly constant for the last 16 years . . .
> . . . Americans do very well in international comparisons of reading—much better, comparatively speaking, than they do on math or science. In a 1992 study comparing reading skill levels among 9-year-olds in 18 Western nations, U.S. students scored among the highest levels and were second only to students in Finland . . .
> (Elley 1992: 97–98)

There is here, of course, already the hint of paradox. The report does not take note of how odd it is (or what implications it might have for reading) that a country could do very well in reading, but poorly in content areas like math and science. For the writers of the report, it is as if content (things like math and science) has nothing to do with reading and vice versa.

However, this paradox is endemic to the report as a whole. Note the report's remarks on the much discussed issue of the "fourth-grade slump":

> The "fourth-grade slump" is a term used to describe a widely encountered disappointment when examining scores of fourth graders in comparison to younger children (Chall *et al.* 1990). . . . It is not clear what the explanation is or even that there is a unitary explanation.
> (p. 78)

The fourth-grade dropoff problem is precisely the problem that lots of children learn to read in the early grades, but then cannot read school-based content (like math, science, and social science) in the later grades (*American Educator* 2003). The fourth-grade slump problem would, on the face of it, lead one to worry about what we mean by "learning to read" in the early grades and how and why this idea can become so detached from "reading to learn." No such worries plague the Academy's report. It assumes throughout that if children learn to engage in what the report calls "real reading" (i.e., decoding) they will thereafter be able to learn and succeed in school. But the fourth-grade slump problem amply demonstrates that this assumption is false.

The report's cavalier attitude towards the content of reading—that is, reading as reading *something* and not just reading generically to develop "reading skills"—can be seen, as well, in the following remark the report makes about comprehension:

> Tracing the development of reading comprehension to show the necessary and sufficient conditions to prevent reading difficulty is not as well researched as other aspects of reading growth. In fact, as Cain (1996) notes, "because early reading instruction emphasizes word recognition rather than comprehension, the less skilled comprehenders' difficulties generally go unnoticed by their classroom teachers.
>
> (p. 77)

Note the paradox here: The report acknowledges Cain's claim that we know too little about comprehension difficulties because research has concentrated on word recognition, but then the report goes on blithely to concentrate on decoding and word recognition, as if we can safely ignore our ignorance about difficulties in comprehension and make recommendations about reading instruction in the absence of such knowledge. Of course, the report does call for teaching comprehension skills, but the teaching it calls for is all generic (things like summarizing or asking oneself questions while reading). It is not rooted in any details about learning specific genres and practices and certainly not about learning different sorts of content (e.g., science, literature, or math).

Yet reading (and, for that matter, speaking) always and only occurs within specific practices and within specific genres in the service of specific purposes or content. And, indeed, it is precisely children's difficulties with using language and literacy within specific practices and genres that fuel the fourth-grade slump.

The Academy's report is well aware that, in the United States, poor readers are concentrated "in certain ethnic groups and in poor, urban neighborhoods and rural towns" (p. 98). In fact, this is the true "crisis" in reading in the United States, though one the report never focuses on. Here, too, we are faced with paradoxes. Let us return to the quote from the report with which we started:

> average reading achievement has not changed markedly over the last 20 years (NAEP 1997). And following a gain by black children from 1970 to 1980, the white–black gap has remained roughly constant for the last 16 years . . .
>
>   . . . Americans do very well in international comparisons of reading—much better, comparatively speaking, than they do on math or science. In a 1992 study comparing reading skill levels among 9-year-olds in 18 Western nations, U.S. students scored among the highest levels and were second only to students in Finland . . .
>
> (Elley 1992: 97–98)

Here the report mentions the now well known and much studied issue that, from the late 1960s to the early 1980s, the black–white gap, in IQ test scores and other sorts of test scores, including reading tests, was fast closing (Neisser 1998; Jencks and Phillips 1998). This heartening progress, especially in regard to achievement tests, ceased in the 1980s. One certainly would have thought that a reading report would care deeply about the factors that had been closing the black–white gap in reading scores. Clearly, these factors were, whatever else they were, powerful "reading interventions," since they significantly increased the reading scores of "at risk" children. But the report shows no such interest, presumably because these factors were social and cultural and not factors only narrowly germane to classroom instructional methods.

Though the matter is controversial (Neisser 1998; Jencks and Phillips 1998), these factors were, in all likelihood, closely connected to the sorts of social programs (stemming originally from Johnson's "War on Poverty") that were dismantled in the 1980s and 1990s (Grissmer *et al.* 1998: 221–223) and which were leading to less segregation in U.S. society. An approach like the Academy's that sees the key issue as "real reading" is not liable to see such social programs as central to a report on reading. Ironically, though, the progress made on reading tests during the time the black–white gap was closing was far greater, in quantitative terms (Hedges and Nowell, 1998), than the results of any of the interventions (e.g., early phonemic awareness training) that the report discusses and advocates.

The following remarks from the report are typical of the sense of paradox bordering on outright contradiction that pervades the report on the issue of poor and minority children:

> for students in schools in which more than 75 percent of all students received free or reduced-price lunches (a measure of high poverty), the mean score for students in the fall semester of first grade was at approximately the 44th percentile. By the spring of third grade, this difference had expanded significantly. Children living in high-poverty areas tend to fall further behind, regardless of their initial reading skill level.
>
> (p. 98)

If these children fall further and further behind "regardless of their initial reading skill level," how, then, can we help them by increasing their initial skill level at "real reading" through things like early phonemic awareness and overt instruction on decoding, as the report recommends?

Finally, we reach the issues of racism and power. It is widely believed that such issues are "merely political," not directly relevant to reading and reading research. The Academy's report is certainly written in such a spirit. But the fact of the matter is that racism and power are just as much cognitive issues as they are political ones. Children will not identify with—they will even disidentify with—teachers and schools that they perceive as hostile, alien, or oppressive to their home-based identities and (Holland and Quinn 1987).

Claude Steele's (Steele 1992; Steele and Aronson 1995, 1998) groundbreaking work clearly demonstrates that in assessment contexts where issues of race, racism, and stereotypes are triggered, the performance of even quite adept learners seriously deteriorates. (See Ferguson 1998 for an important extension of Steele's work.) Steele shows clearly that how people *read* when they are taking tests changes as their fear of falling victim to cultural stereotypes increases. To ignore these wider issues, while stressing such things as phonemic awareness built on controlled texts, is to ignore, not merely "politics," but what we know about learning and literacy, as well.

In fact, one can go further: Given Steele's work, it is simply wrong to discuss reading assessment, intervention, and instruction, as the Academy's report does, without discussing the pervasive *culture of inequality* that deskills poor and minority children and its implications for different types of assessments, interventions, and instruction. This is an empirical point, not (only) a political one.

The Academy's report does not define the "reading crisis" as a crisis of inequality, though it might well have done so. Rather, aware, as it is, that reading scores are not declining among the vast majority of the student population, the report takes the now fashionable tack that the "reading crisis" is really due to the increased demands for higher-level literacy in our technologically driven society:

> Of course, most children learn to read fairly well. In this report, we are most concerned with the large numbers of children in America whose educational careers are imperiled because they do not read well enough to ensure understanding and to meet the demands of an increasingly competitive economy. Current difficulties in reading largely originate from rising demands for literacy, not from declining absolute levels of literacy. In a technological society, the demands for higher literacy are ever increasing, creating more grievous consequences for those who fall short.

While this is a common argument today, it ignores the fact that modern science and technology, in fact, create many jobs in which literacy demands go down, not up, thanks to human skills being replaced by computers and other sorts of technological devices (Aronowitz and Cutler 1998; Aronowitz and DiFazio 1994; Carnoy *et al.* 1993; Mishel and Teixeira 1991). This is true not just for service sector jobs, but also for many higher-status jobs in areas like engineering and bioscience. Indeed, there is much controversy today as to which category is larger: jobs where science and technology has increased literacy demands or those where they have decreased them.

This remark, like the report as a whole, also ignores that fact that, in our technologically driven society, literacy is changing dramatically. What appears to be crucial for success now are abilities to deal with multimodal texts (texts which mix words and images), nonverbal symbols, and with technical systems within specific, and now usually highly collaborative, institutional practices. The Academy's report doggedly focuses on reading at the "Dick and Jane" level (albeit with, perhaps, more interesting texts), while calling for students prepared to work in the twenty-first century. In the coming world, we are going to face not just a fourth-grade dropoff problem, but a "life dropoff problem" as people at every age fail to be able to keep up with fast-paced change requiring multiple new literacies. The Academy's report pales to near insignificance in this context—ironically the only context in which the report acknowledges that we have a "reading crisis."

So what might the deeper problems and fears be—beyond "real reading"—that could explain the paradoxes in this report and the plethora of reports that have followed it? As in the literacy crisis of the 1980s, we still have the problem that school cannot make up for inequities that exist in society. Invention in communities and at the level of economic and social policies is necessary, not just new reading pedagogies. However, today, there is a new wrinkle.

Most developed countries have neo-liberal governments now. Neo-liberalism is a theory that everything should be on the market, that when products or services are offered off-market (for free)—e.g., via the government—they are poor and inefficient (Hayek 1996; von Mises 1997). Only the workings of markets ensure quality. This leaves a real dilemma about institutions like schools and hospitals. It seems cruel, indeed, to charge poor people fees they cannot afford for schooling and health. While there are some neo-liberals who, nonetheless, argue everyone should pay, some argue that we should supply necessary services to the poor (like schooling and health), but only at a basic level (D'Souza 2001). If better or more was offered, then markets for education and health care would be ruined. (Who would buy a good education in a private school or a rich suburb if it was available free?)

There is another issue, as well. In the 1980s, as the world economy became global, people predicted that workers in developed societies would have to become "knowledge workers," adept at producing knowledge, innovation, and dealing with technologies, in order to survive (Gee *et al.* 1996). However, the booming economy of the 1990s was slowed more by the absence of service workers than by the absence of knowledge workers (who could be, and were, imported from places like India). In fact, a great many of the new jobs created in the U.S. economy since the 1990s and into the twenty-first century have been low-level service jobs and other poorly paid jobs, not high-level professional and technical workers (Reich 1992, 2000). Thus, there are people who see the need for public schools to produce service workers, people with basic literacy, numeracy, and communicational skills. Families who want more can buy it from a private school or a good school in a rich suburb—or they can simply supply it themselves at home, as so commonly happens today in privileged homes, often via the use of modern digital technologies, to accelerate their children.

Crisis over literacy tells us that fears about literacy often mask deeper social and moral problems. However, for those of us who have "succeeded" at higher-level school-based literacy, it is hard not to believe that such literacy does not make inherently for better minds, better people (us), and a better society in and of itself. Thus, I turn in the next chapter to a consideration of the history of literacy, a history that makes the links between literacy, values, and politics all the clearer. But, first, here I want to turn to the relationship between literacy and social practices.

Literacy and social practices

You may be convinced by now that talk about "literacy" can often be an indirect way to talk about larger social and political issues. But you may very well see no reason not to consider literacy at the level of an individual as something that primarily concerns that individual's mental abilities. The traditional view of literacy has defined it in rather simple terms: literacy is the ability to read and (sometimes) to write. But, then, what is it to be able to read or write? Again, the traditional view has had a simple answer: to be able to read is to be able to decode writing; to be able to write is to be able to code language into a visual form. Of course, traditionalists realize that the reader has to attribute a meaning to the words and sentences of the text. The reader, that is, has to have an interpretation of the text or parts of it.

For traditionalists, interpretation is a matter of what goes on in the mind, that is, largely a psychological matter. If readers know the language, can decode writing, and have the requisite background "facts" to draw the inevitable inferences any writing requires, they can construct the "right" interpretation in their heads. And this "right" interpretation is (roughly) the "same" for all competent readers.

Of course, traditionalists know that there are "fancy" interpretations of texts like poems, riddles, novels, and sacred texts. But they argue that to read is, at a fundamental level, to have in one's head a "basic" interpretation, something that is often referred to as the "literal" interpretation of the text. "Fancier" interpretations are for "fancier" people, specialists (e.g., literary critics) and priests of various sorts.

In the 1980s a group of scholars began seriously to question such traditional views of literacy and the "literacy myth" as well (and we will discuss the "literacy myth" in the next chapter). They did this by asking anew the questions "What is literacy?" and "What is it good for?" In doing so, they started a new interdisciplinary field of study, one that is now often referred to as "the New Literacy Studies," a name that was first used in the 1990 edition of this book and in my work from the 1980s on which some of that text was based (e.g., see, among many other sources, Barton 1994, Barton and Hamilton 1998; Barton *et al.* 2000; Cazden 1988, 1992; Cook-Gumperz 1986; Gee 1988, 1989a, 1992; Gumperz

1982a, b; Halliday 1978; Halliday and Hasan 1989; Heath 1983; Hymes 1980; Kress 1985; Lankshear 1997; Lankshear with Lawler 1987, Lankshear and Knobel 2007; Luke 1988; Rose 1989; Scollon and Scollon 1981; Street 1984, 1993; Wells 1986; Wertsch 1991; Willinsky 1990; see also Larson and Marsh 2005; Pahl and Rowsell 2005, 2006; for related work from the perspective of social cognition, see Lave 1988; Lave and Wenger 1991; Rogoff 1990; Rogoff and Lave 1984; Scribner and Cole 1981; Tharp and Gallimore 1988).

The New Literacy Studies quickly hit on a paradox: It won't really do to define literacy simply as the ability to write and read. To see why this is so we need to run through a rather simple argument. The argument has something of the structure of a *reductio ad absurdum*. The traditional view of literacy takes literacy to be the psychologically defined ability to read and write. Our little argument starts with the assumption that reading (or writing) is central to literacy only to show that this very assumption itself leads to a view of literacy in which reading (or writing) plays a less central role than one might have thought. We will sketch the argument as it has to do with reading. There is an obvious analogue of the argument that starts with writing, rather than reading.

Here's the argument. Literacy surely means nothing unless it has something to do with the ability to read. "Read" is a transitive verb. So literacy must have something to do with being able to read something. And this something will always be a text of a certain type. Different types of texts (e.g. newspapers, comic books, law books, physics texts, math books, novels, poems, advertisements, etc.) call for different types of background knowledge and require different skills to be read meaning-fully.

To go one step further: No one would say anyone could read a given text if he or she did not know what the text meant. But there are many different levels of meaning one can give to or take from any text, many different ways in which any text can be read. You can read a friend's letter as a mere report, an indication of her state of mind, a prognosis of her future actions; you can read a novel as a typification of its period and place, as vicarious experience, as "art" of various sorts, as a guide to living, and so on and so forth.

Let me elaborate a bit further on this notion of reading texts in different ways by giving a concrete example. Consider the following sentences from a little story in which a man named "Gregory" has wronged his former girl friend Abigail: "Heartsick and dejected, Abigail turned to Slug with her tale of woe. Slug, feeling compassion for Abigail, sought out Gregory and beat him brutally." In one study (Gee 1989b,

1992–93), some readers (who happened to be African-Americans) claimed that these sentences "say" that Abigail told Slug to beat up Gregory. On the other hand, other readers (who happened not to be African-Americans) claimed that these sentences "say" no such thing. These readers claim, in fact, that the African-Americans have misread the sentences.

The African-Americans responded with remarks like the following: "If you turn to someone with a tale of woe, and, in particular, someone named 'Slug', you are most certainly asking him to do something in the way of violence and you are most certainly responsible when he's done it."

The point is that these different people read these sentences in different ways and think that others have read them in the "wrong" way. Even if one thinks that the African-Americans (or the others) have read the sentences "incorrectly," the very act of claiming their reading is incorrect admits that there is another way to read the sentences and that we can dispute how (in what way) the sentences ought to be read (and we can ask who determines the "ought" here, and why). If we say that the African-Americans have gone too far "beyond" the text (or the others not "far" enough), we still, then, are conceding that there is an issue of "how far" to go, what counts as a way (or the way) of reading a text.

Thus, so far, we have concluded that whatever literacy has to do with reading, reading must be spelled out, at the very least, as multiple abilities to "read" texts of certain types in certain ways or to certain levels . There are obviously many abilities here, each of them a type of literacy, one of a set of literacies.

The next stage of the argument asks: How does one acquire the ability to read a certain type of text in a certain way? Here proponents of a sociocultural approach to literacy argue that the literature on the acquisition and development of literacy is clear (Cazden 1992, 2001; Garton and Pratt 1989; Gonzalez *et al.* 2005; Heath 1983; John-Steiner *et al.* 1994; Schieffelin and Gilmore 1985; Scollon and Scollon 1981; Taylor, 1983; Taylor and Dorsey-Gaines 1987; Teale and Sulzby 1986; Lave 1988; Lave and Wenger 1991; Moll 1990; Wenger 1998; Wells 1986): a way of reading a certain type of text is acquired, when it is acquired in a "fluent" or "native-like" way, only by one's being embedded (apprenticed) as a member of a social practice wherein people not only read texts of this type in this way, but also talk about such texts in certain ways, hold certain attitudes and values about them, and socially interact over them in certain ways.

Thus, one does not learn to read texts of type X in way Y unless one has had experience in settings where texts of type X are read in way Y.

These settings are various sorts of social institutions, like churches, banks, schools, government offices, or social groups with certain sorts of interests, like baseball cards, comic books, chess, politics, novels, movies or what have you. One has to be socialized into a practice to learn to read texts of type X in way Y, a practice other people have already mastered. Since this is so, we can turn literacy on its head, so to speak, and refer crucially to the social institutions or social groups that have these practices, rather than to just the practices themselves. When we do this, something odd happens: the practices of such social groups are never just literacy practices. They also involve ways of talking, interacting, thinking, valuing, and believing.

Worse yet, when we look at the practices of such groups, it is next to impossible to separate anything that stands apart as a literacy practice from other practices. Literacy practices are almost always fully integrated with, interwoven into, constituted part of, the very texture of wider practices that involve talk, interaction, values, and beliefs (Barton and Hamilton 1998; Barton et al. 2000; Cook-Gumperz 1986; Heath 1983; Scollon and Scollon 1981; Shuman 1986; Scribner and Cole 1981). You can no more cut the literacy out of the overall social practice, or cut away the non-literacy parts from the literacy parts of the overall practice, than you can subtract the white squares from a chessboard and still have a chessboard.

People who take a sociocultural approach to literacy believe that the "literacy myth"—the idea that literacy leads inevitably to a long list of "good" things—is a "myth" because literacy in and of itself, abstracted from historical conditions and social practices, has no effects, or, at least, no predictable effects. Rather, what has effects are historically and culturally situated social practices of which reading and writing are only bits, bits that are differently composed and situated in different social practices. For example, school-based writing and reading lead to different effects than reading and writing embedded in various religious practices (Kapitzke 1995; Scribner and Cole 1981). And, further, there are multiple school-based practices and multiple religious practices, each with multiple effects.

The aspirin bottle problem

There is a common objection to the sort of approach to literacy I am arguing for here, and, indeed, to "academic" discussions of literacy in general. I call this objection "the aspirin bottle problem." The objection, often made by proponents of "functional literacy" programs and people concerned with "adult literacy," runs as follows: All this "fancy stuff" about types of text and ways of meaning, about social context and ideology, is fine and dandy, but we are dealing with people who can't read the back of an aspirin bottle (because it is written at a tenth-grade level or whatever) and thus could poison themselves or their children. What have fancy theories about "social practices" got to do with the back of an aspirin bottle? It is one thing to talk about the multiple ways of reading, and the depths of, a novel like James Joyce's *Ulysses*, but this isn't relevant to unemployed and underemployed adults who can't read the back of an aspirin bottle. There's only one way to read the warning on a bottle, and fancy theories in linguistics or literary criticism aren't relevant or helpful here.

Actually, I have a fair bit of sympathy for the aspirin bottle problem, and believe that it raises important questions. Hence, let us turn at once to the back of an aspirin bottle. (The warning changes from time to time, see Chapter 5 for another version.)

> WARNING: Keep this and all medication out of the reach of children. As with any drug, if you are pregnant or nursing a baby, seek the advice of a health professional before using this product. In the case of accidental overdosage, contact a physician or poison control center immediately.

Now, apart from whatever level this is written at, it is strange language indeed. First, it says it is a "warning," but it certainly doesn't look like a regular warning. A warning alerts one to danger in a rather more direct fashion than this. This "warning" has other odd aspects as well. For instance, it keeps alluding to the fact that it applies not just to this medication, but to all medication ("and all medication," "as with any drug"). The phrase "as with any drug," in particular, because of its syntactic structure and positioning, implies that the generalization "all drugs, including this one, are dangerous to children and pregnant women" is shared, common knowledge. The whole message in fact implies that it is meant primarily for readers who already know what it has to say.

Note also the contrast between "health professional" in the case of pregnant women, but "physician" in the case of overdosage. Presumably, this contrast assumes that the reader is the sort of person who knows that the category of health providers that work with pregnant women is wider than those that deal with poisonings in emergency rooms. And then note the word "accidental" used before "overdosage": Are we to assume that if someone has taken an overdose on purpose we shouldn't call a physician or poison control?

And, then too, what does "immediately" mean: the dosage information on the bottle says that one should take no more than eight pills in twenty-four hours. Does this mean that if I (inadvertently, of course) take nine or ten in twenty-four hours, I should at once call a doctor? Or should I wait for symptoms? If so, then I am not calling immediately.

And, finally, in my dictionary at least, I can't find the word "overdosage"—why, for heaven's sake didn't the writer of this "warning" use the common English word "overdose," rather than the pretentious "overdosage"?

Of course, we all realize what is going one here. The company does not want to highlight the word "dangerous" on its bottle. It wants to forestall suits by people who do things they know they shouldn't, as well as from people who are sensitive to the medicine and thus could poison themselves by a dose that would be reasonable for others. Further, it wants to create the image that the reader is an intelligent, mainstream person living in a world in which people do not abuse drugs (and "overdose," rather than "overdosage," perhaps suggests too directly the sordid world of drug abusers).

Thus, this warning can be read (interpreted) in the following manner, which, I would argue, is a perfectly "natural" reading (interpretation) of the text (though, of course, not the only one):

> You whom this warning is primarily addressed to already know you shouldn't give adult medication to children, or take medication when pregnant or nursing, or take an "overdosage." You already know in fact that drugs like this one are potent medicine that can do harm. But if you, through negligence, act stupidly and so against your knowledge (as we all do sometimes) don't blame us, we warned you. If you are not this sort of person, then you probably aren't reading or at least paying attention to this label, but don't let your lawyer say in court we didn't warn you (officially speaking). If you are unluckily sensitive to this drug and even a small amount harms you, we did say anything over eight is technically speaking an "overdosage," and so you were warned too. We certainly do not want you to hurt yourself, and we would like the world to be a nice mainstream sort of place: in fact, both these things favor our selling more of this medicine, which is our primary interest.

Now what does "reading the aspirin bottle" mean? I think everyone will agree we must go beyond simple decoding. The way the bottle leaves generalizations about drugs implicit as assumed knowledge would lead us to conclude that, at the very least, we would have to teach someone these generalizations in order for them to "read" the bottle. That is, we would have to teach them the sorts of things which people whom this label is primarily addressed to know, or think they know, about medication in general and aspirin in particular.

But how far beyond this do we go? Do we need to teach them about the ways in which certain aspects of the text are used to set up a particular social relationship, or the ways in which these implicate a whole set of values about people and society? Does one need to know these in order to have "read" the bottle? Do we need, in our "reading lesson," to engage the "reader" in thinking about drug companies, social relations, and the structure of society?

But, it will be said, at once, to answer "yes" to these questions is to render reading and literacy political and ideological. Indeed. To deny the "reader" this way of reading, to pretend that the label has no ideological intent, that it is a "simple" message ("Watch out for aspirin!"), is also political—it is a pretense that only drugs and not drug companies have social effects, enter into possibly harmful relationships with people.

The warnings on the back of aspirin bottles are texts of a certain type that can be read in different ways, more or less deeply, for different interests and concerns, like all texts—they are just as "fancy" as poems and novels. All texts are fully implicated in values and social relations. (In Chapter 5 I discuss the newer and longer warnings on current aspirin bottles.) One learns to read aspirin bottles in the way I did above by being apprenticed to a social group that reads in this way (and talks, acts, and values in certain ways in regard to such texts). Any way of reading the aspirin bottle involves apprenticeship to some social group that reads (acts, talks, values) in certain ways in regard to such texts. (There is no "neutral," "asocial," "apolitical" reading.) So the choice, in any "literacy" program, will always be. What sort of social group do I intend to apprentice the learner into?

So to sum up the main point and to conclude this chapter: Texts and the various ways of reading them do not flow full-blown out of the individual soul (or biology); they are the social and historical inventions of various groups of people. One always learns to interpret texts of a certain type in certain ways only through having access to, and ample experience in, social settings where texts of that type are read in those ways. One is socialized or enculturated into a certain social practice. In fact, each of us is socialized into many such groups and social institutions. (Consider social institutions like churches, banks, schools, government offices; or groups defined around certain interests, whether politics, comic books, or the environment; or groups defined around certain places like the local bar, community centers, the courts, or the street for certain sorts of adolescent peer groups.)

But what about the question as to whether literacy can be used as a tool for liberation, or are we endlessly trapped in replicating the given social *status quo* through enacting the social practices that instantiate it? This question is in reality not a question about literacy, at least as literacy is traditionally conceived. The question comes down to whether the various social groups and institutions that underwrite various types of texts and ways of interpreting them can be changed.

Schools are a crucial instance of these social institutions. It is in school that each of us is socialized into practices which go beyond the home and peer group and initiate us into the "public sphere," at least in much of the Western world (Sennett 1974). Schools mediate (Vygotsky 1978) between what we might call "community-based" social institutions (and their literacies) and public institutions (and their literacies). The question then crucially involves, also, the issue of whether schools can be changed. I don't have the answer, but I believe that the following remark of Raymond Williams's leads the way:

> It is only in a shared belief and insistence that there are practical alternatives that the balance of forces and chances begins to alter. Once the inevitabilities are challenged, we begin gathering our resources for a journey of hope. If there are no easy answers there are still available discoverable hard answers, and it is these that we can now learn to make and share. This has been, from the beginning, the sense and the impulse of the long revolution.
>
> (Williams 1983: 268–269)

Chapter 3

The literacy myth and the history of literacy

The literacy myth

Now and throughout history, language has seemed to us a large part of what makes us human and what distinguishes us from other creatures on earth. Literacy, on the other hand, has played a different role (Gee 2004; Graff 1981a, b; 1987a, b, Goody 1977, 1986; Goody and Watt 1963; Graff and Arnove 1987; Musgrove 1982; Olson 1977; Ong 1982; Pattison 1982; Scribner and Cole 1981). Across history and across various cultures, literacy has seemed to many people what distinguishes one kind of person from another kind of person. Literate people, it is widely believed, are more intelligent, more modern, more moral. Countries with high literacy rates are better developed, more modern, better behaved. Literacy, it is felt, freed some of humanity from a "primitive" state, from an earlier stage of human development. If language is what makes us human, literacy, it seems, is what makes us "civilized."

Claims for the powers of literacy are, indeed, yet more specific than this. Literacy leads to logical, analytical, critical, and rational thinking, general and abstract uses of language, skeptical and questioning attitudes, a distinction between myth and history, a recognition of the importance of time and space, complex and modern governments (with separation of church and state), political democracy and greater social equity, a lower crime rate, better citizens, economic development, wealth and productivity, political stability, urbanization, and a lower birth rate.

This is, indeed, quite a list. But there are those who dispute this omnipotent view of literacy. They refer to it as a "myth"—"the literacy myth" (Graff 1979, 1987a, b). There is, we will see below, precious little historical evidence for these claims about literacy. And where such evidence does exist, the role of literacy is always much more complex and contradictory, more deeply intertwined with other factors, than the literacy myth allows.

As the final products of nearly 4,000 years of an alphabetic literacy, we all tend to believe strongly in the powerful and redeeming effects of literacy, especially in times of complex social and economic crises (Goody and Watt 1963; Goody 1977; Havelock 1963, 1976; Olson 1977; Ong 1982). The literacy myth is, in fact, one of the "master myths" of our society; it is foundational to how we make sense of reality, though it is not necessarily an accurate reflection of that reality, nor does it necessarily lead to a just, equitable, and humane world.

Plato

It is significant that the first shot in the battle against the literacy myth was fired a bare 300 years or so after the invention of alphabetic literacy. And, in many ways the first shot was the best; it was, at any rate, pregnant with implications for the thousands of years of literacy that have followed it. The Greeks invented the basis of Western literacy, and Plato was one of the first great writers in Western culture (in fact, his dialogues were both great literature and great discursive, expository writing).

Plato has also the distinction of being the first writer to attack writing in writing, primarily in his brilliant dialogue the *Phaedrus*. (All quotations, and page and line references, to Plato's dialogue below are from Rowe 1986; see also Burger 1980; Derrida 1972; De Vries 1969; Griswold 1986.) To start with, Plato thought writing led to the deterioration of human memory and a view of knowledge that was both facile and false. Given writing, knowledge no longer had to be internalized, made "part of oneself." Rather, writing allowed, perhaps even encouraged, reliance on the written text as an "external crutch" or "reminder." For Plato, one knew only what one could reflectively defend in face-to-face dialogue with someone else. The written text tempted one to take its words as authoritative and final, because of its illusory quality of seeming to be explicit, clear, complete, closed, and self-sufficient, i.e., "unanswerable" (precisely the properties which have been seen as the hallmarks of the essay and so-called "essayist literacy," see Scollon and Scollon 1981).

In addition to these flaws in writing there are two others which are far more important to Plato. To cite the dialogue, the first of these is:

SOCRATES: ... I think writing has this strange feature, which makes it like painting. The offspring of painting stand there as if alive, but if you ask them something, they preserve a quite solemn silence. Similarly with written words: you might think that they spoke as if they had some thought in their heads, but if you ever ask them about any of the things they say out of a desire to learn, they point to just one thing, the same thing each time.

(275 d 4–e 1)

Socrates goes on immediately to the second charge:

> And when once it is written, every composition is trundled about everywhere in the same way, in the presence both of those who know about the subject and of those who have nothing at all to do with it, and it does not know how to address those it should address and not those it should not. When it is ill-treated and unjustly abused, it always needs its father to help it; for it is incapable of defending or helping itself.

(275 e 1–275 e 6)

These charges are connected: what writing can't do is defend itself; it can't stand up to questioning. For Plato true knowledge comes about when one person makes a statement and another asks, "What do you mean?" Such a request forces speakers to "re-say," say in different words, what they mean. In the process they come to see more deeply what they mean, and come to respond to the perspective of another voice/viewpoint. In one sense, writing can only respond to the question of "What do you mean?" by repeating what it has said, the text itself.

It is at this juncture of the argument that Plato extends his charges against writing to an attack also on rhetoricians and politicians—he referred to both as "speech writers." They sought, in their writing and speeches, to forestall questioning altogether, since their primary interest was to persuade through language that claimed to be logically complete and self-sufficient, standing in no need of supplement or rethinking, authoritative in its own right, not to mutually discover the truth in dialogue.

However, there is a sense in which writing can respond to the question "What do you mean?" It can do so by readers "re-saying," saying in other words, namely their own words, what the text means. But this is a problem, not a solution, for Plato. It is, in fact, part of what he has in mind when he says that writing "does not know how to address those it should address and not those it should not." By its very nature writing can travel in time and space away from its "author" (for Plato, its "father") to be read by just anyone, interpreted however they will, regardless of the reader's training, effort or ignorance (witness what happened to Nietzsche in the hands of the Nazis; to the Bible in the hands of those who have used it to justify wealth, racism, imperialism, war and exploitation). The voice behind the text cannot respond or defend itself. And it cannot vary its substance and tone to speak differently to different readers based on their natures and contexts.

Plato was too sophisticated to make a crude distinction, so popular today, between speech and writing, orality and literacy. He extended his attack on writing, rhetoricians, and politicians yet further to include the poets, in particular Homer, the great representative of the flourishing oral culture that preceded Greek literacy. The oral culture stored its knowledge, values, and norms in great oral epics (e.g., the *Iliad* and the *Odyssey*), passed down from generation to generation. To ensure that these epics were not lost to memory, and with them the cultural knowledge and values they stored, they had to be highly memorable. Thus, they were highly dramatic (built around action) and rhythmical (a species of song), features that facilitate human memory. That is, they had to be a form of poetry (Havelock 1963; Ong 1982). But, Plato argued, the oral tradition via its very drama and poetry lulled the Greeks to sleep and encouraged them to "take for granted" the content of the epics, thus allowing them to accept uncritically the traditional values of their culture.

The oral epic could not stand up to the question "What do you mean?" either. Such a question was a request to poets to "re-say" their words in a different form, to take them out of poetry and put them into prose, and the words thereby lost the power which had lulled the Greeks into a "dream state" (Havelock 1963). In fact, here writing facilitated the critical process. Once written down, the epics could be scanned at leisure, various parts of the text could be juxtaposed, and in the process contradictions and inconsistencies were all the easier to find, no longer hiding under the waves of rhythm and the limitations of human aural memory (Havelock 1963; Ong 1982; Goody 1977, 1986, 1988).

Plato's deeper attack, then, is against any form of language or thought that cannot stand up to the question "What do you mean?" That question is an attempt to unmask attempts to persuade, whether by poets, rhetoricians, or politicians, based on self-interested claims to authority or traditionalism, and not on a genuine disinterested search for truth. In this regard, he reminds one of the currently popular Russian writer, Bakhtin (1981, 1986):

Bakhtin continually sought and found unexpected ways to show that people never utter a final word, only a penultimate one. The opportunity always remains for appending a qualification that may lead to yet another unanticipated dialogue. . . .

Perhaps the sudden and dramatic interest in Bakhtin arises from his emphasis on debate as open, fruitful, and existentially meaningful at a time when our theoretical writings have become increasingly closed, repetitive, and "professional." . . . Genuine dialogue always presupposes that something, but not everything, can be known. "It should be noted," Bakhtin wrote . . . "that both relativism and dogmatism equally exclude all argumentation, all authentic dialogue, by making it either unnecessary (relativism) or impossible (dogmatism)."

(Morson 1986: vii–viii)

Plato, then, thought that only dialogic thought, speaking, and writing were authentic, with the proviso that writing was inherently prone to anti-dialogic properties. Plato's own resolution to this conflict, as a writer, was to write dialogues and to warn that writing of any sort should never be taken too seriously. It should never be taken as seriously as the "writing" that is "written together with knowledge in the soul of the learner, capable of defending itself, and knowing how to speak and keep silent in relation to the people it should" (276 a 5–a 8). In fact, for Plato, authentic uses of language were always educational in the root sense of "drawing out" of oneself and others what was good, beautiful, and true.

All this may make Plato sound like a progressive educator defending discussion, collaboration, and inquiry. He was no such thing. Plato's concerns about writing had a darker, more political side, one pregnant for the future of literacy.

Both Socrates and Plato were opponents of the traditional order of their societies, and in that sense revolutionaries. In the *Republic*, Plato drew a blueprint for a utopian, "perfect" state, the sort which he wished to put in the place of the current order. Plato's perfect state was an authoritarian one based on the view that people are, by and large, born suited to a particular place in a naturally given hierarchy, with "philosopher-kings" (i.e. Plato or people like him) at the top. At the very least, people should be given differential access to higher places in society based on their inborn characteristics and various tests. The philosopher-kings rule in the best interests of those below them, many of whom have no actual say in government, the philosopher-king knowing their interests better than they do.

Homer, the rhetoricians, and the politicians can be seen as Plato's political opposition, competitors to the philosopher-king's assertion to power. In the case of Homer, as long as Greek culture was swept away in rhapsody by Homer's epic verse, its members were not listening to either the oral or the written dialogues of Plato.

In this light, Plato's attack on writing takes on additional meaning. His objection that the written text can get into the wrong hands, that it cannot defend itself, is an objection to the fact that the reader can freely interpret the text without the author ("authority") being able to "correct" that interpretation. In this sense, Plato wants the author to stand as a voice behind the text not (just) to engage in responsive dialogue, but to enforce canonical interpretations. And these canonical interpretations are rendered correct by the inherently higher nature of the philosopher-king, backed up by the advantages (which the *Republic* ensures) of socially situated power and state-supported practice in verbal and literacy skills (which the United States and many other countries today ensure that the children of the economically elite get).

As a writer, Plato also had a resolution to this problem, the problem of how to enforce "correct" interpretations. First, he believed that his writings should by and large be restricted to his own inner circle of students and followers. Second, it appears he may not have actually written down his most serious thoughts, but only spoken them. (None of his dialogues contain a discussion between two equally mature philosophers.) And, finally, he built into his written dialogues various layers of meaning such that they announce their deeper message only to those readers skilled enough to find it, where this skill is tied to being trained (or "initiated") so as to interpret the way one is "supposed" to (Griswold 1986)—the same strategy is used in many sacred writings, e.g. the New Testament (Kermode 1979).

Plato's ultimate solution, however, would have been the instantiation of the society delineated in the *Republic*, where the structure of the state and its institutions would have ensured "correct" interpretations. As we will see, this last solution is the one that has in fact been realized most often in history, though not by states realizing all the other aspects of the *Republic*.

There is a contradiction here. In Plato we see two sides to literacy: literacy as liberator and literacy as weapon. Plato wants to ensure that there is always a voice behind the spoken or written text that can dialogically respond, but he also wants to ensure that this voice is not overridden by respondents who are careless, ignorant, lazy, self-interested, or ignoble. One must somehow empower the voice behind the text, privilege it, at least to the extent of ruling out some interpretations and some interpreters (readers/listeners). And such a ruling out will always be self-interested to the extent that it must be based on some (privileged) view of what the text means, what correct interpretations are, and who are acceptable readers, where acceptable readers will perforce include the one making the ruling.

The ruling is also self-interested in that it has a political dimension, an assertion to power, a power that may reside in institutions that seek to enforce it, whether modern schools and universities or Plato's governing classes in the *Republic*. But then we are close to an authority that kills dialogue by dictating who is to count as a respondent and what is to count as a response.

There is, however, no easy way out of this dilemma: If all inter-pretations ("re-sayings") count, then none does, as the text then says everything and therefore nothing. And if it takes no discipline, expe-rience, or "credentials" to interpret, then it seems all interpretations will count. If they can't all count, then someone has to say who does and who does not have the necessary "credentials" to interpret. A desire to honor the thoughtful and critical voice behind the text, to allow it to defend itself (often coupled with a will to power), leads us to Plato's authoritarianism. In fleeing it we are in danger of being led right into the lap of Plato's poets, speech writers, and politicians. For them, all that counts is the persuasiveness or cunning of their language, its ability to capture readers or listeners, to tell them what they want to hear, to validate the *status quo*. Their interest is decidedly not in the capacity of their language to educate in the root sense discussed above.

Religion and literacy

There have been many facile attempts to get out of Plato's dilemma. But there is no easy way out. Lévi-Strauss has argued that what creates and energizes mythology is the existence of a real contradiction that cannot in reality be removed, e.g., life and death, nature and culture, God and human (Lévi-Strauss 1979). The contradiction can only be continually worked over by the imagination in an ultimately vain, but temporarily satisfying, attempt to remove it. Plato's dilemma is real and the literacy myth can be seen as a response to it.

Virtually every aspect of the history of literacy since Plato can be read as a commentary on Plato's thoughts. This can be seen clearly if we consider the ground-breaking work of Harvey Graff on the history of literacy (1979, 1981a, b, 1987a, b). The central contradiction that emerges in that history is the disparity between the claims in the literacy myth and the actual history of literacy, much of it produced by people who firmly believed in the literacy myth. Let us take one snapshot from the history of literacy, though a particularly revealing one: Sweden (Graff 1987b).

Sweden was the first country in the West to achieve near-universal literacy, having done so before the end of the eighteenth century. It was also unprecedented in that women had equality with men in literacy, an equality that still does not exist in most of the world today. By the tenets of the literacy myth, Sweden should have been an international example of modernization, social equality, economic development, and cognitive growth. In fact it was no such thing.

Sweden's remarkable achievement took place in a land of widespread poverty, for the most part without formal institutional schooling, and it neither followed from nor stimulated economic development. Sweden achieved its impressive level of reading diffusion without writing, which did not become a part of popular literacy until the mid-nineteenth century.

So how did Sweden manage the feat of universal literacy? The Swedish literacy campaign, one of the most successful in the Western world, was stimulated by the Reformation and Lutheran Protestantism. Teaching was done on a household basis (hence the emphasis on the literacy of women), supervised and reinforced by the parish church and clergy, with regular compulsory examinations (Johansson 1977; Graff 1987b: 149).

The goal of literacy in Sweden was the promotion of Christian faith and life; the promotion of character and citizenship training in a religiously dominated state. The campaign was based not just on compulsion, but on a felt religious need on the part of the individual, a need internalized in village reading and family prayers. Religious, social, and political ideologies were transmitted to virtually everyone through literacy learning. The Church Law of 1686 stated that children, farmhands, and maidservants should "learn to read and see with their own eyes what God bids and commands in His Holy Word" (Graff 1987b: 150). Note the phrase "with their own eyes": literally they see it with their own eyes, figuratively they see it through the eyes of the state church, which dictates how it is to be seen.

Plato's dilemma haunts us. The people are given the text for themselves, but then something must ensure they see it "right"—not in reality through their own eyes, but rather from the perspective of an authoritative institution that delimits correct interpretations. Clearly, in this case, the individual reader does not need any very deep comprehension skills, and surely doesn't need to write.

This problem—that people might not see the text in the "right" way—was a problem in both Protestant and Catholic countries, but the two hit on somewhat different solutions. Catholic-dominated countries were much more reluctant to put the Bible and other sacred texts into the hands of the people, for fear they would not interpret them correctly (for example, they might use them as the basis for political or religious dissent). Catholic countries preferred to leave interpretation to the oral word of Church authorities. When the Catholic Church did allow sacred texts into the hands of the people, it attempted to fix their meaning by orthodox exposition and standardized religious illustrations (Graff 1987b: 147).

As a result of these different attitudes, Catholic countries tended to be behind areas of intense Protestant piety (such as Sweden, lowland Scotland, New England, Huguenot French centers, and places within Germany and Switzerland). But we should ask: Is there any essential difference between the sort of literacy in eighteenth and nineteenth-century Sweden and a country with quantitatively more restricted literacy, but equally dominant modes of interpretation ensconced in their powerful religious and civil institutions? Some would argue that there is a difference and that the difference is in the capacity of literacy to give rise to dissent and critical awareness (Plato's liberating, dialogic side to language) and not in the actual reality of eighteenth and nineteenth-century Catholic France and Protestant Sweden, for instance.

Literacy, "higher-order cognitive abilities," and schools

What are the capacities of literacy? That is the heart of the matter. The example of Sweden raises deep questions about the literacy myth, but we are still left with the question: What good does (could?) literacy do? It has been assumed for centuries that literacy gives rise to higher-order cognitive abilities, to more analytic and logical thought than is typical of oral cultures. However, this almost commonsense assumption is disputed by ground-breaking work on the Vai in Liberia, carried out by the psychologists Sylvia Scribner and Michael Cole (1981).

Among the Vai, literacy and schooling don't always go together. There are three sorts of literacy among the Vai, with some people having none, one, two, or all three: (1) English literacy acquired in formal school settings; (2) an indigenous Vai script (syllabic, not alphabetic) transmitted outside an institutional setting (i.e. among peers and family) and with no connection with Western-style schooling; and (3) a form of literacy in Arabic.

Scribner and Cole found that neither syllabic Vai literacy nor Arabic alphabetic literacy is associated with what have been considered higher-order intellectual skills as these are tested by our typical school-based tests. Neither of these types of literacy enhanced the use of taxonomic skills, nor did either contribute to a shift toward syllogistic reasoning. In contrast, literacy in English, the only form associated with formal schooling of the Western sort, was associated with some types of decontextualization and abstract reasoning.

However, after English literates had been out of school a few years, they did better than nonliterates only on verbal explanation tasks ("talking about" tasks). They did no better on actual problem solving, e.g., on categorization and abstract reasoning tasks. School skills, beyond talk, are transitory, unless they are repeatedly practiced in people's daily lives. In the Scribner and Cole study, literacy in and of itself led to no grandiose cognitive abilities, and formal schooling ultimately led to rather specific abilities that are rather useless without institutions which reward "expository talk in contrived situations" (such as schools, courts, bureaucracies).

Any discussion of jobs and education brings us immediately to the question of the point of education. The history of literacy shows that education has not, for the most part, been directed primarily at vocational training or personal growth and development. Rather, it has stressed behaviors and attitudes appropriate to good citizenship and moral behavior, largely as these are perceived by the elites of the society. And this has often meant, especially over the last century, different sorts of behaviors and attitudes for different classes of individuals: docility, discipline, time management, honesty, and respect for the lower classes, suiting them for industrial or service jobs; verbal and analytical skills, "critical thinking," discursive thought and writing for the higher classes, suiting them for management jobs.

While there have been, since the 1970s, rampant changes in global capitalism, it remains to see how these will play out in terms of schooling and access to its "higher forms" (Gee *et al.* 1996). Many industrial jobs have now been out-sourced to low-cost centers (e.g., Mexico, Thailand, India, China), leaving many people to argue our schools are still producing people for an old economic structure that has now changed significantly. I argued above that one reason we leave our school structures intact, at least in urban public schools, is the need for service workers in developed global economies. (Think, for instance, of the economic power of Wal-Mart and other superstores that pay their employees less than living wages.)

There is ample evidence that, in contemporary U.S. schools, tracking systems, which are pervasive, have exactly the effect of distributing different skills and different values to different "kinds" of people. In a massive study of tracking in junior and senior high schools across the United States, Jeannie Oakes found that a student's race, class, or family-based access to knowledge about college and career routes has more to do with what track the student ends up in than does inherent intelligence or actual potential (Oakes 1985; see also Oakes 2005). Once in a lower track, however, a child almost always stays there, and eventually behaves in ways that appear to validate the track the child is in (Rose 1989).

Oakes cites a number of typical interview responses on the part of students and teachers to questions about the teaching and learning that go on in classes at various tracks. These responses eloquently speak to the shaping of social inequality in schools. They demonstrate clearly the way in which two quite different sorts of literacy are being taught, one stressing thinking for oneself and suited to higher positions in the social hierarchy and one stressing deference and suited to lower positions. Some examples, taken at random from the book (Oakes 1985: 85–89):

> What are the . . . most critical things you [the teacher] want the students in your class to learn?

>> Deal with thinking activities—Think for basic answers—essay-type questions.
>>> (High-track English—junior high)

>> To think critically—to analyze—ask questions.
>>> (High-track Social Science—junior high)

>> Ability to use reading as a tool—e.g., how to fill out forms, write a check, get a job.
>>> (Low-track English—junior high)

>> To be able to work with other students. To be able to work alone. To be able to follow directions.
>>> (Low-track English—junior high)

> What is the most important thing you [the student] have learned?

>> To know how to communicate with my teachers like friends and as teachers at the same time. To have confidence in myself other than my skills and class work.
>>> (High-track English—junior high)

I have learned to form my own opinion on situations. I have also learned to not be swayed so much by another person's opinion but to look at both opinions with an open mind. I know now that to have a good solid opinion on a subject I must have facts to support my opinion. Decisions in later life will probably be made easier because of this.

(High-track English—senior high)

I have learned about many things like having good manners, respecting other people, not talking when the teacher is talking.

(Low-track English—junior high)

In this class, I have learned manners.

(Low-track English—junior high)

The most striking continuity in the history of literacy is the way in which literacy has been used, in age after age, to solidify the social hierarchy, empower elites, and ensure that people lower on the hierarchy accept the values, norms, and beliefs of the elites, even when it is not in their self-interest or group interest to do so (Gramsci 1971). Our new global capitalism may well change the sorts of skills and values the society wishes to distribute to "lower" and "higher" "kinds" of people, but, without strong resistance, it will not eradicate these "kinds." Indeed, it can be argued that the new hypercompetitive, science and technology-driven global capitalism will need three classes of workers, leading to three classes of students: poorly paid service workers; "knowledge workers" who must bring technical, collaborative, and communicational skills to the workplace and commit themselves body and soul to the company and its "core values" under conditions of little stability; and, finally, leaders and "symbol analysts" (Reich 1992; see also Reich 2000) who create innovations and "core values" and who will benefit most from the new capitalism (Drucker 1993; Gee et al. 1996). Reich (1992) estimates that three-fifths or more of workers will fall into the first category.

The history of literacy can be looked at as a "great debate." On the one side are elites (whether social, religious, economic, or hereditary) arguing that the lower classes should not be given literacy, because it will make them unhappy with their lot, politically critical and restive, and unwilling to do the menial jobs of society. On the other side are elites who argue that literacy will not have this effect. Rather, they argue, if literacy is delivered in the right moral and civil framework, one that upholds the values of the elites, it will make the lower classes accept those values and seek to behave in a manner more like the middle classes (i.e. they will become more "moral" and "better citizens"). This debate, carried out in quite explicit terms, goes on well into the nineteenth century and the beginning of the twentieth (Donald 1983).

In today's modern "post-industrial" societies the older contrast between literate elites and the nonliterate masses has simply become a highly stratified social ranking based not on literacy *per se*, but on the degree to which one controls a certain type of school-based literacy (in speech and behavior, as well as writing). This school-based literacy is associated with the values and aspirations of what Bernstein has called the "new middle class," that is, elites who do not actually own the sources of production, as the elites of the older capitalism did, but control knowledge, ideas, "culture," and values.

Freire and emancipatory literacy

Up to this point, I have built a somewhat one-sided case, concentrating on the authoritarian side of Plato's dilemma. But there is another side, the liberating side of the dilemma, that is, the use of an emancipatory literacy for religious, political, and cultural resistance to domination (Graff 1987b: 324):

> Literacy was one of the core elements of England's centuries-old radical tradition. In the context of a complex interweaving of political, cultural, social, and economic changes, an essentially new element in literacy's history was formed: the association of literacy with radical political activities, as well as with "useful knowledge", one of the many factors in the making of an English working class. ... Reading and striving for education helped the working class to form a political picture of the organization of their society and their experience in it.

No name is more closely associated with emancipatory literacy than that of Paulo Freire (1970, 1973, 1985; Freire and Macedo 1987). Like Bakhtin and Plato, Freire believes that literacy empowers people only when it renders them active questioners of the social reality around them:

> Reading the world always precedes reading the word, and reading the word implies continually reading the world. ... In a way, however, we can go further and say that reading the word is not preceded merely by reading the world, but by a certain form of writing it or

rewriting it, that is, of transforming it by means of conscious, practical work. For me, this dynamic movement is central to the literacy
process.

(Freire and Macedo, 1987: 35)

In a chapter entitled "The people speak their word: literacy in action"
in his book with Donaldo Macedo, Freire discusses and cites material
from learner Workbooks he helped design for a national literacy campaign in the republic of São Tomé and Principe, a nation that had recently
freed itself from "the colonial yoke to which it was subjected for centuries" (p. 65). He calls attention to the way in which "the challenge to the
critical perception of those becoming literate gradually grows, page
by page" (p. 72). The second Notebook begins by "provoking a debate"
(p. 76) and goes on to say to the learner: "To study is not easy, because
to study is to create and re-create and not to repeat what others say"
(p. 77). The Notebook tells the learner that education is meant to develop
"a critical spirit and creativity, not passivity" (p. 91). Freire says that
in these materials "one does not particularly deal with delivering or
transferring to the people more rigorous explanations of the facts, as
though these facts were finalized, rigid, and ready to be digested. One is
concerned with stimulating and challenging them" (p. 78).

All this sounds open and liberating, much as Plato initially did, and in
not dissimilar terms. But there's another note here as well. Freire comes
up square against Plato's problem: What is to ensure that when people
read (either a text or the world) they will do so "correctly"? Thus, the
second Notebook also reads:

When we learn to read and write, it is also important to learn to think
correctly. To think correctly we should think about our practice in
work. We should think about our daily lives.

(p. 76)

Our principal objective in writing the texts of this Notebook is to
challenge you, comrades, to think correctly. . . .

(p. 87)

Now try to do an exercise, attempting to think correctly. Write on
a piece of paper how you see this problem: "Can the education of
children and adults, after the Independence of our country, be equal
to the education that we had before Independence?"

(p. 88)

Let's think about some qualities that characterize the new man and the new woman. One of these qualities is agreement with the People's cause and the defense of the People's interests. . . . The correct sense of political militancy, in which we are learning to overcome individualism and egoism, is also a sign of the new man and the new woman.

To study [a revolutionary duty], to think correctly, . . . all these are characteristics of the new man and the new woman.

(p. 92)

It is startling that a pedagogy that Freire says is "more a pedagogy of question than a pedagogy of answer," a pedagogy that is radical because it is "less certain of certainties" (p. 54), in fact knows what it is to think correctly. Learners are told not to repeat what others say, but then the problem becomes that in "re-saying" what they read for themselves they may say it wrong, i.e. conflict with Freire's or the state's political perspective. Thus, the literacy materials must ensure that they think correctly, that is, "re-say" or interpret text and world "correctly."

Freire is well aware that no literacy is politically neutral, including the institutionally based literacy of church, state, business, and school that has undergirded and continues to undergird the hegemonic process in Western society. There is no way out of Plato's dilemma. Literacy always comes with a perspective on interpretation that is ultimately political. One can hide that perspective the better to claim it isn't there, or one can put it out in the open. Plato, Sweden, Freire all have a perspective, and a strong one. One thing that makes both Plato and Freire great is that neither attempts to hide his political perspective, or to pretend that politics can be separated from literacy.

In the end, we might say that, contrary to the literacy myth, nothing follows from literacy or schooling. Much follows, however, from what comes with literacy and schooling, what literacy and schooling come wrapped up in, namely the attitudes, values, norms, and beliefs (at once social, cultural, and political) that always accompany literacy and schooling. These consequences may be work habits that facilitate industrialization, abilities in "expository talk in contrived situations," a religiously or politically quiescent population, radical opposition to colonial oppressors, and any number of other things. A text, whether written on paper, or on the soul (Plato), or on the world (Freire), is a loaded weapon. The person, the educator, who hands over the gun hands over the bullets (the perspective) and must own up to the consequences. There is no way out of having an opinion, an ideology, and a strong one, as did Plato, as does Freire. Literacy education is not for the timid. When I wrote this section on Paulo Freire (1921–97) in 1990/96 he was still alive. He was a man I had the great privilege to know personally. Freire was a towering figure, as an intellectual and as a person. Some people have, over the years, taken this section on Freire as a criticism of his work. It was never intended as that: it is reflection on the strength of mind both Plato and Freire had to confront the nature of literacy and the need to acknowledge openly and honestly the role of values, ideology, and world views. Literacy involves real dilemmas and both Plato and Freire confronted them head-on, though from different points of view and different value systems.

Freire in his classic book *The Pedagogy of the Oppressed* (1970) argued for a number of points that are as important today as when he first made them. Indeed, they are integral to the arguments about language and literacy I make in this book:

1   A "banking model" of learning does not "work." By a "banking model," Freire meant a model where learning is seen as a "teacher" transmitting *information* to a "student." Learning involves an active engagement with the world, with words, and with other people. It is not just about information. It is about actions, dialogue, producing knowledge, and changing ourselves and the world, as well.

2   "Reading the world" and "reading the word" are deeply similar—at some level, equivalent—processes. This should have been clear even from our discussion of the aspirin bottle in the last chapter. One cannot learn to "read the word" (make sense of a text) in some domain unless one has learned to "read the world" (make sense of the world that text is about) in that domain. How one "reads the word" and how one "reads the world" are heavily dependent on each other and inextricably interdependent.

3   Dialogue (that is, both face-to-face conversational interaction and conversation-like interaction at a distance through reflection on what one has heard or read) in which diverse viewpoints and perspectives are juxtaposed is, at several levels, essential for learning to "read the world" and to "read the word." Literacy cannot, then, be defined primarily in terms of either "private" individuals (and their mental states) or single isolated texts. Multiple and diverse perspectives juxtaposed in talk or in reflection on multiple texts are essential to literacy for Freire.

4   "Politics" (in the sense of assumptions, attitudes, values, and per-
     spectives about the distribution of "social goods" in society, where,
     by "social goods," I mean anything that is considered "good,"
     "appropriate," or "right" to have, do, or be in the society) doesn't
     stand outside of and is not peripheral to literacy. Rather, politics, in
     the sense just given, and literacy are integrally and inextricably
     interwoven. This is so because "reading the world" always involves
     an interpretation of the "way things are" in terms of what is "appro-
     priate," "normal," "natural," or "right" in regard to the distribution
     of social goods. Since "reading the world" and "reading the word"
     are inextricably interwoven, so, too, then, are politics and literacy.
     This is a point I attempted to make in the first chapter when I pointed
     out that our cultural models determine what and how words will
     mean and in ways that are consequential for us and others in the
     world.

Chapter 4

The New Literacy Studies

Literacy

The last chapter argued that the traditional view of literacy as the ability to read and write rips literacy out of its sociocultural contexts and treats it as an asocial cognitive skill with little or nothing to do with human relationships. It cloaks literacy's connections to power, to social identity, and to ideologies, often in the service of privileging certain types of literacy and certain types of people.

Nonetheless, as we saw in the last chapter, great claims have been made for "literacy" in the traditional sense. In fact, literacy has been argued to be the basis of a "great divide" between cultures: "oral cultures" versus "literate cultures." At the cultural level, literacy is supposed to be the *sine qua non* of "modern," "sophisticated," "complex" cultures; at the individual level it is supposed to lead to higher orders of intelligence. However, the last chapter argued that literacy has different effects in different social settings, and none apart from such settings.

A large body of work, which I referred to in the last chapter as "the New Literacy Studies," has begun to replace the traditional notion of literacy with a sociocultural approach. This chapter will survey some of the key developments that led up to the sociocultural approach. We will see that the New Literacy Studies has its origins in the collapse of the old "oral culture–literate culture" contrast. Out of the deconstruction of this contrast come more contemporary approaches to literacy not as a singular thing but as a plural set of social practices: literacies.

The primitive and the civilized

Humans tend to think in dichotomies, and no dichotomy has played on the popular and the academic mind more insidiously than the contrast between "the primitive" ("the savage") and "the civilized." This contrast has often been used, on the one hand, to trace an evolutionary process, with modern "man" at its pinnacle, and, on the other hand, to romanticize the primitive as an Eden from which Civilization represents a Fall. Neither extreme is warranted.

In anthropological research primitive societies have been characterized as small, homogeneous, nonliterate, highly personal, and held together by a strong sense of group solidarity. They are claimed to be regulated by face-to face encounters rather than by abstract rules (Douglas 1973; Evans-Pritchard 1951; Musgrove 1982). In less sedate terms, they have been said to be "mystical and prelogical" (Levi-Bruhl 1910), incapable of abstract thought, irrational, childlike ("half devil and half child" in Kipling's phrase), and inferior to modern man. ("Man" is used advisedly: modern women were often seen as intermediary between savages/children and modern males, see Gould 1977: 126–135.)

On the other hand, modern urban societies (our best current exemplars of "civilization") are typified by their large and diverse groupings of people, widespread literacy and technology, and sense of science and history. Cities are places where many social relations tend to be impersonal and life is lived within "grids of impersonal forces and rules" (Douglas 1973: 88).

However, this primitive–civilized dichotomy eventually broke down at the hands of modern social anthropology. "Primitive societies" are not primitive in thought, word, or deed, or in any evolutionary sense. Anthropologists like Ruth Benedict and Margaret Mead championed many of the practices of primitive societies (Benedict 1959; Mead 1928). Lévi-Strauss showed that the classification of the natural world amongst South American Indian tribes is as complex and as interesting as those of the academic biologist, at an intellectual as well as a utilitarian level (1963, 1966, 1975). E. E. Evans-Pritchard argued in the 1930s that the views on witchcraft of the Azande of Central Africa, a technologically simple society, were not irrational, illogical or "mystical" (1937). If one accepts the initial premise of statements about witchcraft, the processes of thought involved can be shown to be the same as those involved in scientific thought. Robin Horton broke down the elements of scientific thinking in order to demonstrate that so-called "primitive" peoples such as the Azande did in fact make use of the same elements of thought, although applied to different content (Horton 1967). Sapir in his 1921 classic *Language* demonstrated that there are no primitive languages and that the languages of many primitive cultures are among the world's most complex.

The science of the concrete versus the science of the abstract: recoding the primitive–civilized distinction

The primitive–civilized distinction has repeatedly resurfaced in other guises even in work that ostensibly tried to put it to rest. Claude Lévi-Strauss (1963, 1966, 1975, 1979; all page references following are to Lévi-Strauss 1966), the founder of structuralism in anthropology, demonstrated that there was nothing primitive about thought in primitive cultures. Nonetheless, he reintroduced a dichotomy between primitive and modern cultures in terms of two distinct ways of knowing, what he called "two distinct modes of scientific thought'." These were not a function of different stages of development, but rather of two different levels at which nature is accessible to scientific inquiry:

> Certainly the properties to which the savage mind has access are not the same as those which have commanded the attention of scientists. The physical world is approached from opposite ends in the two cases: one is supremely concrete, the other supremely abstract; one proceeds from the angle of sensible qualities and the other from that of formal properties.
>
> (p. 269)

Primitive cultures use events from the natural world, ordered in myths and totem systems, for instance, to create structures by means of which they can think about, and explain, the world of experience. For example, in a "pure totemic structure" (p. 115), a certain clan associated with a particular species, e.g. the bear, may be viewed to differ from another clan associated with a different species, e.g. the eagle, as the bear differs from the eagle in the natural world. Thus, a type of homology between culture and nature is created. Modern science, on the other hand, manipulates not objects and images from the natural world, but abstract systems, whether numerical, logical, or linguistic, and through these systems seeks to change the world.

In an influential insight, Lévi-Strauss characterized the systems of stories that make up mythical thought as a kind of intellectual *bricolage*. The *bricoleur* (no real English equivalent, but something like a "handyman") is adept at performing a large number of tasks. Unlike modern engineers, bricoleurs do not design tools for the specific task at hand; rather, their universe of instruments is closed and the rules of the game are always to make do with "whatever is at hand." What is at hand is always a contingent result of all the occasions there have been to renew

or enrich the stock or to maintain it with the remains of previous construc-
tions or destructions (p. 17). Mythical thought, with its stories of gods,
animals, and ancestors, is "imprisoned in the events and experiences
which it never tires of ordering and re-ordering in its search to find
meaning" in stories, rather than the sorts of abstract theories our sort of
science trusts in (p. 22).

Literacy: a great divide?

Lévi-Strauss's work raises, without answering, the question as to how cultures move from the science of the concrete to the science of the abstract,
and through which stages. Two influential pieces of work have suggested
that the answer is literacy: Eric Havelock's *Preface to Plato* (1963; see
also Havelock 1982, 1986) and Jack Goody's *The Domestication of the
Savage Mind* (1977; see also 1968, 1986, 1988). I will discuss Havelock
first (all page references below are to Havelock 1963).

Havelock argues that Homeric Greek culture was an oral (nonliterate)
culture. His characterization of that culture has been used both as a
characterization of oral cultures generally and as a cornerstone in the
argument that it is literacy that makes for a "great divide" between human
cultures and their ways of thinking.

The Greek oral epic—such as the *Iliad* and the *Odyssey* in their
original forms—was a storehouse of social directives, an "encyclopedia
of conduct" in the form of contrived and memorized speech. It was the
way the culture passed down its values and knowledge. Havelock argues
that the epic took the form it did due to the demands of human memory
in the absence of writing. It was recited with a heavy metrical rhythm and
constructed out of a large set of pre-given, memorized formulas (short
phrases that would fit the meter), as well as a large set of pre-given motifs
(stereotypical characters, actions and events) and wider themes which
recurred throughout the epic (Finnegan 1977, 1988; Foley 1988; Lord
1960; Parry 1971).

There was, however, scope for creativity in how these building blocks
were arranged and ordered on any occasion of recitation; recitation was
always sensitive to the reactions of the audience. This characterization
reminds one of Lévi-Strauss's view of *bricolage* in mythic thought,
which indeed is what the Homeric epics were.

Oral poetry constituted didactic entertainment, and if it ceased to
entertain, it ceased to be effectively didactic. It was rhythm that underlay
this pleasure, the rhythm of recurrent meter, formulas, motifs, and
themes. Further, since knowledge in an oral culture is compelled to be

obedient to the psychological requirements imposed by memory and the story form, it is couched in the contingent, dealing with actions and actors, not abstractions and principles. Havelock argues that this kind of discourse, since it is the only form of speech in the culture that enjoys a certain autonomy and preservation, represents "the limits within which the mind of the members of that culture can express itself, the degree of sophistication to which they can attain" (p. 182).

Havelock argues—along the same lines, in fact, as Plato did—that the teller of tales and his audience were under a "spell." The epic poet was under the spell of the epic rhythm created by meter and recurrent themes; the hearer in fully identifying with the telling of the tale also entered the spell. The epic was an acting out of, an identification with, the values and beliefs of the society. Innovation in values and ideas was difficult—the cost of giving up what one has memorized and memorizing anew was too great.

As we saw in the last chapter, Plato, one of the first great writers of Greek civilization, sought to reorder Greek society, to relocate power. To do so he had to break the power of the epic poet ("Homer"), because in his care resided the moral and intellectual heritage of society. No surprise then that in Plato's "perfect" society, described in *The Republic*, he excludes poets ("Homer").

What woke the Greeks? Havelock's answer: alphabetic-script literacy, a changed technology of communication. Refreshment of memory through written signs enabled a reader to dispense with most of that emotional identification by which alone the acoustic record was sure of recall. This could release psychic energy, for a review and rearrangement of what had now been written down. What had been written could be seen as an object (a "text") and not just heard and felt. You could, as it were, take a second look.

When Socrates asked the poets what their poems said:

> The poets are his victims because in their keeping reposes the Greek cultural tradition, the fundamental "thinking" (we can use this word in only a non-Platonic sense) of the Greeks in moral, social and historical matters. Here was the tribal encyclopedia, and to ask what it was saying amounted to a demand that it be said differently, non-poetically, non-rhythmically, and non-imagistically. What Plato is pleading for could be shortly put as the invention of an abstract language of descriptive science to replace a concrete language of oral memory.
>
> (p. 209)

Thus, we have returned via Havelock's orality and literacy to something like Lévi-Strauss's contrast between the science of the concrete and the science of the abstract contrasted as two fundamentally different ways of knowing the world.

Literacy as "the domestication of the savage mind"

Jack Goody's *The Domestication of the Savage Mind* (1977) moves beyond ancient Greek culture to modern nonliterate and semi-literate societies. He sees the development and spread of literacy as a crucial factor in explaining how modes of thought and cultural organization change over time.

Goody and Ian Watt (1963), in a now famous earlier paper, laid out some of the outcomes that they saw as linked to the advent of writing and in particular to the invention of the alphabetic system that made widespread literacy possible. They suggested that "logic," in the restricted sense of an instrument of analytic procedures, seemed to be a function of writing, since it was the setting down of speech that enabled humans clearly to separate words, to manipulate their order, to develop syllogistic forms of reasoning, and to perceive contradictions. With writing one could arrest the flow of speech and compare side by side utterances that had been made at different times and places.

Essentially, Goody's procedure is to take certain of the characteristics that Lévi-Strauss and others have regarded as marking the distinction between primitive and advanced cultures, and to suggest that many of the valid aspects of this distinction can be related to changes in the mode of communication, especially the introduction of various forms of writing. Goody relates the development of writing to the growth of individualism, the growth of bureaucracy and of more depersonalized and more abstract systems of government, as well as to the development of the abstract thought and syllogistic reasoning that culminate in modern science. Goody sees the acquisition of writing as effectively transforming the nature of both cognitive and social processes.

Of course, characteristics which Goody attributes to orality persist in societies with literacy. Indeed, this fact might well seem to undermine the case for the "intrinsic" effects of literacy. However, Goody appeals here to a claim that many people in such societies (like ours) have "restricted literacy" as against "full literacy." In fact, Goody comes close to suggesting that "restricted literacy" is the norm in almost all non-technological societies today, and, perhaps, in large pockets of modern technological ones as well.

Orality and literacy as two different worlds

The work of Havelock and Goody is translated into a sweeping philo-sophical, linguistic, and anthropological statement about orality and literacy as a great divide in human culture, thought, and history in Walter Ong's influential and entertaining book *Orality and Literacy* (1982).

Ong argues that work on oral and literate cultures has made us revise our understanding of human identity. Writing—commitment of the word to space—enlarges the potentiality of language "almost beyond measure" and "restructures thought":

> Oral cultures indeed produce powerful and beautiful verbal per-formances of high artistic and human worth, which are no longer even possible once writing has taken possession of the psyche. Nevertheless, without writing, human consciousness cannot achieve its fuller potentials, cannot produce other beautiful and powerful creations. In this sense, orality needs to produce and is destined to produce writing. Literacy, as will be seen, is absolutely necessary for the development not only of science but also history, philosophy, explicative understanding of literature and of any art, and indeed for the explanation of language (including oral speech) itself. There is hardly an oral culture or a predominantly oral culture left in the world today that is not somehow aware of the vast complex of powers forever inaccessible without literacy. This awareness is agony for persons rooted in primary orality, who want literacy passionately but who also know very well that moving into the exciting world of literacy means leaving behind much that is exciting and deeply loved in the earlier oral world. We have to die to continue living.
>
> (pp. 14–15)

Ong goes on to offer a strongly stated characterization of thought and expression in oral cultures. But in doing so he makes a crucial move in claiming that "to varying degrees many cultures and subcultures, even in a high-technology ambiance, preserve much of the mind-set of primary orality" (p. 11). And indeed many of the features he cites have been claimed to be characteristic of, for instance, lower-socioeconomic African-American culture in the United States. Many lower-socioeco-nomic African-American people in the United States still have ties to a former rich oral culture, both from the days of slavery in the United States and from African cultures, and are at the same time less influenced than mainstream middle-class groups by essay-text literacy and the school systems that perpetuate it (Baugh 1983, 1999; Green 2002; Labov 1972a, b; Mufwene *et al.* 1998; Rickford and Rickford 2000; Smitherman 1977; Stucky 1987).

Ong goes on to claim that many modern cultures which have known writing for centuries have not fully interiorized it. He uses as examples Arabic culture and certain other Mediterranean cultures (e.g., ironically, after Havelock's work, including modern Greek culture). He also points out that oral habits of thought and expression, including massive use of formulaic elements of a type similar to those in Homer, still marked prose style of almost every sort in Tudor England some 2,000 years after Plato's campaign in writing against oral poets. Thus, the range of application of Ong's contrast between literacy and orality is greatly expanded by his inclusion of groups with what he refers to as "residual orality" on the oral side of the dichotomy.

Ong offers a set of features that characterize thought and expression in a primary oral culture. The first of these, expanding on Havelock, is "formulaic thought and expression," defined as "more or less exactly repeated set phrases or set expressions (such as proverbs)" (p. 26). Beyond formulaicness, Ong argues that thought and expression in an oral culture are (1) additive (strung together by additive relations like simple adjunction or terms/concepts like "and") rather than subordina-tive; (2) aggregative (elements of thought or expression come in clusters, e.g., not "the princess" but "the beautiful princess") rather than analytic; (3) redundant or "copious"; (4) conservative or traditionalist, inhibiting experimentation; (5) close to the human life world; (6) agonistically toned; (7) empathetic and participatory rather than objectively distanced; (8) situational rather than abstract.

Though Ong restricts these features to primary rather than residually oral cultures, it is striking how similar some of these features are to characterizations linguists have offered of the differences between speech and writing, educators have offered of the differences between "good" and "bad" writers, and sociolinguists have offered of differences between forms of (prosaic versus poetic) storytelling at school and in society at large (Bauman 1986; Bauman and Sherzer 1974; Michaels 1981).

Thus we get to one of the main implications of the Havelock–Goody–Ong line of work: in modern technological societies like the United States something akin to the oral–literate distinction may apply between groups with "residual orality" or "restricted literacy" (usually lower socioeconomic) and groups with full access to the literacy taught in the schools (usually middle and upper middle-class). Lévi-Strauss's recasting of the primitive–civilized distinction in terms of a contrast between concrete and abstract thought, now explained by literacy, comes then to roost in our "modern" society.

Integration versus involvement, not literacy versus orality

The linguist Wally Chafe, in contrasting writing (essays) and speech (spontaneous conversation), suggests that differences in the processes of speaking and writing have led to specific differences in the products (Chafe 1985; see also Gee 2004; Tannen 1985). The fact that writing is much slower than speech, while speaking is much faster, allows written language to be less fragmented, more syntactically integrated, than speech. Writers have the time to mold their ideas into a more complex, coherent, integrated whole, making use of complicated lexical and syntactic devices seldom used in speech, such as heavy use of nominalizations, participles, attributive adjectives, and various subordinating devices (Halliday and Martin 1993).

In addition to its integrated quality, Chafe calls attention to the fact that written language fosters more detachment than speech, which is face-to-face and usually more highly socially involved than writing. Thus, writing is integrated and detached, while speech is fragmented and involved.

Chafe is aware that these are in reality poles of a continuum, and that there are uses of spoken and written language that do not fit these characterizations (e.g. lectures as a form of integrated and detached speech; letters as a form of fragmented and involved writing; literature, where involvement features are used for aesthetic effects). However, integration and detachment are part of the potential that writing offers, thanks to the processes by which it is produced.

It is interesting to note, however, that Richardson *et al.* (1983) argued that in many junior colleges in the United States, given the pervasiveness of multiple-choice tests and note taking, as well as ever present bureaucratic forms to fill out, and a lack of essay writing or discursive exams, literacy has become fragmented, but socially detached. Thus, it partakes of features of both speech (fragmentation) and writing (detachment) in Chafe's terms.

Furthermore, in many oral cultures, there are formal ritual-traditional uses of language that have many of the features of poetry (e.g., rhythm, repetition and syntactic parallelism), but which are also formal and detached (like much writing in our culture). Here, again, we see a case where we get features of both writing (detachment) and speech (in this case, poetry-like features).

As Chafe well knows, these mixed cases show us that the speech–writing or orality–literacy distinction is problematic. What is really involved is different cultural practices that in certain contexts call for certain uses of language, language patterned in certain ways and trading on features like integration/fragmentation and detachment/involvement (and, we might add, prose/poetry) to various degrees. It is better to study the features within their social practices than to stay at the level of writing versus speech. This is one of the major motifs of a contemporary socio-cultural approach to language and literacy.

Literacy and higher-order cognitive skills

The previous section suggests the need for a new approach to the oral–literate divide that studies different uses of language, spoken and written, in their sociocultural contexts. However, there is one major factor that keeps literacy as a personal cognitive skill, apart from any cultural context, in focus: the claim that literacy leads to higher-order cognitive skills.

This claim is founded on a large number of empirical studies that go back to the famous work of Vygotsky and Luria in Soviet Central Asia in the 1930s (Luria 1976; see also Wertsch 1985). Soviet Central Asia in the 1930s was in the midst of collectivization and many previously nonliterate populations were rapidly introduced to literacy and other practices and skills of modern technological society. Vygotsky and Luria compared nonliterate and recently literate subjects on a series of reasoning tasks. The tasks required them to do such things as categorize familiar objects or deduce the conclusion that follows from the premises of a syllogism.

For example, in one task subjects were given pictures of a hammer, a saw, a log, and a hatchet and asked to say which three go together. Literate subjects were generally willing to say that the hammer, hatchet, and saw go together because they are all tools, thus grouping the objects on the basis of abstract word meanings. In contrast, the answers of non-literate subjects indicated a strong tendency to group items on the basis of concrete settings with which they were familiar (saw, logs, hatchet). Thus they said things like "the log has to be here too," and resisted suggestions by the experimenter (based on decontextualized word meanings) that the hammer, hatchet, and saw could be grouped together. Performance on syllogistic reasoning tasks yielded analogous results.

It was concluded that major differences exist between literate and nonliterate subjects in their use of abstract reasoning processes. The responses of nonliterates were dominated by their immediate practical experience and they resisted using language in a decontextualized manner. These results, of course, fit well with the claims of Havelock, Goody, and Ong, as well as with claims made about semi-literate groups in the United States and Britain.

However, there is a major empirical problem in the Vygotsky–Luria work. It is unclear whether the results were caused by "the ability to write and/or read" ("literacy" in the traditional sense), or by schooling, or even the new social institutions to which the Russian revolution exposed these subjects. It is extremely difficult to separate the influence of literacy as "reading and writing" from that of formal schooling, since in most parts of the world the two go together. But school involves much more than becoming literate in the traditional sense: "A student is involved in learning a set of complex role relationships, general cognitive techniques, ways of approaching problems, different genres of talk and interaction, and an intricate set of values concerned with communication, interaction, and society as a whole . . ." (Wertsch 1985: 35–36).

The whole question of the cognitive effects of literacy (defined as the "ability to write and read") was redefined by the ground-breaking work on the Vai in Liberia by Sylvia Scribner and Michael Cole (1981) in *The Psychology of Literacy*, mentioned in the last chapter. Scribner and Cole examine two crucial questions: Is it literacy or formal schooling that affects mental functioning? Can one distinguish among the effects of forms of literacy used for different functions in the life of an individual or a society?

Among the Vai, literacy and schooling are not always coterminous. In addition to literacy in English acquired in formal school settings, the Vai have an indigenous (syllabic, not alphabetic) script transmitted outside an institutional setting and with no connection with Western-style schooling, as well as a form of literacy in Arabic.

Each of these literacies is tied to a particular set of uses: English literacy is associated with government and education; Vai literacy is used primarily for keeping records and for letters, many of them involving commercial matters; Arabic literacy is used for reading, writing, and memorizing the Koran. (Many Arabic literates do not know Arabic, but have memorized and can recite large sections of the Koran in Arabic.)

Since some Vai are versed in only one of these forms of literacy, others in two or more, and still others are nonliterate altogether, Scribner and Cole could disentangle various effects of literacy from effects of formal schooling, which affected only the English literates. If literacy is what is affecting mental abilities, then all literates (English, Vai, and Arabic) should show the same effects, but if schooling is responsible, then only schooled literates will show the effects.

Scribner and Cole examined subjects' performance on categorization and syllogistic reasoning tasks similar to those used by Vygotsky and Luria. Their results call into question much work on the cognitive consequences of literacy. Neither syllabic Vai script, nor Arabic alphabetic literacy, was associated with what have been considered higher-order intellectual skills. Neither literacy enhanced the use of taxonomic skills, nor did either contribute to a shift toward syllogistic reasoning. In contrast, literacy in English, the only form associated with formal schooling, was associated with some types of decontextualization and abstract reasoning.

But schooling does not give rise to "higher intelligence" or "higher mental abilities" in any general or global sense. Rather, it has quite narrow and specific effects:

> A convenient way of grasping the role of school is to consider first those tasks on which it was the highest ranking determinant of performance. These were: explanation of sorting, logic explanation, explanation of grammatical rules, game instructions (communication), and answers to hypothetical questions about name switching. All of these are "talking about" tasks.
> . . . Once we move away from verbal exposition, we find no other general patterns of cross-task superiority.
> . . . school fosters abilities in expository talk in contrived situations (Scribner and Cole, 1973). All primary influences of schooling in the present research fit this description.
>
> (pp. 242–243)

Scribner and Cole did not find that schooled, English-literate subjects, many of whom had been out of school a number of years, differed from other groups in their actual performance on categorization and abstract reasoning tasks. They simply talked about them better, providing informative verbal descriptions and justifications of their task activity. However, those who had recently been in school did do better on the tasks, suggesting that both task performance and verbal description of task performance improved as a result of schooled literacy, but the former was transient, unless practiced in the years after school.

There is another very important finding in the Scribner and Cole work. Each literacy was associated with some quite specific skills. For example,

Vai script literacy was associated with specific skills in synthesizing spoken Vai in an auditory integration task (repeating back Vai sentences decomposed, by pauses between syllables, into their constituent syllables), in using graphic symbols to represent language, in using language as a means of instruction, and in talking about correct Vai speech. All of these skills are closely related to everyday practices of Vai script literacy. For instance, the ability to synthesize spoken Vai appears to follow from the practice Vai readers get in synthesizing language when they decode a syllabic script that does not mark word divisions. To construct meaning out of a chain of syllables, Vai script readers must often hold a sequence of syllables in working memory until they can determine what words they belong to. Or, to take another example: the Vai, in writing letters, often discuss the quality of the letters and whether they are written in "good Vai." This practice appears to enhance their ability to talk about correct speech on a grammar task.

Scribner and Cole, on the basis of such evidence, opt for what they call "a practice account of literacy." A type of literacy enhances quite specific skills that are practiced in carrying out that literacy. Grandiose claims for large and global cognitive skills resulting from literacy are not, in fact, indicated. One can also point out that the effect of formal schooling—being able to engage in expository talk in contrived situations—is itself a fairly specific skill practiced a good deal in school. Thus, we might extend Scribner and Cole's "practice account" to schooling as well as literacy.

In summing up, Scribner and Cole bring out another variable, beside schooling, that enhances some cognitive skills that have been attributed to literacy, namely living in a city:

> Our results are in direct conflict with persistent claims that "deep psychological differences" divide literate and nonliterate populations . . . On no task—logic, abstraction, memory, communication—did we find all nonliterates performing at lower levels than all literates. . . . We can and do claim that literacy promotes skills among the Vai, but we cannot and do not claim that literacy is a necessary and sufficient condition for any of the skills we assessed.
>
> One explanation for the variegated pattern of nonliterate performance is that other life experiences besides school and literacy were potent influences on some of our tasks. Principal among these was urban residency. Living in cities was a major influence in shifting people away from reliance on functional modes of classification to use of taxonomic categories . . .

The evidence we have summarized . . . strongly favors the conclusion that literacy is not a surrogate for schooling with respect to
its intellectual consequences.

(pp. 251–252)

The Scribner and Cole research clearly indicates that what matters is not
"literacy" as some decontextualized "ability" to write or read, but the
social practices into which people are apprenticed as part of a social
group, whether as "students" in school, "letter writers" in the local community, or members of a religious group.

Literacy: the ideological model

The work of Scribner and Cole calls into question what Brian Street, in
his book *Literacy in Theory and Practice* (1984), calls "the autonomous
model" of literacy: the claim that literacy (or schooling for that matter)
has cognitive effects apart from the context in which it exists and the
uses to which it is put in a given culture. Claims for literacy, in particular
for essay-text literacy values, whether in speech or writing, are thus
"ideological." They are part of "an armoury of concepts, conventions and
practices" that privilege one social formation as if it were natural, universal, or, at the least, the end point of a normal developmental progression
(achieved only by some cultures, thanks either to their intelligence or
their technology).

Street proposes, in opposition to the "autonomous model" of literacy,
an "ideological model." The ideological model attempts to understand
literacy in terms of concrete social practices and to theorize it in terms of
the ideologies in which different literacies are embedded. Literacy—of
whatever type—has consequences only as it acts together with a large
number of other social factors, including political and economic conditions, social structure, and local ideologies.

Any technology, including writing, is a cultural form, a social product
whose shape and influence depend upon prior political and ideological
factors. Despite Havelock's brilliant characterization of the transition
from orality to literacy in ancient Greece, it now appears that the Greek
situation has rarely if ever been replicated. The particular social, political,
economic and ideological circumstances in which literacy (of a particular
sort) was embedded in Greece explain what happened there. Abstracting
literacy from its social setting in order to make claims for literacy as
an autonomous force in shaping the mind or a culture simply leads to a
dead end.

There is, however, a last refuge for someone who wants to see literacy as an autonomous force. One could claim that essay-text literacy, and the uses of language connected with it, lead, if not to general cognitive consequences, to social mobility and success in the society. While this argument may be true, there is precious little evidence that literacy in history or across cultures has had this effect either.

Street discusses, in this regard, Harvey Graff's (1979) study of the role of literacy in nineteenth-century Canada. While some individuals did gain through the acquisition of literacy, Graff demonstrates that this was not a statistically significant effect and that deprived classes and ethnic groups as a whole were, if anything, further oppressed through literacy. Greater literacy did not correlate with increased equality and democracy nor with better conditions for the working class, but in fact with continuing social stratification.

Graff argues that the teaching of literacy in fact involved a contradiction: illiterates were considered dangerous to the social order, thus they must be made literate; yet the potentialities of reading and writing for an underclass could well be radical and inflammatory. So the framework for the teaching of literacy had to be severely controlled, and this involved specific forms of control of the pedagogic process and specific ideological associations of the literacy being purveyed.

While the workers were led to believe that acquiring literacy was in their benefit, Graff produces statistics that show that in reality this literacy was not advantageous to the poorer groups in terms of either income or power. The extent to which literacy was an advantage or not in relation to job opportunities depended on ethnicity. It was not because you were "illiterate" that you finished up in the worst jobs but because of your background (e.g. being black or an Irish Catholic rendered literacy much less efficacious than it was for English Protestants).

The story Graff tells can be repeated for many other societies, including Britain and the United States (Donald 1983; Levine 1986). In all these societies literacy served as a socializing tool for the poor, was seen as a possible threat if misused by the poor (for an analysis of their oppression and to make demands for power), and served as a technology for the continued selection of members of one class for the best positions in the society. We have discussed this issue in the last chapter.

Differing world views replace the orality–literacy contrast

Literacy has no effects—indeed, no meaning—apart from particular cultural contexts in which it is used, and it has different effects in different contexts. Two founding works that helped initiate the contemporary project of looking at orality and literacy in the context of the social practices and world views of particular social groups were Ronald and Suzanne Scollon's *Narrative, Literacy and Face in Interethnic Communication* (1981) and Shirley Brice Heath's *Ways with Words* (1983). Both of these works realize that what is at issue in the use of language is different ways of knowing, different ways of making sense of the world of human experience, i.e. different social epistemologies.

The Scollons believe that discourse patterns—ways of using language to communicate, whether in speech or writing—in different cultures reflect particular reality sets or world views adopted by these cultures. Discourse patterns are among the strongest expressions of personal and cultural identity. The Scollons argue that changes in a person's discourse patterns—for example, in acquiring a new form of literacy—may involve a change in identity. They provide a detailed study of the discourse practices and world view of Athabaskans in Alaska and northern Canada, and contrast these with the discourse patterns and world view in much of Anglo-Canadian and Anglo-American society (see also Wieder and Pratt 1990a).

Literacy as it is practiced in European-based education, "essay-text literacy" in the Scollons' phrase, is connected to a reality set or world view the Scollons term "modern consciousness." This reality set is consonant with particular discourse patterns, ones quite different from the discourse patterns used by the Athabaskans. As a result, the acquisition of this sort of literacy is not simply a matter of learning a new technology, it involves complicity with values, social practices, and ways of knowing that conflict with those of the Athabaskans.

Athabaskans differ at various points from mainstream Canadian and American English-speakers in how they engage in discourse. A few examples: (1) Athabaskans have a high degree of respect for the individuality of others and a careful guarding of their own individuality. Thus, they prefer to avoid conversation except when the point of view of all participants is well known. On the other hand, English-speakers feel that the main way to get to know the point of view of people is through conversation with them. (2) For Athabaskans, people in subordinate positions do not display, rather they observe the person in the superordinate position. For instance, adults as either parents or teachers are supposed to display abilities and qualities for the child to learn. However, in mainstream American society, children are supposed to show off their abilities for teachers and other adults. (3) The English idea of "putting your best foot forward" conflicts directly with an Athabaskan taboo. It is normal in situations of unequal status relations for an English-speaker to display oneself in the best light possible. One will speak highly of the future, as well. It is normal to present a career or life trajectory of success and planning. This English system is very different from the Athabaskan system, in which it is considered inappropriate and bad luck to anticipate good luck, to display oneself in a good light, to predict the future, or to speak ill of another's luck.

The Scollons list many other differences, including differences in systems of pausing that ensure that English-speakers select most of the topics and do most of the talking in interethnic encounters. The net result of these communication problems is that each group ethnically stereo-types the other. English-speakers come to believe that Athabaskans are unsure, aimless, incompetent, and withdrawn. Athabaskans come to believe that English-speakers are boastful, sure they can predict the future, careless with luck, and far too talkative.

The Scollons characterize the different discourse practices of Athabaskans and English-speakers in terms of two different world views or "forms of consciousness": bush consciousness (connected with sur-vival values in the bush) and modern consciousness. These forms of consciousness are "reality sets" in the sense that they are cognitive orientations toward the everyday world, including learning in that world.

Anglo-Canadian and American mainstream culture has adopted a model of literacy, based on the values of essayist prose style, that is highly compatible with modern consciousness. In essayist prose, the important relationships to be signaled are those between sentence and sentence, not those between speakers, nor those between sentence and speaker. For a reader this requires constant monitoring of grammat-ical and lexical information. With the heightened emphasis on truth value, rather than social or rhetorical conditions, comes the necessity to be explicit about logical implications.

A further significant aspect of essayist prose style is the fictional-ization of both the audience and the author. The "reader" of an essayist text is not an ordinary human being, but an idealization, a rational mind formed by the rational body of knowledge of which the essay is a part. By the same token the author is a fiction, since the process of writing and editing essayist texts leads to an effacement of individual and idiosyncratic identity. The Scollons show the relation of these essayist values to modern consciousness by demonstrating that they are variants of the defining properties of the modern consciousness as given by Berger *et al.* (1973).

For the Athabaskan, writing in this essayist mode can constitute a crisis in ethnic identity. To produce an essay would require the Athabaskan to produce a major display, which would be appropriate only if the Athabaskan was in a position of dominance in relation to the audience. But the audience, and the author, are fictionalized in essayist prose and the text becomes decontextualized. This means that a contextualized, social relationship of dominance is obscured. Where the relationship of the communicants is unknown, the Athabaskan prefers silence.

The paradox of prose for the Athabaskan then is that if it is communication between known author and audience it is contextualized and compatible with Athabaskan values, but not good essayist prose. To the extent that it becomes decontextualized, and thus good essayist prose, it becomes uncharacteristic of Athabaskans to seek to communicate. The Athabaskan set of discourse patterns are to a large extent mutually exclusive of the discourse patterns of essayist prose.

The Scollons go on to detail a number of narrative and non-narrative uses of language in Athabaskan culture, showing how each of these is in turn shaped by the Athabaskan "reality set," especially their respect for the individual and care about not overly intervening in others' affairs (including their knowledge and beliefs). For example, riddles are an important genre in Athabaskan culture. Riddles are seen as schooling in guessing meanings, in reading between the lines, in anticipating outcomes and in indirectness. In short, riddles provide a schooling in non-intervention. And in the best telling of a narrative "little more than the themes are suggested and the audience is able to interpret those themes as highly contextualized in his own experiences" (Scollon and Scollon 1981: 127). This is, of course, just the reverse of the decontextualization valued by essayist prose.

Different ways with words

Shirley Brice Heath's classic *Ways with Words* (1983) is an ethnographic study of the ways in which literacy is embedded in the cultural context of three communities in the Piedmont Carolinas in the United States: Roadville, a white working-class community that has been part of mill life for four generations; Trackton, a working-class African-American community whose older generation were brought up on the land but which now is also connected to mill life and other light industry; and mainstream middle-class urban-oriented African-Americans and whites (see also Heath 1994).

Heath analyzes the ways these different social groups "take" knowledge from the environment, with particular concern for how "types of literacy events" are involved in this taking. Literacy events are any event involving print, such as group negotiation of meaning in written texts (e.g. an ad), individuals "looking things up" in reference books, writing family records in the Bible, and dozens of other types of occasions when books or other written materials are integral to interpretation in an interaction.

Heath interprets these literacy events in relation to the larger sociocultural patterns which they may exemplify or reflect, such as patterns of care-giving roles, uses of space and time, age and sex segregation, and so forth. Since language learning and socialization are two sides of the same coin (Schieffelin and Ochs 1986), Heath concentrates on how children in each community acquire language and literacy in the process of becoming socialized into the norms and values of their communities.

As school-oriented, middle-class parents and their children interact in the pre-school years, adults give their children, through modeling and specific instruction, ways of using language and of taking knowledge from books which seem natural in school and in numerous other institutional settings such as banks, post offices, businesses, or government offices. To exemplify this point, Heath analyzes the bedtime story as an example of a major literacy event in mainstream homes (Heath 1982, all page references below are to this article).

The bedtime story sets patterns of behavior that recur repeatedly through the life of mainstream children and adults at school and in other institutions. In the bedtime story routine, the parent sets up a "scaffolding" dialogue (Cazden 1979) with the child by asking questions like "What is X?" and then supplying verbal feedback and a label after the child has vocalized or given a nonverbal response. Before the age of two, the child is thus socialized into the "initiation–reply–evaluation" sequences so typical of classroom lessons (Cazden 1988, 2001; Mehan 1979).

In addition, reading with comprehension involves an internal replaying of the same types of questions adults ask children of bedtime stories. Further, "What is X?" questions and explanations are replayed in the school setting in learning to pick out topic sentences, write outlines, and answer standard tests. Through the bedtime story routine, and similar practices, in which children learn not only how to take meaning from books, but also how to talk about it, children repeatedly practice routines which parallel those of classroom interaction: "Thus, there is a deep continuity between patterns of socialization and language learning in the home culture and what goes on at school" (p. 56).

Children in both Roadville and Trackton are unsuccessful in school despite the fact that both communities place a high value on success in school. Roadville adults do read books to their children, but they do not extend the habits of literacy events beyond book reading. For instance, they do not, upon seeing an event in the real world, remind children of similar events in a book, or comment on such similarities and differences between book and real events.

The strong Fundamentalist bent of Roadville tends to make parents view any fictionalized account of a real event as a lie; reality is better than fiction and they do not encourage the shifting of the context of items and events characteristic of fictionalization and abstraction. They tend to choose books which emphasize nursery rhymes, alphabet learning, and simplified Bible stories. Even the oral stories that Roadville adults tell, and that children model, are grounded in the actual. The sources of these stories are personal experience. They are tales of transgression which make the point of reiterating the expected norms of behavior.

Thus, Roadville children are not practiced in decontextualizing their knowledge or fictionalizing events known to them, shifting them about into other frames. In school, they are rarely able to take knowledge learned in one context and shift it to another; they do not compare two items or events and point out similarities and differences.

Trackton presents a quite different language and social environment. Babies in Trackton, who are almost always held during their waking hours, are constantly in the midst of a rich stream of verbal and nonverbal communication that goes on around them. Aside from Sunday School materials, there are no reading materials in the home just for children; adults do not sit and read to children. Children do, however, constantly interact verbally with peers and adults.

Adults do not ask children "What is X?" questions, but rather analogical questions which call for non-specific comparisons of one item, event, or person with another (e.g., "What's that like?"). Though children can answer such questions, they can rarely name the specific feature or features which make two items or events alike.

Parents do not believe they have a tutoring role, and they do not simplify their language for children, as mainstream parents do, nor do they label items or features of objects in either books or the environment at large. They believe children learn when they are provided with experiences from which they can draw global, rather than analytically specific, knowledge. Heath claims that children in Trackton seem to develop connections between situations or items by gestalt patterns, analogs, or general configuration links, not by specification of labels and discrete features in the situation. They do not decontextualize, rather they heavily contextualize nonverbal and verbal language.

Trackton children learn to tell stories by rendering a context and calling on the audience's participation to join in the imaginative creation of the story. In an environment rich with imaginative talk and verbal play, they must be aggressive in inserting their stories into an on-going stream of discourse. Imagination and verbal dexterity are encouraged.

Indeed, group negotiation and participation are a prevalent feature of the social group as a whole. Adults read not alone but in a group. For example, someone may read from a brochure on a new car while listeners relate the text's meaning to their experiences, asking questions and expressing opinions. The group as a whole synthesizes the written text and the associated oral discourse to construct a meaning for the brochure.

At school, most Trackton children not only fail to learn the content of lessons, they also do not adopt the social interactional rules for school literacy events. Print in isolation bears little authority in their world and the kinds of questions asked of reading books are unfamiliar (for example, what-explanations). The children's abilities to metaphorically link two events or situations and to recreate scenes are not tapped in the school. In fact, these abilities often cause difficulties, because they enable children to see parallels teachers did not intend and, indeed, may not recognize until the children point them out. By the time in their education, after the elementary years for the most part, when their imaginative skills and verbal dexterity could really pay off, they have failed to gain the necessary written composition skills they would need to translate their analogical skills into a channel teachers could accept.

Heath's characterization of Trackton, Roadville, and Mainstreamers leads us to see not a binary (oral–literate) contrast, but a set of features that cross-classifies the three groups in various ways. The groups share various features with each other group, and differ from them in yet other regards. The Mainstream group and Trackton both value imagination and fictionalization, while Roadville does not; Roadville and Trackton both share a disregard for decontextualization not shared by Mainstreamers. Both Mainstreamers and Roadville, but not Trackton, believe parents have a tutoring role in language and literacy acquisition (they read to their children and ask questions that require labels), but Roadville shares with

Trackton, not the Mainstream, an experiential, nonanalytic view of learning. (Children learn by doing and watching, not by having the process
broken down into its smallest parts.) As we added more groups to the
comparison, e.g. the Athabaskans (which share with Trackton a regard
for gestalt learning and storage of knowledge, but differ from them in the
degree of self-display they allow) we would get more complex cross-
classifications.

Heath suggests that in order for a non-mainstream social group to
acquire mainstream, school-based literacy practices, with all the oral and
written-language skills this implies, individuals, whether children or
adults, must "recapitulate," at an appropriate level for their age, of course,
the sorts of literacy experiences the mainstream child has had at home.
Unfortunately, schools as currently constituted tend to be good places to
practice mainstream literacy once you have its foundations, but they are
not good places to acquire those foundations.

Heath suggests that this foundation, when it has not been set at
home, can be acquired by apprenticing the individual to a school-based
literate person, e.g., the teacher in a new and expanded role. Heath has
had students, at a variety of ages, engage in ethnographic research with
teachers, studying, for instance, the uses of language or languages, or
of writing and reading, in their own communities. This serves as one
way for students to learn and practice in a meaningful context the various
sub-skills of essay-text literacy, e.g., asking questions, taking notes, discussing various points of view—often among people with whom the
student doesn't share a lot of mutual knowledge—writing discursive
prose, and revising it with feedback, often from non-present readers.

This approach obviously fits perfectly with Scribner and Cole's practice account of literacy. And, in line with Street's ideological approach
to literacy, it claims that individuals who have not been socialized into the
discourse practices that constitute mainstream school-based literacy must
eventually be socialized into them if they are ever to acquire them. The
component skills of this form of literacy must be practiced, and one
cannot practice a skill one has not been exposed to, cannot engage in a
social practice one has not been socialized into, which is what most non-
mainstream children are expected to do in school.

But at the same time we must remember the Scollons' warning that for
many social groups this practice may well mean a change of identity
and the adoption of a reality set at odds with their own at various points.
There is a deep paradox here—and there is no facile way of removing it,
short of changing our hierarchical social structure and the school systems
that by and large perpetuate it.

I have, in this chapter, sketched the way in which sociocultural approaches to language and literacy emerged out of earlier anthropological approaches to "orality" and "literacy." We have seen how "orality" and "literacy" as autonomous categories disappear into a myriad of social practices and their concomitant values and world views. Sociocultural approaches to literacy have come mainly from linguists, sociologists, and anthropologists. During the same period, some cognitive psychologists began to abandon asocial individualist views of thinking and problem solving and to develop insightful approaches to "socially distributed cognition." They began to see thinking as something that is carried out by—distributed across—people, tools, technologies, and social settings working together in intricate alignments (Gee 2004; Hutchins 1995; Lave 1988; Lave and Wenger 1991; Newman *et al*. 1989; Rogoff 1990; Rogoff and Lave 1984).

Though it has different origins, work on "social cognition" is beginning to come together with work on sociocultural approaches to language and literacy (Gee 1992, 2004; Hutchins 1995; Wertsch 1991). The goal for the future is an integrated view of mind, body, and society. But it is to be hoped that this enterprise will not abandon the social activism and calls for social justice that are an inherent part of work on sociocultural approaches to literacy. We ought to be much less interested in creating a "new science" than in creating a new society.

Chapter 5

Meaning

Language and social languages

We have now looked at the background to sociocultural approaches to language and literacy. Chapters 7 and 8 will develop a specific theory of language and literacy in society. Before that, however, we need to discuss the nature of language and ways of analyzing it. This chapter deals with meaning in its sociocultural contexts, the next with the analysis of coherent stretches of language such as arguments and stories. In both cases, our concern is with the sociocultural nature of meaning and communication, but with due deference to human agency and responsibility.

At the outset, however, we need to be clear that any language—English, for example—is not one monolithic thing. Rather, each and every language is composed of many sub-languages, which I will call "social languages." Social languages stem from the fact that any time we act or speak, we must accomplish two things: (1) we must make clear *who* we are, and (2) we must make clear *what* we are doing (Wieder and Pratt 1990a, b). This sounds simple, but it is not. First, we are all, despite our common illusions about the matter, not a single *who* but a great many different *whos* in different contexts. Second, one and the same speaking or acting can count as different things in different contexts. We accomplish different *whos* and *whats* through using different social languages.

To exemplify these points, consider an example involving an upper middle-class Anglo-American young woman—let us use "Jane" as a pseudonym for her. Jane was attending a college course of mine on language and communication. The course had discussed the ways in which each of us, when we are talking to different sorts of people, shift the style of our speech. During a class discussion, Jane had claimed that she herself did not shift her language when speaking to different people, but, rather, was consistent from context to context. In fact, to do otherwise, she said, would be "hypocritical," a failure to "be oneself."

In order to support her claim, Jane decided to record herself talking to her parents and to her boyfriend. In both cases, she decided to talk about a story her class had read and discussed, so as to be sure that, in both contexts, she was talking about the same thing. The story had been used in the class to focus discussion on the different ways in which people argue about moral values. In the story, a woman named Abigail wants to get across a river to see her lover, Gregory. A river boat captain (Roger) says he will take her only if she sleeps with him. In desperation she does so—only to see her true love, Gregory. But when she arrives and tells Gregory what happened, he disowns her and sends her away. There is more to the story (Abigail seeks revenge), but this is enough for our purposes here.

In explaining to her parents why she thought Gregory was the worst character in the story, the young woman said the following:

Well, when I thought about it, I don't know,
it seemed to me that Gregory should be the most offensive.
He showed no understanding for Abigail,
when she told him what she was forced to do.
He was callous.
He was hypocritical,
in the sense that he professed to love her,
then acted like that.

Earlier, in her discussion with her boyfriend, in an intimate setting, she had also explained why she thought Gregory was the worst character. In this context she said:

What an ass that guy was, you know, her boyfriend.
I should hope,
if ever I did that to see you,
you would shoot the guy.
He uses her and he says he loves her.
Roger never lies,
you know what I mean?

It was clear—clear even to Jane   that Jane had used two very different forms of language, one to her parents and another to her boyfriend. These different forms of language are, of course, both English. But they are quite different, nonetheless. We can say that they constitute different social languages. Different social languages (and there are, for any one language, like English, a great many) make visible and recognizable two different social identities, two different versions of who one is. The linguistic differences are everywhere to be seen in the two texts. To her parents, Jane carefully hedges her claims ("I don't know," "it seemed to me"); to her boyfriend, she makes her claims straight out. To her boyfriend, she uses terms like "ass" and "guy," while to her parents she uses more formal (and "school"-like) terms like "offensive," "understanding," "callous," "hypocritical," and "professed." She also uses more school-like syntax to her parents ("it seemed to me that . . ." "He showed no understanding for Abigail, when . . ." "He was hypocritical in the sense that . . .") than she does to her boyfriend (". . . that guy, you know, her boyfriend"; "Roger never lies, you know what I mean?"). She repeatedly addresses her boyfriend as "you," and thereby notes his social involvement as a listener, but does not directly address her parents in this way. To her parents, she explicitly introduces each character by name (e.g., Gregory) and then re-refers to the introduced character by a pronoun (e.g., "he"), the way we would in school-based writing. This contrasts with how she singles out and refers back to Gregory in the text to her boyfriend: "that guy . . . you know, her boyfriend . . . you would shoot the guy . . . he uses her . . . he says he loves her." In this latter case, the first "that guy" stands for Gregory and the second "the guy" stands for the hypothetical guy that might do to Jane what Roger did to Abigail. While the "he" pronouns all refer to Gregory, Gregory is introduced as "that guy," thus, not by his name, but by the role—"her boyfriend'"—he shares with her listener. This use of the two "guy"s, by the way, effectively equates the moral standing of Gregory and Roger. In the text to her boyfriend, she leaves several points to be inferred, points that she spells out more explicitly to her parents (e.g., her boyfriend must infer that Gregory is being accused of being a hypocrite from the information that though Roger is bad, at least he does not lie, which Gregory did in claiming to love Abigail).

All in all, Jane appears to use more "school-like" language to her parents. Her language to her parents stands on its own, requiring little inferencing on their part. It distances them as listeners from social and emotional involvement with herself or what she is saying, while stressing, perhaps, their cognitive involvement with the information she is "transmitting" and their judgment of her and her "intelligence." Her language to her boyfriend stresses, on the other hand, social and affective involvement, solidarity, and co-participation in meaning making.

This young woman is making visible and recognizable two different versions of who she is—one for her parents and one for her boyfriend. None of us speaks a single, uniform language, nor is any one of us a single, uniform identity. The different social languages we use allow us to render multiple *whos* (we are) and *whats* (we are doing) socially visible. Different people use different social languages on different occasions. Had the same sort of social language been used by someone from a different social or cultural group than Jane's at dinner with their parents, it might very well have come across as rude and distant. Additionally, Jane would not have used the same sort of social language she used with her boyfriend in a different context, for example during her college classroom discussions. Finally, Jane might well use a different social language altogether when talking to her parents in a different context. In some sociocultural groups, like Jane's, dinner has become habituated as a time when children display public-sphere and school-based intelligence and accomplishments to parents.

So what we see here—and it is a crucial point—is that the who we are and the what we are doing are really enacted through a three-way simultaneous interaction among (1) our social or cultural group memberships (e.g., Jane's class, ethnic, social, cultural, educational, and gender-based group memberships); (2) a particular social language or mixture of them (e.g., the one Jane used to her parents); and (3) a particular context, that is, set of other people, objects, and locations (e.g., at home at dinner with one's parents).

Heteroglossia

It is important to extend our discussion of social languages by pointing out that they are very often "impure." That is, when we speak or write, we very often mix together different social languages. This is a practice that the Russian literary theorist Mikail Bakhtin (1981, 1986; see also Ball and Freedman 2004) called "heteroglossia" (multiple voices). In fact, it is arguable that Jane's social language to her parents is actually a mixture of a form of "everyday" language and aspects of the sorts of social languages used in schools and academic work. There are historical reasons why such a heteroglossic mixture has arisen and survived— having to do with specific ways in which certain sociocultural groups have sought to give their children a "head start" for, and a continuing advantage in, school.

To see a clear example of such heteroglossia, and its ties to sociopolitical realities, consider the following warning(s) taken from a bottle of aspirin. (In Chapter 2 we discussed an earlier version of this warning.)

> Warnings: <u>Children and teenagers should not use this medication for chicken pox or flu symptoms before a doctor is consulted about Reye Syndrome, a rare but serious illness reported to be associated with aspirin</u>. Keep this and all drugs out of the reach of children. In case of accidental overdose, seek professional assistance or contact a poison control center immediately. As with any drug, if you are pregnant or nursing a baby, seek the advice of a health professional before using this product. IT IS ESPECIALLY IMPORTANT NOT TO USE ASPIRIN DURING THE LAST 3 MONTHS OF PREGNANCY UNLESS SPECIFICALLY DIRECTED TO DO SO BY A DOCTOR BECAUSE IT MAY CAUSE PROBLEMS IN THE UNBORN CHILD OR COMPLICATIONS DURING DELIVERY. See carton for arthritis use* and Important Notice.

This text starts with a sentence of very careful and very specific information indeed: the initial sentence talks (in bolded language) about "children and teenagers"; it specially says "this medication"; gives us an exclusive list of two relevant diseases, "chicken pox or flu"; mentions a specific syndrome, "Reye Syndrome," and explicitly tells us that it is "rare but serious." Then, all of a sudden, with the second sentence we enter a quite different sort of language, marked both by the phrasing of the language and by the disappearance of the bolding. Now, the text talks not about aspirin specifically, as in the first sentence, but about "this and all drugs" (second sentence) and "any drug" (fourth sentence). We are told to keep "this and all drugs" out of the reach of "children," but what now has happened to the teenagers? We get three different references to the medical profession, none of them as direct and specific as "doctor" (which was used in the first sentence): "professional assistance," "poison control center," and "health professional." We are told to seek help in case of "accidental overdose" (note that "overdosage" is now gone, see Chapter 2), making us wonder what should happen if the overdose wasn't accidental. The language of this middle part of the text speaks out of a (seemingly not all that dangerous) world where institutional systems (companies, professionals, centers) take care of people who only through ignorance (which these systems can cure) get themselves into trouble.

Then, all of a sudden, again, we make a transition back to the social language of the opening of the text, but this time it is shouted at us in bolded capitals. We are confronted with the phrase "especially important." We return to quite specific language: we again get "aspirin," rather than "all drugs" or "any drug," time is handled quite specifically ("last 3 months"), we no longer "seek assistance or advice" from "professionals," rather we once again "consult" with our "doctor" and do not take the aspirin "unless specifically directed." This is, once again, a dangerous world in which we had better do what (and only what) the doctor says. This dire warning about pregnancy, however, does make us wonder why a rather general and gentle warning about pregnancy and nursing is embedded in the more moderate language of the middle of the text. The text ends with small print, which appears to tell us to look on the carton for an "Important Notice." (Weren't these "warnings" the important notice?)

So, in this text we have at least two rather different social languages (voices) intermingled, juxtaposed rather uncomfortably side by side. Why? At one time, the aspirin bottle had only (a version of) the middle text (sentences 2, 3, and 4) on it as a "warning" (singular). Various medical, social, cultural, and political changes, including conflicts between and among governmental institutions, medical workers, consumers, and drug companies, have led to the "intrusion" of the more direct and sharper voice that begins and ends the "warnings." Thus, we see, the different social languages in this text are "sedimented" there by social, political, and cultural happenings unfolding in history. In fact, even what looks like a uniform social language—for example, the moderate middle of this text—is very often a compendium of different social languages with different historical, social, cultural, and political sources, and looks to us now to be uniform only because the workings of multiple social languages have been forgotten and effaced.

Similarity in the "eye of the beholder"

One of the key ways humans think about the world is through seeking out similarities (Hofstadter *et al.* 1995; Holyoak and Thagard 1995). We try to understand something new in terms of how it resembles something old. We attempt to see the new thing as a "type," thus, like other things of the same or similar type. And very often a great deal hangs on these judgments. For example, is spanking a child a type of discipline or a type of child abuse? When we answer this question we claim either that spanking a child is more similar to paradigmatic instances of discipline or to paradigmatic instances of child abuse.

Judgments like whether spanking is discipline or child abuse are still "open" and widely discussed in the culture thanks to on-going social changes. However, any language is full of such similarity judgments that have been made long ago in the history of the language—in another time and another place—and which are now taken for granted and rarely reflected upon by current speakers of the language.

Let me take another example that is relevant to those of us interested in language and learning. Consider a sentence like "The teacher taught the students French" (see also Birch 1989: 25–29; Halliday 1976b). This sentence has the same grammar as (the language treats it the same as) sentences like "John handed Mary the gun," "John gave Mary the gun," "John sent Mary the gun" (and many more). This type of sentence seems to mean (if we consider prototypical cases like "give," "hand," and "send") that an agent transfers something to someone. The structure of these sentences is: subject–verb–indirect object–direct object. In each case, there is an alternative version using the preposition "to": "The teacher taught French to the students"; "John handed the gun to Mary"; "John gave the gun to Mary"; "John sent the gun to Mary."

And so we are led to think of teaching French as transferring something (French) from one person (the teacher) to someone else (the student), though this transfer is a mental one, rather than a physical one. This suggestion (about the meaning of teaching languages), which we pick up from our grammar, happens to fit with one of the most pervasive ways of thinking (what I will later call a master myth) embedded in our language and in culture. We tend to think of meaning (whether in transmitting our native language or learning a foreign one) as something speakers or writers take out of their heads (its original container), package, like a gift, into a "package" or "container" (i.e., words and sentences), and convey (transfer) to hearers, who unpackage it and place its contents (i.e., "meaning") into their heads (its final container).

This container/conveyor metaphor (Lakoff and Johnson 2003; Reddy 1979) is, as we will see below, a fallacious view of meaning. It gives rise to idioms like "I catch your meaning," "I can't grasp what you are saying," "I've got it," "Let me put the matter in plain terms," "I can't put it into words," and a great many more. So, it is easy for us to accept the suggestion of our grammar and see teaching languages as a form of mental transference of neatly wrapped little packages (drills, grammar lessons, vocabulary lists) along a conveyor belt from teacher to student.

At a more subtle level, the fact that "The teacher teaches the students French" has the same grammar as "The teacher teaches the students history (physics, linguistics, algebra)" suggests that teaching a language (like French) is a comparable activity to teaching a disciplinary content like physics (Halliday 1976b). Our schools, with their classrooms, curricula, discrete class hours (five times a week for an hour we learn French), encourage us further to think that, since all these "teachers" are standing in the same sort of space, playing the same sort of role in the system, they must be or even could be doing the same (sort of) thing.

We can note, as well, that the driving instructor spends too much time in a car and the coach spends too much time on the field to be respected as teachers. Consider, too, that we don't say things like "The coach teaches football"—football can't be taught, one can only help someone master it in a group with other apprentices. Our "cultural model" of teaching makes us compare "teaching French" to "teaching history" and not "coaching football" or "training someone to drive," despite the fact that it may well be that learning a language is a lot more like learning to drive a car or play football than it is like learning history or physics.

What we see here, then, is that language encapsulates a great many "frozen" theories ("cultural models"), generalizations about what is similar to what—we have just witnessed frozen theories of communication (meaning is transmitted from head to head) and language acquisition (a foreign language is transmitted from the teacher's head to the student's head). We do not have to accept the theories our various social languages offer us. Though we can hardly reflect on them all, we can reflect on some of them and come to see things in new ways. Chapter 1 suggested two principles that help indicate where we are under a moral obligation to engage in such reflection.

Meaning

Having established the context of social languages, we can turn directly to "meaning." "Meaning" is one of the most debated terms in linguistics, philosophy, literary theory, and the social sciences. To start our discussion of meaning, let us pick a word and ask what it means. Say we ask: "What does the word 'sofa' mean?"

Imagine that my friend Susan and I go into my living room, where I have a small white, rather broken-down seat big enough for more than one person, and a larger and nicer one. I point to the larger, nicer one and say, "That sofa has a stain on it." Susan sees nothing exceptional about what I have said, assumes we both mean the same thing by the word "sofa," and points to the smaller object, saying, "Well, that sofa has a lot more stains on it." I say, "That's not a sofa, it's a settee." Now Susan realizes that she and I do not, in fact, mean the same thing by the word "sofa."

Why? The reason is that I am making a distinction between two words, "sofa" and "settee," where something is either the one or the other, and not both, while Susan does not make such a distinction, either because she does not have the word "settee" or because she uses it in the same way as she uses "sofa." When I use the word "sofa," I mean it to exclude the word "settee" as applicable; when I use the word "settee," I mean it to exclude the word "sofa." Susan, of course, does not exactly know the basis on which I make the distinction between "sofa" and "settee" (how and why I distinguish "sofa" and "settee"), a matter to which we will turn in the next section.

Now someone else comes in, let's call her Kris, who has overheard our conversation, and says, "That's not a settee, nor a sofa, it's a couch." I and Susan now realize that when Kris uses the word "couch," she distinguishes among the words "sofa," "settee" and "couch." Perhaps someone else comes along and offers up the term "divan."

What is emerging here is that what we mean by a word depends on which other words we have available to us and which other words our use of the word (e.g., "sofa") is meant to exclude or not exclude as possibly also applying (e.g., "sofa" excludes "settee," but not "couch"). It also depends on which words are "available" to me in a given situation. For example, I may sometimes use the word "love seat," which I consider a type of settee, but in the above situation with Susan and Kris I may have not viewed this as a possible choice, perhaps because I am reluctant to use the term in front of close friends who might think it too "fancy." This is to say that I am currently using a social language in which "love seat" is not available.

The sorts of factors we have seen thus far in our discussion of "sofa" reflect one central principle involved in meaning, a principle I will call the exclusion principle. Susan, Kris, and I all have the word "sofa," but it means different things to each of us because each of has a different set of related words.

The exclusion principle says that the meaning of a word is—in part, because there are other principles, as well—a matter of what other words my use of a given word in a given situation is intended to exclude or not exclude as also possibly applicable (though not actually used in this case). Meaning is always (in part) a matter of intended exclusions and inclusions (contrasts and lack of contrasts) within an assumed semantic field.

I should point out that in a given situation my choices always include both words (like "sofa" or "settee") and phrases ("my old piece of furniture" or "my new piece of furniture"). Indeed, where someone doesn't have a given word, they can often substitute a phrase (e.g., "small sofa," "down-scale sofa," "old sofa"), though these phrases will rarely (probably never) mean exactly what a given word does. However, to keep matters simple, I will continue to talk just about words.

Notice that the exclusion principle implies that we speakers of the same language can (and usually) do mean different things by the words we use, or, at least, we can never really be sure that this is not so in any given case. This fact undoubtedly leads to misunderstanding and miscommunication, but by the nature of the case we can, in fact, never be sure how much. When people differ significantly enough in the sets of words available to them, in the distinctions they are making, they are speaking different social languages. But the borders between social languages are not rigid and entirely discrete—they are often a matter of degree.

Now, in the above example, when Susan heard me say that what she had pointed to was not a sofa, but a settee, she knew I meant to distinguish between "sofa" and "settee." But she did not know what my basis for this distinction was (though she may have guessed, say, that it was size). In fact, there is no way for her to know for sure, even if she asks me—I might not be consciously aware of my basis, I may even be wrong about the matter, misreporting what I unconsciously think. We can all, in fact, continually learn more about the basis for our exclusions and inclusions of other words. That is, we can continually discover new things about what we mean.

Susan can guess my basis only by watching my behavior. Even if I say that "settees" are small and "sofas" are large, Susan may through watching my behavior (watching what I do and do not call what) come to guess (as I may too) that settees are (for me) small seats for more than one person that are not very "upscale" or "trendy," and that sofas are larger such seats or smaller ones that are "upscale." But it is always possible that further observation will show that even this is not the basis on which I make the distinction and that the basis is somewhat different. My meanings can be ascertained (and, then, only for a time) only by watching the social practices in which I engage.

Call this the guessing principle, a second central principle operative in meaning. We can make judgments about what others (and ourselves) mean by a word used on a given occasion only by guessing what other words the word is meant to exclude or not exclude (however conventionalized or not, however conscious or unconscious the guess may be). And we can make judgments about what others (and ourselves) mean by a word, not just in a given context, but in general or usually, only by guessing what other words that word is meant to exclude or not exclude across a wide array of different occasions wherein they (or we) normally or regularly use the word. Of course, people who belong to the same or similar social groups, who speak the same or similar social languages, make better "guesses" about each other.

In fact, as the philosopher John Austin (1953) pointed out, we may not know what we would say, what word we would use or not, on a given occasion until we have confronted that occasion. In this sense, we can always discover something new about what we mean by a word. An example that is commonly discussed is what we would say if a computer engaged in all the sorts of behaviors we associated with thinking and displayed emotions to boot—would we say that the computer could "think," that it had "feelings"? Confronted with such a situation (or even just thinking about it) we can discover new aspects of what we mean by words like "think" and "feel." We would also discover, in this case, how central having a body is to our notions of thinking, feeling, and being human.

What the guessing principle says, in part, is that we discover what others and ourselves mean by operations that are—though they are sometimes carried out consciously and sometimes unconsciously—not in principle different from the operations scientists use to investigate and make intelligent guesses about the world. They (and we) simply build theories and "test" them by how well they make sense of past and future experience, revising them as the need arises. Philosophers of science usually use the word "induction" where I am using the word "guess" (Holland et al. 1986).

There is more to meaning than the exclusion principle and the guessing principle. We can make good guesses about what other words a given word is meant to exclude or not exclude as applicable on a given occasion only by consideration of the context of the communication (Duranti 1997; Duranti and Goodwin 1992; Garnham 1985: 134–182). By context I mean the other words used, or liable to be used, in the situation, the physical setting, and the assumed knowledge and beliefs of the speaker (writer, signer). However, we should be clear on the fact that whenever we speak, context is not really something that can be seen and heard, it is actually something people make assumptions about (Cazden 1992: ch. 4). They assume that just so much of the preceding speech (or writing) is relevant to what is being said now; they assume that just so much of the available physical setting is relevant to what is being said; they assume that the speaker believes so-and-so and has such-and-such values.

To see how context helps to determine meaning, consider the following example: if I show you a comic book, a magazine, and a hard-cover novel, and ask you to "pick out the book," you will probably select the hard-cover novel. On the other hand, if I show you a radio, a table, and a comic book, and ask you to "pick out the book," you will select the comic book and would even have selected the magazine had that been a choice with the radio and table, instead of the comic book.

Or, to take other examples, in the context of looking at stuffed animals, "cat" in "I'll take the cat" means an inanimate object, but in the context of an animal shelter, "cat" in "I'll take the cat" means a living being. In the context of a discussion about ancient Egyptian thought, "cat" in "The cat was considered a sacred symbol" means living beings and images of them (pictures, statues, and so forth). And in the context of looking at two clouds, one of which looks like a cat and the other like a star, "cat" in "The cat is moving faster than the star" means a cat-shaped cloud.

Call this the context principle: guesses about what words mean (what other words they are intended to exclude or not as applicable) are always relative to assumptions about what the relevant context is, and, thus, change with assumptions about the context.

Our three principles—the exclusion principle, the guessing principle, and the context principle—imply claims about meaning that are deeply opposed to our common sense (and many academic) beliefs about the matter. Words have no meaning in and of themselves and by themselves apart from other words. They have meanings only relative to choices (by speakers and writers) and guesses (by hearers and readers) about other words, and assumptions about contexts.

Now, you might say that this is precisely why scientists use formal languages like mathematics and formal symbols like "H_2O"—in order to avoid meanings involving other words and contexts. But this will not get us into a realm of non-contextual absolutes. The scientist still has to choose where to draw the lines: Is this different enough to be a different species? Is this different enough in chemical composition to get a different symbol? Should we take into consideration for our symbols not just which atoms are present, but their "handedness" as well, or other properties physics has or will discover? Anything has innumerable properties that could be relevant and thus could enter into a choice about just what we symbolize. These choices just are choices about what other possible symbols to exclude or not in what contexts.

When we get outside "scientific" terms, and even outside terms for material objects altogether, we come to "abstract" terms like "honesty," "love," "good," "immoral," or "correct." While people have struggled to give absolute "definitions" for these sorts of words too, here it is yet more apparent that we have nothing but the exclusion principle, the guessing principle, and the context principle. One could spend a lifetime figuring out what someone else (or one's self) means by "love," "friendship," or "honesty."

It is important to be clear about the nature of our choices and guesses. They are not, of course, completely free, rather they are constrained by the formal system that constitutes the language. Consider the following example in this regard. I show you a picture of an African-American woman, a Native American woman, a Chinese-American woman, and a Mexican-American woman, and ask, "Who are these people?" The question word "who" requires the answer to be a noun, and in particular a noun naming a person. The way the vocabulary of English is structured makes available only so many and only certain families of words, though these do not have absolutely rigid borders. The vocabulary of English makes available families of words for people germane to ethic groups, "colors," gender, humanity in general, and many more.

My choice of a word here, then, is partially constrained by the structure of the language, but obviously, within these constraints, there is much room left for choice in what word I select and this choice will be partly contingent on what I take (assume) the relevant context to be. Within this freedom, I can say "people of color," "U.S. minorities," "women," "people," "groups that have been oppressed in the United States," and many more. Note, too, that saying "people of color" has a different meaning than saying "colored people." (When there are two choices, there are two possible meanings, thanks to the different histories of these phrases.)

It is also the case that the choices and guesses we make may be more or less conscious and more or less conventionalized (routinized, a matter of habit). But nothing stops us, in principle, from trying to bring unconscious aspects of our choices and guesses to consciousness and from questioning our conventionalized, routinized, habitualized choices. We do this not by inspecting the insides or our heads, but by observing and reflecting on the social practices of ourselves and other people.

Of course, if we always engaged in such reflective activity, communication would quickly slow to the breaking point. Everyday social activity requires us to leave most choices we make to the routine established by conventional habits, habits we have picked up as part of the socialization involved in acquiring the language, various social languages within it, and becoming members of our society. As Mary Douglas (1986) has argued, we allow social institutions (including language) to do much of our thinking for us. We could not live if we consciously made every decision involved in communication and other social behavior, no more than we could dance if we thought out each step as we did it. But this does not remove the moral obligation we have to sometimes investigate the basis of our choices, especially in the case of what I called in Chapter 1 socially contested terms, or when we have reason to suspect that our choices are harming us or others.

Cultural models as the basis of meaning choices and guesses

So far I have left out one crucial principle of meaning. This is the principle that determines the basis of the distinctions we make (e.g., "sofa" versus "settee" versus "couch" applicable to both). This basis is, as we have argued, ultimately the social practices in which we and others engage. However, we bring "theories" to those social practices, based on the fact that, in many cases, we have engaged in such practices over and over again. We have picked up certain ideas and assumptions about them, ideas and assumptions that we use to make things go smoothly in the practices.

To get at such ideas and assumptions—our "theories"—let us consider what the word "bachelor" means (Fillmore 1975; Quinn and Holland 1987). All of us think we know what the word means (see Chapter 1 as well). Dictionaries say it means "an unmarried man" (*Webster Handy College Dictionary* 1972), because it seems clear that in its most contexts in which the word is used it excludes as applicable words like woman, girl, boy, and married.

Let me ask you, then, is the Pope a bachelor? Is a thrice-divorced man a bachelor? Is a young man who has been in an irreversible coma since childhood a bachelor? What about a eunuch? A committed gay man? An elderly senile gentleman who has never been married? The answer to all these questions is either "no" or "I'm not sure" (as I have discovered by asking a variety of people). Why? After all, all these people are unmarried men.

The reason why the answer to these questions is "no," despite the fact that they all involve cases of clearly unmarried males, is that in using the word "bachelor" we are making exclusions we are unaware of and are assuming that the contexts in which we use the word are clear and transparent when they are not. Context has the nasty habit of almost always seeming clear, transparent, and unproblematic, when it hardly ever actually is.

Our meaningful distinctions (our choices and guesses) are made on the basis of certain beliefs and values. This basis is a type of theory (in the terms I used in Chapter 1), in the case of many words a social theory. The theories that form the basis of such choices and assumptions have a particular character. They involve (usually unconscious) assumptions about models of simplified worlds. Such models are sometimes called cultural models, folk theories, scenes, schemas, frames, or figured worlds (D'Andrade and Strauss 1992; Gee 2005; Holland *et al.* 1998; Holland and Quinn 1987). I will call them "cultural models."

I think of cultural models as something like "movies" or "videotapes" in the mind (Gee 2004). We all have a vast store of these simulations, each of which depicts prototypical (what we take to be "normal") events in a simplified world. We conventionally take these simplified worlds to be the "real" world, or act as if they were. We make our choices and guesses about meaning in relation to these worlds.

These cultural models are emblematic visions of an idealized, "normal," "typical" reality, in much the way that, say, a Clint Eastwood movie is emblematic of the world of the "tough guy" or an early Woody Allen movie of the "sensitive but klutzy male." They are also variable, differing across different cultural groups, including different cultural groups in a society speaking the same language. They change with time and other changes in the society, but we are usually quite unaware we are using them and of their full implications.

These cultural models are, then, pictures of simplified worlds in which prototypical events unfold. The most commonly used cultural model for the word "bachelor" is (or used to be) something like the following (Fillmore 1975): Men marry women at a certain age; marriages last for life; and in such a world, a bachelor is a man who stays unmarried beyond the usual age, thereby becoming eminently marriageable. We know that this simplified world is not always true, but it is the one against which we use the word "bachelor," that is, make choices about what other words are excluded as applicable or not, and make assumptions about what the relevant context is in a given case of using the word. Thus, the Pope is not a bachelor because he just isn't in this simplified world, being someone who has vowed not to marry at any age. Nor are gay men, since they have chosen not to marry women.

Such cultural models involve us in exclusions that are not at first obvious and which we are often quite unaware of making. In the case of "bachelor" we are actually excluding words like "gay" and "priest" as applying to ("normal") unmarried men, and in doing so, we are assuming that men come in two ("normal") types: ones who get married early and those that get married late. This assumption marginalizes all people who do not want to get married or do not want to marry members of the opposite sex. It is part of the function of such cultural models to set up what count as central, typical cases, and what count as marginal, non-typical cases.

Such hidden exclusions are, in the sense in which we defined the term in Chapter 1, ideological. They involve social theories (remember, cultural models are a type of theory), quite tacit ones involving beliefs about the distribution of "goods" in society—prestige, power, desirability, centrality. Furthermore, the fact that we are usually unaware of using these cultural models and of their full implications means that the assumptions they embody about the distribution of social goods appear to us "natural," "obvious," "just the way things are," "inevitable," even "appropriate." And this is so despite the fact that cultural models vary across both different cultures and different social groups in a single society, and change with time and changes in the society.

We also pointed out in Chapter 1 that it was a moral imperative to question and investigate tacit social theories that have a reasonable potential to (or actually do) harm people. Thus, it follows that it is a moral imperative to render conventionalized or unconscious choices and assumptions less habitualized when they involve cultural models which reasonably could or do harm people.

Due to cultural changes, partly the result of the greater assertion and visibility of gays and women, as well as changing attitudes towards marriage, many people are beginning to use "bachelor" differently. Some people apply the word to women as well men, while others use it as a term of abuse for men who think a certain life style makes them attractive to women. Yet others are beginning to use "spinster" as a term of praise for women who have accepted their marginality in the eyes of certain segments of society as a badge not only of honor, but as a sign of their lack of complicity with sexist values.

As we pointed out in Chapter 1, when we discussed Patricia Williams's (1991) law case involving what was and was not sausage, meaning is embedded in social practices, tied to social theories (cultural models), and open to negotiation and contestation. I don't have to accept your use of "bachelor" or your exclusion of gay marriage as marriage. In turn, you don't have to accept my refusal to accept your use of "bachelor." It is always interesting to see where people will stop the flow of conversation and interaction to object to meanings (and exclusions). At times, the matter puts all of us into a moral dilemma.

Cultural models in action

I will give one final example of cultural models operating, an example that brings out rather clearly the role cultural models play in creating and upholding stereotypes. Consider, then, a study of middle-class parents in Cambridge, Massachusetts, in the United States (Harkness *et al.* 1992). When these parents talked about their children, two cultural models were highly salient. One was tied to the notion of "stages of development" through which children pass. The other was tied to the notion of the child's growing desire for "independence" as the central theme giving point and direction to these stages.

For example, consider how one mother talked about her son David:

> he's very definitely been in a stage, for the last three or four months, of wanting to help, everything I do, he wants to help. . . . And now, I would say in the last month, the intensity of wanting to do every- thing himself is . . . we're really into that stage. . . . I suppose they're all together . . . ya, I suppose they're two parts of the same thing. Independence, reaching out for independence. Anything he wants to do for himself, which is just about everything, that I move in and do for him, will result in a real tantrum.
>
> (pp. 165–166)

David's mother later gave as an example of his "wanting to do things for himself" an episode where she had opened the car door for him when he was having a hard time getting out of the car: "He was very upset, so we had to go back and . . . close the door" (p. 166). She also attributed David's recent dislike of being dressed or diapered to his growing sense of independence: ". . . he's getting to the point where it's insulting, and he doesn't want to be put on his back to have his diaper changed."

However, in the same interview, David's mother also mentioned another behavior pattern. To get David to sleep, she straps him into his car seat and pretends to be taking him for a drive. He almost immediately falls asleep, and then she returns home, leaving him in the car, with a blanket, to take a nap: "But he goes to sleep so peacefully, without any struggle, usually" (p. 167).

Though this latter pattern is a repeated daily routine, nonetheless David's mother does not talk about this behavior as part of a "stage." Rather, she says, the behavior "just sort of evolved." This is somewhat remarkable. Being strapped into a car seat and taken for a ride that inevitably ends in a nap might be seen as inconsistent with David's need for "independence"—just as having his diaper changed is—and thus equally cause for being "insulted."

Ironically, another pair of parents in the same study use their daughter's active resistance to being put in a car seat as an example of "this whole stage of development" and "the sort of independence thing she's into now," but in the same interview say "the thing that's interesting is that she allows you to clean her up, after changing her, a lot more easily than she used to. She used to hate to be cleaned up. She would twist and squirm." So, here, too, parents appear to be inconsistent. They take the child's desire not to be manipulated into a car seat as a sign of a growing desire for "independence," but are not bothered by the fact that this desire doesn't seem to carry over to the similar event of having her diaper changed. And, oddly, this little girl exemplifies just the reverse pattern from David (who resents having his diaper changed, but willingly gets strapped into the car seat, even to take a nap).

Many parents, and many others in our culture, consider stages to be "real" things that are "inside" their children. Further, they interpret these stages as signposts on the way to becoming an "independent" (and a rather "de-socialized") person. But, it appears, parents label behaviors part of a stage only when these behaviors represent new behaviors of a sort that both could be seen as negative or difficult and that require from the parents new sorts of responses. Behaviors that are not problematic in the parent–child relationship—e.g., David yielding to naps in his car seat or the little girl yielding peacefully to being diapered—are not labeled as stages. Furthermore, the parents interpret these potentially negative behaviors which get labeled as stages in terms of a culturally valued notion of "independence," a notion that other cultures, even different social groups within our culture, may well view as socially disruptive or as "antisocial."

And where do these parents get their notions of "stages" and "independence"? To answer this question, we need only turn to Rudolph Fleck's seminal 1943 book *Genesis and Development of a Scientific Fact*. Fleck argued that words that we take to name "private" mental states ("believe," "recognize," "know") do not, in fact, name individual processes, but social ones:

> Cognition is therefore not an individual process of any theoretical "particular consciousness." Rather it is a result of a social activity, since the existing stock of knowledge exceeds the range available to any one individual.

The statement, "Someone recognizes something," whether it be a relation, a fact, or an object [that they recognize], is therefore incomplete. It is no more meaningful as it stands than the statements "This book is larger," or "Town A is situated to the left of Town B." Something is still missing, namely the addition, "than that book," to the second statement, and either "to someone standing on the road between towns A and B while facing north," or "to someone walking on the road from town C to town B" to the third statement. The relative terms "larger" and "left" acquire a definite meaning only in conjunction with their appropriate components.

Analogously, the statement "Someone recognizes something" demands some such supplement as "on the basis of a certain fund of knowledge," or, better, "as a member of a certain cultural environment," and, best, "in a particular thought style, in a particular thought collective."

(pp. 38–39)

What Fleck is saying, put into terms relevant to our discussion here, is that a statement like "Cambridge parents recognize that (or believe that, or think that) their child is in a certain stage" only appears to be about their private minds or about an internal process going on in their child, a "stage." In fact, the statement is better taken to mean something like "In the set of social practices through which these parents render visible and recognizable who they are as parents and who their child is as a child and what they are doing when they parent, such and such words, deeds, actions and interactions count as a child undergoing a stage toward further independence, a highly valued trait within these social practices." Talking and acting in terms of stages is, within these social practices, part of what it is to do being a parent or child, or, better put, to do being in a parent–child relationship. This is not necessarily true of other groups' social practices. (For a quite different set of social practices in regard to parent–child relationships, see Philipsen 1975, 1990.)

These notions of "stage" and "independence" are partially conscious and partially unconscious cultural models these parents hold and act on as part and parcel of a set of related social practices (what I will call in Chapters 6 and 7 a "Discourse," with a capital "D"). These cultural models need not be fully in any parent's or child's head, consciously or unconsciously, because they are available in the culture in which the parents live—through the media, through written materials, and through interaction with others in the society.

Cultural models, self-judgments, and actual behavior

The different cultural models of different social and cultural groups of people always involve competing notions of what counts as an "acceptable" or "valuable" person or deed. In fact, we can, at times, enforce on ourselves the negative judgment of other groups' cultural model. A particularly clear example of this phenomenon can be seen if we consider for a moment a common American cultural model of "success" or "getting ahead," as discussed by D'Andrade (1984), a cultural model that is deeply embedded in U.S. society, in particular:

> It seems to be the case that Americans think that if one has ability, and if, because of competition or one's own strong drive, one works hard at achieving high goals, one will reach an outstanding level of accomplishment. And when one reaches this level one will be recognized as a success, which brings prestige and self-satisfaction.
>
> (p. 95)

So pervasive is this cultural model in American culture that D'Andrade goes on to say: "Perhaps what is surprising is that anyone can resist the directive force of such a system—that there are incorrigibles" (p. 98). However, people from different social groups within American society relate to this cultural model in quite different ways.

Claudia Strauss (1988, 1990, 1992) in a study of working-class men in Rhode Island (U.S.) talking about their lives and work found that they accepted the above cultural model of success. For example, one working man said:

> I believe if you put an effort into anything, you can get ahead. . . . If I want to succeed, I'll succeed. It has to be, come from within here. Nobody else is going to make you succeed but yourself . . . And, if anybody disagrees with that, there's something wrong with them.
>
> (1992: 202)

However, most of the men Strauss studied did not, in fact, act on the success model in terms of their career choices or in terms of how they carried out their daily lives. Unlike many white-collar professionals, these men did not choose to change jobs or regularly seek promotion. They did not regularly sacrifice their time with their families and their families' interests for their own career advancement or "self-development." These men recognized the success model as a set of values and, in fact, judging themselves by this model, concluded that they had not really been "successful," and thereby lowered their self-esteem.

The reason these men did not actually act on this model was due to the influence of another cultural model, a model which did affect their actual behaviors. This was the cultural model of "being a breadwinner." Unlike the individualism expressed in the success model, these workers, when they talked about their actual lives, assumed that the interests of the family came ahead of the interests of any individual in it, including themselves. For example, one worker said:

> [The worker is discussing the workers' fight against the company's proposal mandating Sunday work.] But when that changed and it was negotiated through a contract that you would work, so you had to change or keep losing that eight hours' pay. With three children, I couldn't afford it. So I had to go with the flow and work the Sundays.
>
> (1992: 207)

This is in sharp contrast to the white-collar professionals studied in Bellah *et al.* (1996), professionals who carried their individualism so far as to be unsure whether they had any substantive responsibility to their families if their families' interests stood in the way of their "developing themselves" as individuals. The Rhode Island workers accepted the breadwinner model not just as a set of values with which to judge themselves and others. They saw the model not as a matter of choice, but rather as an inescapable fact of life (e.g., "had to change," "had to go with the flow"). Thus, the values connected to this model were much more effective in shaping their routine daily behaviors. In fact, this very distinction—between mere "values" and "hard reality" ("the facts")—is itself a particularly pervasive cultural model within Western society.

In contrast to these working-class men, many white-collar professionals work in environments where the daily behaviors of those around them conform to the success model more than daily behaviors on the factory floor conform to this model. For these professionals, then, their daily observations and social practices reinforce explicit ideological learning in regard to the cultural model for success. For them, in contrast to the working-class men Strauss studied, the success model, not the breadwinner model, is seen as "an inescapable fact of life," and, thus, for them, this model determines not just their self-esteem, but many of their actual behaviors.

The working-class men Strauss studied are, in a sense, "colonized" by the success model. They use it, a model which actually fits the observations and behaviors of other groups in the society, to judge themselves and lower their self-esteem. But, as we have seen, since they fail to identify themselves as actors within that model, they cannot develop the very expertise that would allow and motivate them to practice it. In turn, they leave such expertise to the white-collar professionals, some of whom made the above worker work on Sunday against his own interests and wishes. On the other hand, many of the white-collar professionals fail to see that their very allegiance to the success model is connected to their failure to be substantive actors in their families or larger social and communal networks.

Cultural models and master myths

I have argued that one of the bases for our choices and guesses about meaning are cultural models. The various cultural models that a particular social group or whole society uses often share certain basic assumptions. These shared assumptions form what I will call "master myths" of the social group or society. These master myths are often associated with certain characteristic metaphors or "turns of phrase and thought" in which the group or society encapsulates its favored wisdom (Lakoff 1987, 2002; Lakoff and Johnson 2003). At the same time, these myths hide from us other ways of thinking, even ways that actually coexist in society with the master myths. They come to seem "inevitable," "natural," "normal," "practical," "commonsense," though other cultures and people at other times in history have found them "odd," "unnatural," violations of common sense.

To see an example of one of our master myths at work, let's play a little game. Below, I give lists of words designating various concepts. In each list I have underlined a given concept, and I have given two lists for each italicized concept. True to what we have seen about context, each italicized concept takes on a somewhat different meaning in each list (context). You should ask yourself what this meaning is and how it differs from the alternative meaning (in the other list) for each italicized concept. In each case, I have appended to the second list (the "b" list) an idiomatic expression that we all regularly use and which seems to be closely associated with the meaning of the italicized concept in the second ("b") list.

1   a   garden, home, *work*, dust, dishes
      b   profit, wage, *work*, unions, management
          idiom: work for money (also: work for a living)

2   a   shower, dinner-date, beach, *time*, bed
    b   waste, spend, save, *time*, clock
       idiom: time is money

3   a   food, clothes, apartment, *money*, car
    b   interest-rate, bank, stock, *money*, investment
       idiom: it takes money to make money

In 1a, "work" takes on the meaning of a human activity that is part of everyday life, the effort it takes to go about daily life. In 1b, on the other hand, "work" names an abstract commodity that is bought, sold and negotiated within social institutions, and which generates profit. In 2a, "time" names the flow of human experience within which certain activities are appropriately embedded and ordered in relation to each other in terms of human desire and need. In 2b, "time" names an abstract entity that is analogized to a substance that can be measured out, wasted, and saved. In 3a, "money" names a thing that can be "traded for" other useful things (like food, clothes, or fun). In 3b "money" names an abstract thing which, situated within the economic system, is hoarded in and for itself and generates more of itself.

The second ("b") lists represent perspectives on the underlined concepts (work, time, money) which situate them in one of the master myths of our society (Marx 1967, 1973; Taussig 1980). In all three "b" lists, the three concepts are actually seen in a similar way. They are abstracted away from the context of human activity and human relationships, and set up as quantifiable entities, entities that can be measured out, stored, saved, wasted, bought, sold, invested. Furthermore, in addition to their attenuated tie to human beings and human relationships, they become intertranslatable in terms of each other: so much work = so much (work) time = so much money (wages) = so much profit = so much invested = so much capital.

The idioms I have placed beside the "b" lists show these intertranslations quite clearly, if we quit taking their meanings for granted and actually think about them. "Work for money" implies that work can be translated, quantity by quantity, into money (and "a day's work for a day's pay" shows that this translation can be computed in units of time); "time is money" equates time and money; and "it takes money to make money" implies that money somehow, like a living being, can generate, give birth to, yet more of itself.

The "a" lists above show us a perspective on our underlined concepts (work, time, money) that is different from that encouraged by our master myth, but a perspective which is often ignored, forgotten, or hidden from us through the operations of the master myth. The "a" lists contextualize our three concepts in terms of human activities and human relationships. Time is the way humans experience the socially appropriate ordering of events; work is the effort people put into their daily lives; and money is an object that can be traded for other objects, objects that satisfy human needs, desires, and interests, not something of any use in and of itself. This money doesn't self-generate more money, it is meant to be given up for "real things" (things which are meaningful in human lives).

To most of us in our daily lives, the perspectives of the master myth we have looked at, and the idioms that support it, seem natural, obvious, appropriate, and "right." But these perspectives and idioms do not really stand up very well under critical ethically focused thought. Think, for instance, of what the idiom "earn a living" means. This idiom denotes the work I do for money. It implies I need to earn by living-ness (alive-ness) by working for money (usually so that someone else can earn "profit"). But there is another, much older perspective: people don't trade work for life and they do not need to "earn" their own lives, rather work in the sense of their own willed activity and effort, like play, is just part of being alive. Idioms like "work for a living," "earn a living," and the master myth they are part of (not to mention the work realities they help to uphold and naturalize), alienate work from life, indeed, alienate people from their very lives. What could be less natural than that?

Cultural models in education

Cultural models have deep implications for the teaching of language and literacy to people new to a culture and to non-mainstream students who wish to master the "standard," "dominant" cultural models in the society, despite the fact that many of these models marginalize non-mainstream people. It is entirely unlikely that anyone could overtly teach the whole network of cultural models for any one culture. One learns cultural models by being acculturated, by being open to and having experiences within a culture or social group, by practicing language and interaction in natural and meaningful contexts. Of course, not all students are open to such experiences. Acculturation carries with it real risk. Cultural models carry within them values and perspectives on people and on reality. Cultural models from different sociocultural groups can conflict in their content, in how they are used, and in the values and perspectives they carry.

The cultural models of non-mainstream students, rooted in their homes and communities, can conflict seriously with those of mainstream culture (Heath 1983; Gonzalez *et al.* 2005; Ogbu 1978; Trueba 1987, 1989). The values of mainstream culture are, in fact, often complicit with the oppression of non-mainstream students' home cultures and other social identities. This is true, for instance, in the case of many African-American and Latino students, as well as many students from non-Western cultures. It is true for many women, as well as for many people with alternative sexual orientations.

These conflicts are real and cannot be wished away. They are an integral part of the language teacher's job. The teacher can, however, allow these conflicts to become part of the instruction. Brought to the student's attention, allowed to become part of on-going discussion with teacher and peers, they can themselves serve to focus students' attention on relevant aspects of cultural models, in the students' home culture, in their multiple other social identities, and in mainstream and school culture.

The teacher's job, in my view, is to properly focus attention. Any student faced with the myriad aspects of reality in a culture which might be relevant to the cultural models used by members of that culture could well take forever to master the meaning of language. The typical second-language learner does not have the great amount of time available to the infant and young child learning a first language. The teacher, then, can, at the right time, in the midst of the student's on-going practice within the culture, and with culturally relevant materials in the classroom, point to the relevant data, focus the student's attention on the relevant aspects of experience that will make the system, the network of cultural models, begin to gel.

There is no knowing a language without knowing the cultural models that constitute the meaning of that language for some cultural group. But all cultural models tend ultimately to limit our perception of differences and of new possibilities. They allow us to function in the world with ease, but at the price of stereotypes and routinized thought and perception. It is the job of the teacher to allow students to grow beyond both the cultural models of their home cultures and those of mainstream and school culture.

Just as many women have sought to replace our cultural models of gender roles with new ways of thinking, interacting, and speaking, so humans at their best are always open to rethinking, to imagining newer and better, more just and more beautiful words and worlds. That is why good teaching is ultimately a moral act.

Chapter 6

Discourse analysis

Introduction

In the last chapter we looked at the meanings of words, the cultural models connected to them, and the diverse social languages in which they are embedded. This chapter and the next deal with how meaning works in extended stretches of talk like arguments and stories. To accomplish our task we will use one approach to "discourse analysis" (Gee 2005). By "discourse" I mean stretches of language which "hang together" so as to make sense to some community of people, such as a contribution to a conversation or a story. At the limit, such "stretches" can be just one word—for example, if I say "Chocolate" to a sales clerk in an ice-cream store. Here the single word "hangs together" with the interactional sequence it is part of ("What will you have?"). Making sense is always also a social and variable matter: what makes sense to one community may not make sense to another. Thus, to understand sense making in language it is necessary to understand the ways in which language is embedded in society and social institutions (such as families and schools).

It is not only linguists who are interested in language and society. Novelists, too, have often had a keen ear for the social workings of language. For instance, in the following conversation between Jonathan Harker and Count Dracula (from Bram Stoker's novel *Dracula*, 1897/ 1981, p. 19), Count Dracula shows himself a sophisticated student of language in society:

"But, Count," I said, "you know and speak English thoroughly!" He bowed gravely.

"I thank you, my friend, for your all-too-flattering estimate, but I fear that I am but a little way on the road I would travel. True,

> I know the grammar and the words, but yet I know not how to speak them."
> "Indeed," I said, "you speak excellently."
> "Not so," he answered. "Well, I know that, did I move and speak in your London, none there are who would not know me for a stranger. That is not enough for me. Here I am noble . . . the common people know me, and I am master. But a stranger in a strange land, he is no one; men know him not—and to know not is to care not for. I am content if I am like the rest, so that no man stops if he see me, or pauses in his speaking if he hear my words . . . I have been so long master that I would be master still—or at least that none other should be master of me."

Of course, Dracula has a special reason for wanting to give no pause as he moves about London: he is about to travel to London to collect fresh blood. It would not do to stick out too conspicuously. Nonetheless, Dracula here argues in terms of a sophisticated theory of language.

First, Dracula realizes that there are two major motivations underlying language use: status and solidarity. Dracula says, "I have been so long master that I would be master still," indicating that he wants status in the community. By "status" I want to name things like respect, dignity, and social distance. At the same time Dracula says, ". . . a stranger in a strange land, he is no one; men know him not—and to know not is to care not for. I am content if I am like the rest." Here Dracula indicates he also desires solidarity with others. Status and solidarity are the competing, conflicting, and yet intimately related fields of attraction and repulsion within which all uses of language are situated.

Second, Dracula realizes that it is not grammar alone (or primarily) that carries out the work of achieving status and solidarity, but the ways in which words are spoken, or, we might say, how one "designs" one's utterances: "True, I know the grammar and the words, but yet I know not how to speak them."

Variations to demarcate social identities

Before we look at extended texts, I want to discuss briefly how social identity works in relation to status and solidarity. In the last chapter, I pointed out that there are a great many different social languages, that is, different ways of speaking or writing a language like English. However, if speakers are to be able to vary their style of speaking, they must have a language that essentially gives them options between equivalent ways of saying the same thing, but that differ in terms of their associations with various socially defined groups (e.g., class, gender, ethnic group, work group, area of expertise, etc.).

For example, English-speakers can pronounce the *-ing* affix of the progressive either as *-ing* or *-in'* (e.g., "I am looking into it," "I'm lookin' into it"; note also the options in regard to the contraction of "am"). The *-ing* pronunciation is more "formal"; it denotes that one is taking on a more formal, more "public" identity. The *-in'* pronunciation is less formal and more colloquial; it denotes that one is taking on a more local, casual, intimate identity (Milroy and Milroy 1985). Speakers of English tend to use *-ing* when they are more concerned with status and "keeping their distance" and *-in'* when they are more concerned with solidarity and bonding with those to whom they are speaking.

There are literally hundreds of such variable elements in English pronunciation, morphology, and syntax. This reservoir of variability is used to mark out various styles or social languages (Labov 1972a, b, 1980, 2006; Milroy 1987a, b; Milroy and Gordon 2003). These styles can be ranged in a continuum from more formal and status-oriented styles to less formal and more solidarity-oriented styles, with a good many styles in between. Furthermore, the use that English-speakers make of this variability is a subtle indicator of their social class and social aspirations. Table 1, which contains data on the use of *-ing* versus *-in'* in Norwich, England, indicates a typical way in which such variability patterns in a speech community, a pattern that has been replicated many times over for a number of variables in a wide variety of speech communities in Great Britain and the United States (Milroy and Milroy 1985: 95).

In Table 1 we see data on the percentage of *-in'* forms used by speakers from different socioeconomic classes, speaking in various styles defined in terms of degrees of formality. The styles range from reading word lists, a very formal style in which one monitors one's speech very carefully, to casual style, in which one is socially comfortable and is not closely monitoring speech, with several styles in between. The more speakers monitor their speech—the more formal the context—the more their speech reflects the norms for what they believe is "prestige-ful" language in the wider society. These norms are determined by how speakers perceive the higher social classes to speak (Finegan 1980; Milroy and Milroy 1985; Labov 1972a, b; Milroy and Gordon 2003).

Thus, note that the lowest social class (lower working class) in their most formal style (word list style) approximate (29 percent) the behavior of the middle class in their casual speech (28 percent). This is because,

118   Social Linguistics and Literacies

Table 1 Percentage of *-in'* in Norwich, shown according to style and class

Class	WLS	RPS	FS	CS
Middle middle	0	0	3	28
Lower middle	0	10	15	42
Upper working	5	15	74	87
Middle working	23	44	88	95
Lower working	29	66	98	100

Note:
WLS word list style, RPS reading passage style, FS formal style (direct questions in interview), CS casual style (attention diverted away from recording).
Source: Chambers and Trudgill (1980: 71).

as the lower-class speakers monitor their speech more (as they move to more formal styles), they apply to their behavior the norms they have internalized about language, norms formed by their (unconscious) observation of the more or less everyday behavior of the middle class, a class whose behavior they associate with status and prestige.

But this raises a rather deep paradox: If the lower classes are aware of the prestige norm and are capable of meeting it when they monitor their speech, why do they progressively raise their percentage of the less prestigious form (*-in'*) as they engage in more casual styles? The answer is in the trade-off between status and solidarity.

Every speaker in the speech community, regardless of class, uses the variation between *-ing* and *-in'* to distinguish more formal (public) from less formal (intimate) styles. However, the degree to which one uses the less prestigious form in more casual styles also marks one's membership in and solidarity with one's local social group(s). As lower-class speakers enter more formal, public contexts, many of them want to achieve respect and status, as defined by the wider society, by using prestigious forms. As they enter more local, informal contexts, they want to identify with and achieve solidarity with their peers, whose values and norms they identify with at the more local level. In intermediate contexts, they may well be (unconsciously) torn between the two and seek a satisfying balance and compromise.

Table 1, however, may give a deceptively simple picture: Speakers are actually manipulating hundreds of variables at the same time, and all speakers are actually signaling, in many subtle ways, identification with a number of different "social networks" to which they belong, ranging from the society as a whole through a number of intermediate groups to the family unit. Each such group or social network defines a different identity that speakers signal in their language, with sidelong glances at other identities they adopt in other contexts, as well as glances at the identities their hearers are assuming in the interaction. Any speaker who did not have variability in his or her language, variability with which to indicate different social identities, would be a "social isolate," not part of any community. But note, also, that members of the "elites" in the society tend to adopt more formal styles in any situation than do people from less socially powerful groups. Part of their power, in fact, resides in this "vigilance" to "keep up appearances"—to attempt to signal allegiance to the centers of power and status in their society even when they are "at ease" (Bourdieu 1991, 2002).

A sample discourse analysis of an argument

We turn now to actual instances of people "making sense" using particular social languages. We will study sense making through the application of one approach to discourse analysis. Discourse—the design of language-in-use—is constituted by five interrelated linguistic systems (for various approaches, see Brown and Yule 1983; Fairclough 2003; Gee 2005; Rogers 2004; Schiffrin 1994; Schiffrin et al. 2003; Stubbs 1983; Wodak and Myers 2002). Working together, these five systems constitute the sensefulness of a text. I use the word "text" for any stretch of oral or written language such as a conversation, story, argument, report, and so forth. The five systems that make up discourse can be briefly characterized as follows:

1 *Prosody* covers the ways in which the words and sentences of a text are said: their pitch, loudness, stress, and the length assigned to various syllables, as well as the way in which the speaker hesitates and pauses.

2 *Cohesion* covers all the multifarious linguistic ways in which sentences are connected or linked to each other. It is the "glue" that holds texts together.

3 *The overall discourse organization* of a text. This covers the ways in which sentences are organized into higher-order units (bigger than single sentences), for example the scenes and episodes making up a story or the arguments and sub-arguments making up an overall argument for a particular position.

4 *Contextualization signals* by means of which speakers and writers "cue" listeners and readers into what they take the context to be. Communication is senseless unless people share some view of what

the context is within which they are communicating. But context is not "just there"; it is something people actively construe, negotiate over, and change their minds about (Duranti 1997; Duranti and Goodwin 1992; Gumperz 1982a).

5 *The thematic organization of the text.* This covers the ways in which themes (images, contrasts, focal points of interest) are signaled and developed.

These five systems are interrelated: for instance, the devices in the first three systems are used to accomplish the functions of the last two systems. In order to see the forest rather than the trees, we will look at a short text in order to gain an overview of the basic workings of the five systems. The text we will investigate, reprinted below, is an "everyday" argument in which a speaker (a young adult lower middle-class Jewish woman from Philadelphia) is defending her belief in fate.

People often think that "everyday" argumentation, carried out in informal styles, is "irrational" in comparison with the more formal styles of argumentation found in schools and academic disciplines. We will see, using discourse analysis, that "everyday" argumentation has deeper purposes than just validating a claim (winning a point) and that it is quite "rational" in its own terms.

When an English-speaker wishes to communicate an extended amount of material, she must break it up into what I will call "lines" and "stanzas." Lines are usually "clauses" (simple sentences); stanzas are sets of lines about a single minimal topic, organized rhythmically and syntactically so as to hang together in a particularly tight way. The stanza takes a particular perspective on a character, action, event, claim, or piece of information. Each stanza has a particular point of view such that when character, place, time, event, or the function of a piece of information changes (whether in an argument, report, exposition or description), the stanza must change (see also Scollon and Scollon 1981: 111–121). I will discuss lines and stanzas in more detail later.

I reprint our argument in terms of its lines and stanzas, numbering both for ease of reference later. A period indicates falling intonation followed by a noticeable pause. A comma denotes continuing intonation: there may be a slight fall or rise of contour; it may be followed by a short pause.

An argument within a conversation

Stanza 1: Position to be argued for

1   I believe in that.
2   Whatever's gonna happen is gonna happen.
3   I believe that y'know it's fate.
4   It really is.

Stanza 2: Support for position by giving personal experience

5   Because my husband has a brother, that was killed in an auto-
    mobile accident,
6   And at the same time there was another fellow, in there, that
    walked away with not even a scratch on him.

Stanza 3: Position to be argued for (repeated)

7   And I really feel—I don't feel y'can push fate,
8   and I think a lot of people do.
9   But I feel that you were put here for so many years or whatever
    the case is,
10 and that's how it is meant to be.

Stanza 4: Support for position by giving personal experience

11 Because like when we got married, we were supposed t'get
    married like about five months later.
12 My husband got a notice t'go into the service and we moved it
    up.
13 And my father died the week after we got married.
14 While we were on our honeymoon.

Stanza 5: Conclusion: position to be argued for (repeated)

15 And I just felt that move was meant to be, because if not, he
    wouldn't have been there.
16 So y'know it just seems that that's how things work out.
    (Text from Schiffrin 1987: 49–50. Stanza markings are my own)

We will look briefly at how the five systems that constitute discourse
work in this text. Speakers do not just "say what they mean" and get it
over with. They lay out information in a way that fits with their viewpoint
on the information and the interaction. They are always communicating

much more than the literal message. And to do this they use prosody, cohesion, discourse organization, contextualization signals, and thematic organization. In discussing each of these below, I will try also to give some flavor for how they are mutually interconnected.

Since we have written down an oral text, we have lost most of the prosody of the text, the way in which the speaker's voice rose and fell in pitch, the way in which she lengthened and shortened her syllables, the way in which she speeded up and slowed down her rate of speech, and the places she hesitated and paused (Bolinger 1986; Brazil 1997; Halliday 1976a; Ladd 1980). Nonetheless, we can still get a bit of a feeling for some of these rhythmical matters, and how they function in the text as a whole.

In the transcript above, a period at the end of a line stands for a fall in the pitch of the voice. Such a fall signals closure ("a closure contour"), that is, that an idea is considered by the speaker to be complete, closed off, finished. A comma at the end of a line, on the other hand, stands for only a slight fall or rise in pitch ("a continuation contour"). Such a pitch movement signals that the information in a line is considered by the speaker to be not closed off or finished, but is intended to be supplemented by information that is to follow. Whether information is finished or in need of supplement is not a matter that is determined by the nature of the information itself, rather it is a decision (choice) that the speaker makes in rhetorically structuring her text so as to achieve the viewpoint she wishes.

In this regard, consider stanza 4 in the above text. Line 13 ("And my father died the week after we got married") ends with a "closure contour," as does line 14 ("While we were on our honeymoon"). Clearly, however, these could have been said differently. Lines 13 and 14 could have been said with line 14 continuing or supplementing line 13: "And my father died the week after we got married, while we were on our honeymoon."

By placing a "full stop" at line 13, the speaker isolates and, thus, stresses the death of the father only a week after the marriage (which is supposed to be a main example of the operation of fate). Leaving line 14 as a closed-off line in its own right, separated from line 13 by the closure contour ending line 13, brings home the irony of the juxtaposition of the father's death (a closing of life) and a honeymoon (a beginning of mutual life and possible birth). If line 14 had been more closely tied to line 13, the honeymoon would have served as no more than a temporal background for the foregrounded event of the father's death.

But the separation of 13 and 14, despite a syntax that can tie them together, does more as well: it stresses the very theme of the text. In the text, the father's death (line 13) looks closed off from the honeymoon (line 14), and, indeed, to the "rational" mind these events are not, in fact, connected. But the speaker's argument is that such a lack of connection is only apparent; at a deeper level they are in fact connected by the workings of fate. The speaker's language, throughout the text, as we will see, constantly enacts and plays with the theme of connection and disconnection.

Cohesion (Halliday and Hasan 1976) is the way in which the lines and stanzas of a text are linked to or interrelated to each other. Cohesion is achieved by a variety of linguistic devices, including conjunctions, pronouns, demonstratives, ellipsis, various sorts of adverbs, as well as repeated words and phrases. In fact, any word, phrase, or syntactic device that causes two lines (clauses) to be related (linked together) makes for cohesion in the text. Such links are part of what stitches a text together into a meaningful whole; they are like threads that tie language and, thus, also, sense together.

We can see the operation of cohesion particularly clearly in how the word "because" functions in our text. Words like "because" (Schiffrin 1987) have two functions in English: one is to tie parts of "sentences" together, the other is to tie two stanzas (or even parts) together. The word "because" in line 15 is a typical intrasentential [within sentence] cohesive use of "because," simply connecting two clauses of a single "sentence." But the two other instances of the word "because" in this text are functioning differently. They are not intrasentential uses of cohesion, but rather what we might call inter-stanza uses.

Stanza 2 begins with the word "because," which here relates not two parts of a single sentence, but two stanzas (stanzas 1 and 2); it is a discourse connector, not an intrasentential connector. "Because" here signals that stanza 2 is support or evidence for the view expressed in stanza 1 as we switch from the generalized language of personal belief and feeling in stanza 1 to the narrative-based language of specific action and event in stanza 2.

Stanza 3 returns to the generalized language of personal belief and feeling, whereas stanza 4 again uses "because" to introduce specific supporting data from action and event for the speaker's position. Thus, stanzas 3 and 4 have a parallel structure to stanzas 1 and 2: "general position (stanzas 1 and 3); because specific case (stanzas 2 and 4)," creating a large-scale parallelism that ties the text together as a whole (helping to signal and develop its thematics). These uses of "because" not only stitch the text together, they help constitute its very sense: the brother's accident (in stanza 2) and the wedding that has been moved forward in time (stanza 4) are not just isolated events, as they at first seem, but rather the concrete, specific realizations of the generalized principles of fate (stanzas 1 and 3).

Both the prosody of the text and its cohesive devices contribute, along with its grammar and content, to the overall discourse organization of the text (Gee 2005; Hinds 1979; Hymes 1981; Longacre 1979, 1983; van Dijk 1980). By "discourse organization" I mean the organization of the text into lines and stanzas, as well as the way language patterns within and across these lines and stanzas.

As we have seen, stanza 1 states the general theme ("fate") in the generalized language of belief and feeling, while stanza 2 exemplifies this theme in the specific narrative-based language of action and event. Stanza 3 returns to the generalized language of belief and feeling. Then, once again, stanza 4 returns us to the specific narrative-based language of action and event. Stanza 5 concludes by returning to the more generalized language of belief and feeling about fate. The text, in deftly interweaving these two forms of language, makes its thematic "point": the world of concrete event and action is but a reflection (at a deeper level) of the general workings of "fate," workings open to feeling/belief, though not necessarily "reason."

We can look also at how language is distributed within and across the stanzas. Notice how stanza 2 uses the passive voice ("was killed") and relative clauses to introduce the husband's brother and "another fellow" in a parallel fashion, thus "mimicking" the speaker's point that though their role in the accident was the same, fate capriciously treated them differently. One of the speaker's major themes is that what looks the same (connected) or different (unconnected) at a superficial level may be just the opposite at the "deeper" level of the workings of fate:

| my husband has | a brother | [that was killed] |
| there was | another fellow | [that walked away . . .] |

Now we move to the contextualization sub-system of the discourse system (Gumperz 1982a, b). Speakers must signal to hearers what they take the context to be, and how they want their hearers to construct that context in their minds. These contextualization signals essentially tell the hearer what sort of person the speaker takes (or wants) the hearer to be (for this particular communication), what sort of person the speaker takes herself to be (for this communication) and what the speaker assumes the world (of things, ideas, and people) to be like (for this communication).

We will look at the speaker's use of terms of feeling and belief, her use of the adverbs "really" and "just," as well of the ritualistic phrase "y'know" as contextualization signals. These elements set up a persona for the speaker, situate a place for the "appropriate" hearer, and signal a world within which the text makes sense and finds its grounding. The first stanza just says literally, "I believe in fate," but it says it in such a way that we know the speaker expects some skepticism on the hearer's part ("it really is"), that she is more or less forced to the view that she holds (repetition of "believe"), and that she knows that she is on sensitive ground, given the spiritual and metaphysical implications of her topic ("y'know" before "it's fate"). Stanza 3 returns to these themes: the "really" in "I really feel" in line 7 once again signals that the speaker is forced to her view, that she is tapping the wellspring of intuitive feeling beneath superficial levels of "rational" thought. In this stanza (stanza 3) she goes on to repeat "I think" and "I feel," which, together with "really," stresses her belief/feeling against not only superficial "rationality," but the implied skepticism of others who "push fate." In the concluding stanza, stanza 5, the speaker once again uses the language of feeling, saying, "I just felt that move was meant to be," the little word "just" setting up a tacit contrast of her basic and rationally inexplicable feelings as against an implied rationality that cannot explain such "coincidences."

To be an appropriate hearer for this text (to accept its contextualization signals) is to adopt a sympathetic skepticism that is "overcome" in the face of the striking evidence offered by the speaker, in much the way the speaker herself is "forced" to acknowledge the workings of fate. We are in a world of (implied) contrasts between feelings and rationality, between the loose logic of the speaker's discourse-level *becauses* and the stricter logic of science and rationality, though these latter are never explicitly named. An appropriate hearer dare not advance that rationality and stricter logic. Such a move would only place the hearer with those who "push fate," and will run smack into the speaker's "that's just how I really feel."

The only appropriate place to "hear from" is to accept the loose logic of the text, which is precisely the logic of fate, and thus the argument of the text. The concluding line says, "it just seems that that's how things work out," and though "seems" is normally a term of implied doubt, this text has created a context in which what "seems" (what I "just" or "really" feel/believe) is true. Thus, the "seems" in the last line is, far from a term of doubt, a term of "evidence" (the truth of what is "evident," "felt," "believed").

Our fifth sub-system, thematic organization, has been less studied in linguistics than the other four sub-systems we have studied (but see Fairclough 1989, 1992, 2003; Gee 2005; Hodge and Kress 1988), though it has been extensively studied in literature, myth, and folklore (e.g., Barthes 1972; Birch 1989; Jakobson 1980; Lévi-Strauss 1966, 1979; Stahl 1989). Most—perhaps, all—instances of sense making in language are organized around contrasts, usually binary contrasts. These contrasts are signaled in a variety ways by a speaker, including word and syntax choice, the use of other sub-systems of the discourse system, and patterns of repetition and parallelism in the text.

We have already seen that the text trades on an implied contrast of feeling/belief, on the one hand, and rational evidence, on the other (the latter never overtly named). We have also seen that it trades on the contrast between what appears to be unconnected and what is "really" connected at a deeper level by the workings of fate.

The text also works with the contrast between "and that's how it is meant to be" (line 12), which seems to imply a purpose or goal (an intention), and "whatever's gonna happen is gonna happen" (line 2), which seems to imply that things are determined to happen in a certain way, but to no set purpose or intention. This contrast is carried over in the ambiguity of "So y'know it just seems that that's how things work out" (line 21), which, in the context of the text, can mean either "things just happen mechanically" (the brother's death in stanza 2) or "things work out for the best" (the father's presence at the wedding in stanzas 4 and 5).

Within the themes and contrasts which organize a text, often one side "wins out" over or "subordinates" the other. In our text, the "apparent" disconnection of events is subordinated to the "deeper" connection made by fate. The claims of "reason" (never explicitly allowed a voice in the text) are subordinated to the "basic" claims of feelings/beliefs (remember the workings of "really" and "just"). But, of course, it is this "winning out" here that allows this text to function as an "argument."

However, not uncommonly, this process of subordination of one side of a contrast to the other, is "undermined" in the workings of the text. The "winning out" process is not fully resolved. The subordinated side raises its head uncomfortably, leaving us with a residue of paradox and/or contraction. The contrast in our text above between intentional determination (well intentioned determination, in fact) and mechanical determinism (the universe, like a clock, just works the way it works, once started) is an example.

The text clearly "attempts" to resolve this contrast in "favor" of intentional (well intentioned) determination in that it ends on the presence of the father at the wedding before his death. But the resolution is not complete; we are still left with the "contradiction" between the brother's "ill fortune" and the father's "good fortune." Of course, the brother's "ill fortune" is the "good fortune" of the stranger (who walked away unharmed from the accident). But this "relativity" of fate will undermine the whole argument of the text: if any event is "good fortune" from someone's perspective and "ill fortune" from someone else's, then fate is always "ill intentioned" and "well intentioned" at one and the same time, depending on the perspective from which we view (feel) it. This leads us directly into the hands of the deprivileged, subordinated side of the contrast: mechanical determination—or worse yet, subordinates both sides of the contrast to fate as fickle.

Such irresolutions exist in texts like ours precisely because at a deeper level such texts are attempts to come to terms with, make sense of, very real paradoxes and contradictions, ones that cannot in reality be removed, and thus, perforce, not removed by the texts that seek to efface them. This was just the function Lévi-Strauss (1979) argued for myth. Though our text is not part of a traditional "myth system," it does trade on historically and socioculturally shared motifs, discourse devices, and themes. It, too, seeks to privilege one side of a contrast over another in order to resolve paradox and contradiction. In fact, historical and scientific texts often engage in similar devices.

The sorts of indeterminacies that we have just discussed serve as a fertile base for the work of human interpretation, on the part of speakers (in regard to themselves and their own meanings), hearers, and analysts (us). Thus, in this regard, note again the indeterminacy in our text around the irresolved contrast between well intentioned and mechanistic determination. The speaker has two "arguments" for fate. The first, in stanza 3, is that "another fellow" (a stranger, non-kin) lives and "walks away," while her brother (kin) dies. The second, in stanza 4, is that the speaker and her new husband (initially non-kin) live (and are on their "honeymoon") while her father (kin) dies. Is the "deep" problem of the text that the speaker "feels guilty" because she has "deserted" her father, both by being with her new husband when he died and by marrying the husband in the first place and thus leaving the father (the way the stranger "walked away" from her brother)? Is her argument for fate an attempt to assuage this guilt by having "fate" redeem the father's death, her absence from the death on her honeymoon, and her separation from the father through marriage? Note that stanza 4 never says the father was at the wedding, rather we are told it indirectly in stanza 5 in a very backgrounded clause. The father is both present and absent in a very strange way. Is the text then really and finally about the presence/absence (contrast) of the father, a presence/absence as much signaled by wedding/honeymoon as by death?

Have I now gone too far? There are always, in principle, many interpretations of a text, a text can always be interpreted at different levels (more or less "deeply"), and interpretations can never be "proven." This is not to say that "anything goes": we can offer more or less satisfying arguments for interpretations (but only "more or less," never definitive), and some interpretations are, indeed, just wrong (the speaker of the above text is not talking about ice cream).

This multiplicity of interpretation follows from the very way sense making functions. Contrasts are often not explicitly stated in texts, but set up or implied by a variety of syntactic and discourse devices (of the sort we have looked at here). But there really is no end to implication; different hearers can, with good reason, draw further and further, more and more subtle, implications from a text. It will, thus, always be indeterminate (arguable) how far and in exactly what way a given contrast is functioning in a text. And this cannot (always) be settled by appeal to what the speaker "intended." The speaker often "discovers" meaning while making it, and can, on reflection, come to see that she meant "more" than she thought (Gee 1993b). She can often be "unaware" of the full ramifications of what she has said, though she may come to "see" them upon reflection or under analysis, linguistic or otherwise.

In fact, the speaker is not really in a radically different position in determining the meaning of her own text than is the hearer. If asked (by herself or others) what she meant, all she can do is consult her text or the representation of it in her head. She must, in a sense, "read" (decode) her own text, the way any listener must. She may know more about herself than most other hearers (though there is also self-deception and so in some regards she can know less), but she never knows enough to render the text completely determinate or to rule out further discoveries about herself or the world that would lead her to take a different view on what she meant.

Multiplicity of interpretation also follows from the sorts of irresolutions we looked at above when we considered the contrast between well intentioned determination and mechanical (or even ill intentioned) determinism. When a contrast is not fully resolved, when its resolution is undermined to some extent by the text, when the supposedly subordinated side raises its head, we can always ask why, and the answer to this "why" will always be multiple and indeterminate. Indeed, the answer will be indeterminate to the speaker as well, since these are points of very real paradox, contraction, tension, confusion, "murk" for the speaker, the very problems that in all likelihood generated the attempt to make sense in the first place.

It is through attempts to deny this inevitable multiplicity and indeterminacy of interpretation that social institutions (like schools) and elite groups in a society often privilege their own version of meaning as if it were natural, inevitable, and incontestable. It is by stressing this multiplicity and indeterminacy—in the context of searching and on-going investigations of meaning—that the rest of us can resist such domination (Faigley 1992; Taussig 1987).

All texts—spoken or written—construct a favored position from which they are to be received (Fairclough 1989, 1992, 2003; Hodge and Kress 1988; Lemke 1995). We have seen how the text above constructs a space for "appropriate hearers." In this sense, all texts—even ones in quite formal language which seek status in the wider society—are also about solidarity, that is, the construction of the "right" sorts of listeners and readers, ones that are sufficiently like the social identity the speaker or writer has adopted for the construction of that particular text. Of course, we can choose to be "resistant" hearers or readers, reading "against the grain" of the text and disavowing solidarity with the (implied) speaker and/or writer and her text.

The woman who constructed the argument we have analyzed uses a form of language and a style of argumentation that seek solidarity with people and viewpoints at some variance with the academic and "professional" centers of status and power in our society and their views of "rationality." Most of us use such forms of argumentation when we are bonding to others outside the wider spheres of social power and prestige, even if we switch to other forms in other contexts. Such "everyday" forms of argumentation help us deal with the complexities of experience by making a form of "deep sense" that is, in many respects, akin to both myth and literature. Many people have stressed the role of stories and storytelling as a form of deep sense making for humans (Bruner 1987, 2003), as we do in the next chapter, but humans use other genres—for example, the type of argumentation we have studied here—to make deep sense of their experiences, as well.

Chapter 7

Discourse analysis: stories go to school

Discourse analysis of stories and their contexts

Now I turn to a different genre, stories. Like the argument above, "everyday" stories very often make "deep sense" in quite literary ways. In my analysis here, though, I want to stress both a way of engaging in the discourse analysis of stories, as well as focus on placing the stories that I will analyze in their wider social contexts.

I argued above that speech is organized into lines and stanzas. Lines and stanzas are, I believe, universal, the products of the mental mechanism by which humans produce speech (Gee 1986, 1989c, 1991, 2005). At the same time, how different people organize language within these lines and stanzas is socially and culturally variable (Gee 1989c; Hymes 1981; Scollon and Scollon 1981; Tedlock 1983).

To discuss the role of lines and stanzas in sense making, I will concentrate on two school "sharing time" stories of a seven-year-old African-American girl whom I will call "Leona" (not her real name). Because she comes from a culture that has retained substantive ties with an "oral culture" past (Edwards and Steinkewicz 1990; Rickford and Rickford 2000; Smitherman 1977), Leona's stories are very rich in "literary-like" markings of discourse structures.

After analyzing Leona's stories, I will discuss why they were not accepted by her teacher as "successful" sharing-time turns at school. I will also eventually contrast them with a "successful" sharing-time turn. This will allow us to see the workings of sense making in social contexts with all their political and ideological ramifications.

I reprint the two stories below. But before preceding further, let me say something more about how the transcripts of these two stories were prepared. All speech is produced in "little spurts" which the linguist Wallace

Chafe has called "idea units" (Chafe 1980, 1994). Each spurt has a unitary intonation contour and is often bounded by short pauses or hesitations. For Chafe (1980) an idea unit is a single focus of consciousness, analogous to the single focus of the eye as it scans a scene through many rapid focuses. The vast majority of these idea units are a single clause, with one piece of new information towards the end of the clause. It is only when the subject of the clause, or an adverbial element, is new information that it constitutes an idea unit by itself. (This is a simplification, see Chafe 1994; Gee and Grosjean 1983; Kreckel 1981.) Some examples of idea units taken from the stories printed below are (each idea unit is printed on a separate line):

today
it's Friday the 13th

an' . . . my mother
my mother
my mother's bakin' a cake

last night
my grandmother snuck out

my puppy
he always be following me

Once the agent or an adverbial element is introduced as an idea unit, the speaker can then incorporate it as old information in the following idea unit(s). Once this happens, idea units tend to be clauses with an old or given agent, and with new information at or towards the end of the clause. This is, of course, a very typical discourse pattern in English (and across languages). Thus, it appears that speech aims at a series of short clauses as ideal idea units.

If we remove obvious false starts and repairs from the text and collapse the few subject nouns or noun phases that are idea units by themselves into the clauses they belong to, we get an ideal realization of the text, which is printed below. Each of the idea units in this ideal text I will refer to as a "line." (In Gee 1991, 2005 I define "line" somewhat differently in order to deal with the more complex texts produced by adults.)

The puppy story

Section 1 Home

Section 1a Opening scene: breakfast

Stanza 1

1   Last yesterday in the morning
2   there was a hook on the top of the stairway
3   an' my father was pickin' me up
4   an' I got stuck on the hook up there

Stanza 2

5   an' I hadn't had breakfast
6   he wouldn't take me down
7   until I finished all my breakfast
8   cause I didn't like oatmeal either

Section 1b The puppy and the father

Stanza 3

9   an' then my puppy came
10 he was asleep
11 he tried to get up
12 an' he ripped my pants
13 an' he dropped the oatmeal all over him

Stanza 4

14 an' my father came
15 an' he said "Did you eat all the oatmeal?"
16 he said "Where's the bowl?"
17 I said "I think the dog took it"
18 "Well I think I'll have t'make another bowl"

Section 2 School

Section 2a Going to school

Stanza 5

19 an' so I didn't leave till seven
20 an' I took the bus

21 an' my puppy he always be following me
22 my father said "He—you can't go"

Stanza 6

23 an' he followed me all the way to the bus stop
24 an' I hadda go all the way back
    ([aside] by that time it was seven-thirty)
25 an' then he kept followin' me back and forth
26 an' I hadda keep comin' back

Section 2b Non-narrative section

Stanza 7

27 an' he always be followin' me when I go anywhere
28 he wants to go to the store
29 an' only he could not go to places where we could go
30 like to the stores he could go but he have to be chained up

Section 3 Hospital

Section 3a The hospital

Stanza 8

31 an' we took him to he emergency
32 an' see what was wrong with him
33 an' he got a shot
34 an' then he was crying

Stanza 9

35 an' last yesterday, an' now they put him asleep
36 an' he's still in the hospital
37 an' the doctor said he got a shot because
38 he was nervous about my home that I had

Section 3b ending

Stanza 10

39 an' he could still stay but
40 he thought he wasn't gonna be able to let him go

The cakes story

Frame

   Stanza 1

1   Today
2   it's Friday the 13th
3   an' it's bad luck day
4   an' my grandmother's birthday is on bad luck day

Section I   Making cakes

   Stanza 2

5   an' my mother's bakin' a cake
6   an' I went up my grandmother's house while my mother's bakin' a cake
7   an' my mother was bakin' a cheesecake
8   my grandmother was bakin' a whipped cream cupcakes

   Stanza 3

9   an' we both went over my mother's house
10   an' then my grandmother had made a chocolate cake
11   an' then we went over my aunt's house
12   an' she had make a cake

   Stanza 4

13   an' everybody had made a cake for Nana
14   so we came out with six cakes

Section 2   Grandmother eats cakes

   Stanza 5

15   last night
16   my grandmother snuck out
17   an' she ate all the cake
18   an' we hadda make more

Stanza 6

([aside] she knew we was makin' cakes)

19   an' we was sleepin'
20   an' she went in the room
21   an' gobbled em up
22   an' we hadda bake a whole bunch more

Stanza 7

23   she said mmmm
24   she had all chocolate on her face, cream, strawberries
25   she said mmmm
26   that was good

Stanza 8

27   an then an' then all came out
28   an' my grandmother had ate all of it
29   she said "What's this cheesecake doin' here?"—she didn't like
     cheesecakes
30   an' she told everybody that she didn't like cheesecakes

Stanza 9

31   an' we kept makin' cakes
32   an' she kept eatin' 'em
33   an' we finally got tired of makin' cakes
34   an' so we all ate 'em

Section 3 Grandmother goes outside the home

Non-narrative section (35–41)

Stanza 10

35   an' now
36   today's my grandmother's birthday
37   an' a lot o'people's makin' a cake again
38   but my grandmother is goin' t'get her own cake at her bakery
39   an' she's gonna come out with a cake
40   that we didn't make
41   'cause she likes chocolate cream

Return to narrative

    Stanza 11

42   an' I went t'the bakery with her
43   an' my grandmother ate cup cakes
44   an' an' she finally got sick on today
45   an' she was growling like a dog cause she ate so many cakes

Frame

    Stanza 12

46   an' I finally told her that it was
47   it was Friday the 13th bad luck day

Leona uses a good deal of syntactic and semantic parallelism between her lines, just as do biblical poetry (e.g., in the Psalms), the narratives of many oral cultures (e.g., Homer), and much "free verse" (e.g., the poetry of Walt Whitman). Leona groups her lines into stanzas wherein each line tends to have a parallel structure with some other line in the stanza and to match it in content or topic. Furthermore, prosodically the lines in a stanza sound as if they go together, by tending to be said with the same rate and with little hesitation between the lines. Leona's stanzas are very often four lines long, though they are sometimes two lines long. Thus, Leona's stanzas show intricate structure and patterning, taking on some of the properties of stanzas in poetry.

Let's look at some examples of the patterns within Leona's stanzas. The first example is stanza 2 of the Cakes story:

> An' my mother's bakin' a cake
> An' I went up my grandmother's house while my mother's bakin' a
>   cake
> An' my mother was bakin' a cheesecake
> My grandmother was bakin' a whipped cream cupcakes

Notice that every line here ends with "cake." Further, the stanza has an a b a b structure (like an a b a b rhyme structure in poetry): the first and third line involve "my mother" and the second and fourth lines involve "my grandmother." But they also have an a a b b structure: the second line ends by repeating the first ("my mother's bakin' a cake"), the fourth "echoes" the third: "(grand)mother bakin' a type of cake."

Thus, the lines are fully saturated with pattern, and are tightly knit together. That this parallelism is really part of Leona's production process is shown by the speech error in the fourth line. The line end pattern that Leona is using in this stanza is essentially: . . . bakin' a cake / . . . bakin' a cake / . . . bakin' a TYPE of cake / . . . bakin' a TYPE of cake (an a a b b "rhyme" scheme). However, her fourth line ends on a plural noun ("cupcakes"), and so cannot take the singular article "a" required by the formal pattern. Nonetheless, driven by the pattern, Leona says in the fourth line "bakin' a whipped cream cupcakes." It is as if she is operating with slots that are to be filled in ways partially determined by what has come before (this type of composing process is common in "oral poetry").

Let's take another example, stanza 3 of the Cakes story:

An' we both went over my mother's house
An' then my grandmother had made a chocolate cake
An' then we went over my aunt's house
An' she had made a cake

This stanza has a clear a b a b structure: lines 1 and 3 are "we . . . went over my X's house," while in lines 2 and 4 someone "had made a cake." Notice, too, the lines end "house . . . cake . . . house . . . cake" (a b a b).

Another example, involving a pair of related stanzas, is stanzas 3 and 4 from the Puppy story:

An' then my puppy came
He was asleep
He tried to get up
An' he ripped my pants
An' he dropped the oatmeal all over him
An' my father came
An' he said "Did you eat all the oatmeal?"
He said "Where's the bowl?"
I said "I think the dog took it"
"Well I think I'll have t'make another bowl"

Here Leona introduces one stanza by the line "an' my puppy came" and the next by "an' my father came," setting puppy and father into contrast. The first stanza has four actions, while the second has four speakings. Notice that in the second stanza the first two lines have "he said" and are questions, while the last two lines repeat "I think," giving it something of an a a b b structure.

I do not argue that all stanzas are so transparently patterned as these. Rather, I argue that these transparently patterned stanzas give us the clue we need to identify stanzas as operative in the production of the text. We can then go on to identify stanzas that are not so transparently patterned. For example, stanza 13 in the Cakes story:

> An' I went t'the bakery with her
> An' my grandmother ate cupcakes
> An' she finally got sick on today
> An' she was growling like a dog cause she ate so many cakes

These lines are clearly set off in the text. They are preceded by a series of non-narrative statements, the first line of the stanza constitutes a change of location in the story, and the stanza ends on a falling pitch contour. The stanza is followed by a concluding couplet that parallels the opening of the story. Thus, we can be reasonably sure the four lines belong together. One line leads to another in the stanza by simple relations of cause and effect. We do not get much overt patterning, though the first two lines are about the bakery and the last two about the sickness. Nonetheless, we can clearly identify a four-line unit here.

There are levels of organization in Leona's stories beyond lines and stanzas. If we look at the content of Leona's narratives as wholes, they clearly fall into larger units that we could call "episodes." However, in keeping with the terminology of lines and stanzas we have adopted so far, I will refer to them as "sections." Talking about sections involves talking about the whole text. In the texts above, I label each of the sections. The breakdown into sections in terms of topics or themes is fairly straight-forward and obvious. In turn it is confirmed by other structural properties of the texts.

In Cakes, the first section is about baking cakes, the second about the grandmother eating the cakes, and the third is about the bakery. The second section begins on a temporal adverb ("last night"), the third does also ("an' now"). The first section, of course, is understood to be in the scope of the opening adverb in the opening frame ("today").

I should, however, note at this point that I am not claiming that Leona knows the overall structure of her story before she starts. (The stories are not memorized.) Rather I am claiming that that structure is emergent by a process of incremental addition that is somewhat broken or thrown into "crisis" at larger breaks in the text.

The Cakes story gives us a good insight into the relationship between the story as a whole and its emergence part by part. In the actual telling of the story there was a great deal of hesitation, and there were a number of false starts and repairs in the final section of the story and in the concluding couplet. Leona seems to be trying both to carry the story forward and to plan its ending. She manages to construct the final narrative event and to conclude with a couplet that immediately returns us full circle to the opening frame, thereby constructing a closed and unified structure—but the hesitation seems to indicate that this is partly an on-line and reflective decision. Leona both has structural schemata that helps drive production and discovers aspects of her structure, as she proceeds.

This dynamic combination of pre-given resources and real-time discovery can be seen if we look at other stories Leona told in school. On occasion, at sharing time, Leona would start a story and not finish it (either because she didn't want to go on or because the teacher stopped her). These "story starts" are interesting, as many of them contain structural elements that remind one of structural aspects of Leona's "finished" stories. For example, consider the relation of the story start below to both the Cakes story and the Puppy story:

Stanza 1

Yesterday
an' we had a teacher
an' we hadda go to gym with her

Stanza 2

an' then we went outside
an' played dodgeball

Stanza 3

an' then I went home
an' my mother was there
an' yesterday was my mom's birthday
an' my mom ? made a cake

Stanza 4

an' when I got home
the party was all over
an' everybody had ate the whole cake
and my mother made another cake

Stanza 5

an' my aunt came back
and ? both went to sleep
an' she ate it again

Stanza 6

an' an' then and I got up
early this morning
and I ate a piece of cake for breakfast
an' my mother said "Where's the other piece?"

Stanza 6 above is reminiscent of the opening stanzas of the Puppy story, as well as stanza 4 of that story. Stanzas 3, 4, and 5 above are reminiscent of several of the stanzas and the initial development of the Cakes story. Add the on-line creative discovery that occurred as Cakes was produced to the structural elements that underlie story starts like the one above (and many others), and you get the masterpiece that the Cakes story is. The same phenomenon, though more "routinized" at the structural level, seems to have occurred with the Homeric poems, and in the case of a great many oral cultural practices across the world (Finnegan 1977, 1988; Foley 1988).

It is probably the case that Leona has structural resources (strategies for production) beyond the local level of lines and stanzas. The Cakes and Puppy stories display similar strategies at a global level as well. They both open with a temporal adverb, they both have three major sections, they both have a non-narrative portion close before the ending (labeled as such in the texts), and they both conclude by a rapid switch to a new and different locale (the bakery, the hospital).

Further, they both have themes that run like strongly colored threads throughout the entire text—for example, baking and eating in the Cakes story, and coming and going in the Puppy story. These global or abstract strategies may be schemas or global templates that Leona does, in fact, have as a pre-given resource or plan in constructing the story, a resource that is used together with her strategies of incremental addition, parallelism, and lingering over an image, as well as her individually and culturally given sources of creativity and discovery.

Before moving on, I would like to comment on the non-narrative portions of the two texts, which are reprinted below:

Cakes

An' now
Today's my grandmother's birthday
An' a lot o'people's makin' a cake again
But my grandmother is goin' t'get her own cake at her bakery
An' she's gonna come out with a cake
That we didn't make
'Cause she likes chocolate cream

Puppy

An' he always be followin' me when I go anywhere
He wants to go to the store
An' only he could not go to places where we could go
Like to the stores he could go but he have to be chained up

These portions involve generic statements, stative verbs, or statements lumping many discrete events together, all of which depart from the narrative line (which involves statements of discrete events). There are several things to note about the language of these portions. First, it is more complicated syntactically than the other parts of the text. Second, it does not by any means fit as nicely the line and stanza structures we have been using. Third, the language gets rather "meandering," as if Leona is delaying.

I would suggest the following hypotheses: These sections come close to the end of the stories. They serve as what the sociolinguist William Labov (1972a) has called "evaluation" (which he points out often occurs before the ending in the narratives of African-American teenagers), giving an indication of the point of the stories and what Leona considers makes them "tellable." Further, they serve as transitions between the body of the story and the ending, giving Leona space and time to plan the endings. They, thus, serve as aids both to the listener and to the speaker. If I am right about this, these parts of the stories are crucial to their interpretation (see below).

There is a great deal of similarity between the structures we have found in Leona's stories and those that have been found in oral narratives from oral cultures around the world (Foley 1988; Finnegan 1977, 1988). But why do these structures of lines, stanzas, and sections exist across so many diverse cultures and genres? It seems to me that the beginnings of an answer are to be found in the hypothesis that these structures reflect units of human narrative/discourse competence. Of course, they will be marked in surface performance in different ways in different cultures, and here oral cultures and cultures influenced by an oral tradition may be more perspicuous than some others. Thus, in the end, what we see is that Leona—though only seven years old—is very much part of a specific cultural tradition of sense making, a tradition rooted in African-American history in the United States and Africa (Baugh 1999, 2000; Heath 1983; Hecht *et al.* 1993; Kochman 1972; Rickford and Rickford 2000; Smitherman 1977; Stucky 1987).

The overall sense of a text

We have not, thus far, gotten at the "deeper meanings" of Leona's stories. The line and stanza structure of a text (what we called above its discourse organization) works together with the other aspects of the discourse system (prosody, cohesion, contextualization signals, thematics) to generate the sense of the text, a sense with many (and not completely determinate) layers of meaning.

I will briefly discuss the sense of one of Leona's stories, the Cakes story. The purpose of this discussion is both to understand some of the specific aspects of how this single child makes sense, within the parameters of her primary social group, and to see, once again, the workings of contrasts in the creation of sense (the thematic organization of the text).

Given the amount of parallelism and repetition in her text, clearly Leona is not primarily interested in making rapid and linear progress to "the point." Rather, she is interested in creating a pattern out of language, within and across her stanzas, a pattern which will generate meaning through the sets of relationships and contrasts which it sets up, like the multiple relationships and contrasts—the points of contact and stress—in a painting or a poem (Frank 1963).

And what might that meaning be? Of course, there are always multiple plausible interpretations of a text (and many non-plausible ones as well). But if we follow the clues or guides the child has placed in the organization of her text, and are sensitive to the child's culture, we can offer a "reading" that accepts the invitations of her language.

The non-narrative "evaluative" section in stanza 10 suggests that there is something significant in the fact that the grandmother is going to get a cake at the bakery and thus "come out with a cake that we [the family] didn't make." And, indeed, the story as a whole places a great deal of emphasis on the production of cakes within the family, a production that doesn't cease even when the grandmother keeps eating them.

The grandmother, the matriarch and repository of the culture's norms, is behaving like a child, sneaking out and eating the cakes and rudely announcing that she doesn't like "cheesecake," even though the cake has been made by her relatives for her birthday. It must intrigue the child narrator that the grandmother can behave this way and, far from getting in trouble, the family simply makes more cakes. Surely the story carries some messages about family loyalty and respect for age. But it also, I would argue, raises a problem: the matriarch, the guardian of culturally normative behavior, is behaving in such a way as to violate the home and culture's canons of polite behavior. What might the sanctions be for such a violation? And what is the deeper meaning of the grandmother's violation? Like all real stories, this one raises real problems, problems that the story attempts to resolve in a satisfying manner.

We can get to this deeper level of the text if we consider the constant use of and play on the word "cake" in the story. The story, in fact, contains a humorous paradox about cakes: the grandmother eats innumerable (normal size) cakes at home, made by her relatives, and never gets sick. Then she goes outside the home, buys little cakes ("cupcakes") at the bakery, and, not only does she get sick, she "growls like a dog," that is, loses her human status and turns into an animal. Why?

What I would argue is this: The grandmother is learning, and the child narrator is enacting, a lesson about signs or symbols. A birthday cake is a material object, but it is also an immaterial sign or symbol of kinship, when made within the family—a celebration of birth and family membership. The cake at the bakery looks the same, but it is a duplicitous symbol—it is not actually a sign of kinship, rather it is a commodity that non-kin have made to sell, not to celebrate the birth of someone they care about. To mistake the baker's cake as a true symbol of birth and kin is to think, mistakenly, that signs have meaning outside the contexts that give them meaning.

In the context of the family, the cake means kinship and celebration; in the context of the bakery and market society, it signals exchange and commodities. The grandmother, in her greed, overvalues the material base of the sign (its cakehood) and misses its meaning, undervaluing the network of kin that gives meaning to the cakes. This is particularly dangerous when we consider that the grandmother is a senior representative of the family and culture. Her penalty is to momentarily lose her human status, that is, the status of a giver and taker of symbolic meaning—she becomes an animal, merely an eater.

And now, of course, I must face the inevitable question: could this seven-year-old really have meant this? Could she really have this sophisticated a theory of signs? I would argue that these questions seem so compelling to us because we think meaning is a matter of privatized intentions locked in people's heads and indicative of their individual "intelligence" or "skill." But once we deny this view of meaning, the questions lose most of their force; in fact, they become somewhat odd.

This little girl has inherited, by her apprenticeship in the social practices of her community, ways of making sense of experience that, in fact, have a long and rich history going back thousands of years. This enculturation/apprenticeship has given her certain forms of language, ranging from devices at the word and clause level, through the stanza level, to the story level as a whole, forms of language which are intimately connected to forms of life (Wittgenstein 1958). These forms of language are not merely structural: rather they encapsulate, carry through time and space, meaning, meanings shared by and lived out in a variety of ways by the social group. The girl speaks the language, engages in the social practices, and gets the meanings "free."

Why Leona's stories failed at school

Leona's sharing-time stories are clearly in a language rooted in her home community—it is, in fact, a language of solidarity with that community. This is not say that its use excludes the non-African-American children in the class. As Leona tells the Cake story, for instance, the children in the class participate with sound effects and glee. Leona's language is an invitation to the other children to participate with her in sense making, to achieve solidarity with her, and they readily accept this invitation. The teacher did not. Leona was regularly told to sit down because she was either "rambling on" or "not talking about one important thing" (a sharing-time rule in this class).

To see why Leona's sharing-time turns did not "succeed" at school, we need to look at a "successful" sharing-time text. The text below comes from an Anglo-American middle-class seven-year-old girl whom I will call "Mindy." Mindy was also engaged in a school "sharing-time" session. Mindy was interrupted by the teacher several times, and this is indicated in the text below (see Gee *et al.* 1992 for a fuller discussion of this text):

Mindy's sharing-time turn

MINDY: When I was in day camp,
    we made these, um candles,
TEACHER: You made them?

MINDY: And uh, I-I tried it with different colors,
with both of them but,
one came out, this one just came out blue,
and I don't know, what this color is,
TEACHER: That's neat-o.
Tell the kids how you do it from the very start.
Pretend we don't know a thing about candles.
OK.
What did you do first?
What did you use?
Flour?
MINDY: Um, there's some, hot wax,
some real hot wax,
that you, just take a string,
and tie a knot in it.
And dip the string in the um wax.
TEACHER: What makes it uh have a shape?
MINDY: Um, you just shape it.
TEACHER: Oh you shaped it with your hand. mm.
MINDY: But you have, first you have to stick it into the wax,
and then water,
and then keep doing that
until it gets to the size you want it.
TEACHER: OK.
Who knows what the string is for?

Mindy's school sharing-time turn was considered appropriate and successful by the teacher; Leona's turns were not. Let us start with Leona's text. Sharing time in the sorts of classrooms where this data was collected was an activity meant to apprentice children to the sorts of explicit language used in literate-style talk and writing, though the children could not yet read or write (Michaels 1981). Children in these classrooms were encouraged to "talk about one important thing" and to be completely explicit in their language, relying as little as possible on the ability of their audience to draw inferences. Sharing time in these sorts of classrooms, then, was, in a sense, early school-based or "essayist" (prosaic) literacy training for children who could not necessarily yet write or read (Scollon and Scollon 1981).

Leona is telling a story out of a social language that the teacher does not recognize, and that "goes against the grain" of the social language to which sharing time is intended to apprentice children (though they are never, of course, told this overtly). In many cases, even African-American teachers who are elsewhere adept at Leona's sort of style do not "recognize" it once they shift, in school, to their school-based social languages and identities. As teachers, they are listening through their school-based "ears." Leona's text doesn't count as "doing/being in school," and this despite its obvious ties to literature (which is sealed off in another part of the curriculum in other practices).

Let us, then, turn to Mindy's report on candles, a "successful" and "appropriate" sharing-time turn. Mindy and the teacher manage to be "in sync": Mindy immediately announces her topic in her first two lines, while holding up two small candles for the class to see. The teacher, then, uses an echo question to show how impressed and interested she is: "You made them?" said with surprise. Without missing a beat, Mindy continues. However, her following talk about the color of the candles is lexically inexplicit and not elaborated; it relies heavily on the fact that the whole class can see the candles. Furthermore, the coloring of the candles is a rather peripheral part of the process of candle making, one that, however, lends itself to the visual presentation of the candles in this face-to-face setting. All of this is not the sort of talk that the teacher wants to encourage at sharing time, though it is typical of informal, face-to-face talk in the here-and-now to peers.

However, the teacher waits until Mindy pauses (after a low falling tone on the world "color") and reiterates her interest in the actual process, but this time does so more explicitly. She provides a clear and elaborate set of guides for how she wants Mindy to talk about making candles. "Tell the kids about how you did it from the very start. Pretend we don't know anything about candles." The last remark is of course an instruction to assume no shared knowledge and to be as explicit as possible, i.e. to abandon the assumption that this is informal talk to peers who can obviously see the candles and who may well know as much as Mindy does about candle making. The teacher then pauses and gets no response. She rephrases her instruction as a question, "What did you do first?" She pauses again and follows with an additional clue by offering an obviously wrong answer to the question, which nonetheless suggests to Mindy an example of the type of answer she has in mind. "What did you use? . . . Flour?" At this point Mindy responds, building upon the base that the teacher's questions have provided. She describes what she used ("hot wax") and the steps involved. In addition to a description of the sequencing of activities involved in the business of making candles, this passage introduces several context-free lexical items ("some hot wax," "a string," "a knot"). This use of these lexical items provides explicit information about the activity and the materials used in candle making. This contrasts with the use in the preceding talk of anaphoric and deictic items that rely on the context for interpretation. Additionally the use of definite and indefinite articles grammaticalizes the distinction between new and old information: "some wax" and "a string" become "the string" and "the wax."

The teacher and Mindy are able to coordinate their interaction in a smooth and flowing way so that Mindy, the apprentice, is scaffolded and supported by the teacher's greater expertise. Mindy's discourse in response to the teacher's questions and comments is far more complex than the spontaneous utterances she produced at the beginning of her sharing-time turn without the teacher's guidance. Thus, we see in this example how a synchronization of exchanges enables the student and teacher to collaborate in develop a lexically explicit, coherent, and school-based account of a complex activity. Mindy is engaged not so much in overt learning as in coming to be "in sync" with the resources of the sorts of school-based social practices.

This interaction between Mindy and the teacher is very reminiscent of a type of verbal interaction between much younger children and their parents that has been extensively studied in middle-class homes, and which appears to occur much less frequently in non-mainstream homes (Heath, 1982, 1983; Wells, 1986). For example, consider the following breakfast-table conversation between a twenty-nine-month-old and his parents (from Snow 1986: 82):

CHILD: Pancakes away.
    Duh duh stomach.
MOTHER: Pancakes away in the stomach, yes, that's right.
CHILD: Eat apples.
MOTHER: Eating apples on our pancakes, aren't we?
CHILD: On our pancakes.
MOTHER: You like apples on your pancakes?
CHILD: Eating apples.
    Hard.
MOTHER: What?
    Hard to do the apples, isn't it?
CHILD: More pancakes.
FATHER: You want more pancakes?
CHILD: Those are Daddy's.
FATHER: Daddy's gonna have his pancakes now.
CHILD: Ne ne one a Daddy's.

Ne ne one in the plate.
Right there.
FATHER: You want some more on your plate?

Much research on child language development (e.g., Dickinson 1994; Dickinson and Neuman 2006; Garton and Pratt 1989) has shown that verbal interactions like the one above, coupled with certain types of interactive story-book reading, enhance a child's chance of later school success. There is a sense in which both the teacher's interaction with Mindy and the conversation above between parents and child are interactive slot-and-filler activities centered around adding more and more descriptive and lexically explicit detail around a single topic. Here we see one social group building into their home-based "culture" practices that resonate with the practices and values of a certain type of schooling. Children like Mindy certainly do not fully know the sharing-time schema, nor do they know in any detailed way the nature of school-based literacy practices, but they are experts in engaging in the sorts of adult–child verbal scaffolding that we see in Mindy's sharing-time turn and in the above conversation about pancakes.

What is striking about the poor reception that Leona's stories received at school during sharing time is that her stories have deep meanings when she tells them in her own community or when we situate them in the interpretive setting of "poetics" and "linguistic stylistics" (as we have done here), yet they have no very deep meaning when they are situated in school at sharing time (Cazden 1988, 2001; Michaels 1981; see also Collins and Bolt 2003). Sharing time in these classrooms was early "essayist (reportive, linear, 'the facts') literacy" training (Michaels 1981, 1985). Leona's text does not "resonate" well with that practice, while other sorts of texts do.

However, we can ask: While the sorts of "literary" stories that Leona told are not encouraged or recruited at sharing time (in the sorts of sharing-time sessions we have discussed here—where, in fact, "fantasy" is banned), why aren't they recruited within other school-based practices where "creativity" and "literariness" in language are being encouraged? Leona's sort of story, the sort told by many African-American children— with its rich ties to the historical base of literature and its many creative and literary features—is but rarely encouraged and recruited in school. Why? The answer, of course, has partly to do with the fact that Leona uses a different social language within which to engage in "poetic practices" than does "high literature." It has also to do with the fact that what counts is not simply linguistic features (after all, Leona's language has many features that could be easily recruited for an apprenticeship into poetry and other "high literature"), but who we are and what we are doing. And Leona's community-based *who* and *what* are, at best, not visible to the school, and, at worse, opposed by the school, which, in turn, fails to render visible and accessible to children like Leona the sorts of *whos* and *whats* that do count there.

Leona's "failure" at sharing time is a denigration of her community-based social identity, which is constructed, in part, in the social language she has used in her stories. It also rebuffs her attempt to achieve solidarity with teacher and her fellow pupils. At the same time, the school has failed to apprentice Leona to the sorts of language through which she could gain status in academic practices. Such an apprenticeship could have (Gallas 1994)—and should have—been based on a engagement with and recruitment of her storied language and the social identity it betokens.

Chapter 8

Discourses and literacies

The New Literacy Studies

In Chapter 4, I argued that a new field of study has emerged around the notion of literacy, a field I called "the New Literacy Studies." It is a problem, of course, to call any enterprise "new," because, of course, it soon becomes "old." Were it not so cumbersome, it would be better to call the field something like "integrated social-cultural-political-historical literacy studies," which names the viewpoint it takes on literacy. However, for better or worse, the term New Literacy Studies has become well known and widely used, so, reluctantly, I will continue to use the term.

In this chapter, I develop a particular viewpoint on literacy and the New Literacy Studies by alternating theoretical discussion with specific case studies meant to exemplify the theory. One way we can begin to develop a sociocultural approach to literacy is to engage in the rhetorical conceit of imagining that we have been asked: "What does the word 'literacy' mean?" Immediately we will see that in order to define "literacy" adequately we must first discuss a few other concepts which are commonly misconstrued. One of these is "language."

"Language" can be a misleading term: It is often used to mean the grammar (structure, the "rules") of a language. However, it is a truism, but one we nonetheless must hold constantly in mind, that a person can know the grammar of a language and still not know how to use that language (Gumperz 1982a, b; Hanks 1996; Scollon and Scollon 1995; Wolfson 1989). What is important in communication is not speaking grammatically, but saying the "right" thing at the "right" time and in the "right" place. If I enter my neighborhood biker bar and say to my tattooed drinking buddy, as I sit down, "May I have a match please?" my grammar is perfect, but what I have said is wrong nonetheless. The situation requires something more like "Gotta match?"

Research on second language acquisition both inside and outside classroom settings indicates that some speakers can have quite poor grammar and still function in communication and socialization quite well (Huebner 1983). They know how to use the language, even if all their forms are not "correct." So what counts is use, not grammar *per se*. However, it is less often remarked that a person could even be able to use a language perfectly and still not make sense. Use alone is not enough. Paradoxically put: a person can speak a language grammatically, can use the language appropriately, and still get it "wrong." This is so because what is important is not just how you say it, not just language in any sense, but *who* you are and *what* you're doing when you say it.

If I enter my neighborhood biker bar and say to my drinking buddy, as I sit down, "Gotta match?" or "Gimme a match, wouldya?" while placing a napkin on the bar stool to avoid getting my newly pressed designer jeans dirty, I have said the right thing. My "language-in-use" is just fine. But my "saying–doing" combination is, nonetheless, all wrong. My words, however appropriately formulated for the situation, do not "fit" with my actions, and, in the case of socially situated language, "fit" between words and actions is all important (Gee 1992; Goffman 1959, 1967, 1981; Gumperz 1982a, b; Hanks 1996).

In fact, the matter goes further: It is not just language and action which must "fit" together appropriately. In socially situated language use one must simultaneously say the "right" thing, do the "right" thing, and in such saying and doing also express the "right" beliefs, values, and attitudes.

Any time we act or speak, we must accomplish two things: (1) We must make clear *who* we are, and (2) we must make clear *what* we are doing (Wieder and Pratt 1990a). We are each of us not a single *who*, but different *whos* in different contexts. In addition, one and the same act can count as different things in different contexts, where context is something people actively construe, negotiate over, and change their minds about (Duranti 1997; Duranti and Goodwin 1992).

An example of language use and types of people

Let me give a concrete example of the way in which language must not only have the right grammar and be used appropriately, but must also express the right values, beliefs, and attitudes—the "right *who*," the right "type" of person. In a paper arguing the importance of using language appropriately, F. Niyi Akinnaso and Cheryl Seabrook Ajirotutu (1982) present "simulated job interviews" (practice sessions) from two African-American mothers in a US job training program. I reprint these two interviews below.

Though the interviews are from two different women, Akinnaso and Ajirotutu present these two interviews as "before and after" cases. That is, the first one is presented as an example of how not to carry out an interview, and the second is presented as the correct way to do it, the successful result of having been properly trained in the job training program. In the texts below, material between two slashes represents one "tone group"—a set of words said with one unitary intonational contour—and dots represent pauses, with the greater number of dots equaling a longer pause:

Job interview text 1

Question: Have you had any previous job experience that would demonstrate that you've shown initiative or been able to work independently?

1   Well / . . . yes when I / . . . OK / . . . there's this Walgreen's Agency /
2   I worked as a microfilm operator / OK /
3   And it was a snow storm /
4   OK / and it was usually six people / workin' in a group /
5   uhum / and only me and this other girl showed up /
6   and we had quite a lot of work to do /
7   and so the man / he asked us could we / you know / do we / . . . do we thinks we could finish this work /
9   so me 'n' this girl / you know / we finished it all /

Job interview text 2

Question: One more question was that ah, this kind of work frequently involves using your own initiative and showing sort of the ability to make independent judgment. Do you have any . . . can you tell me about any previous experience which you think directly show .. demonstrates that you have these qualities?

1   Why / .. well / as far as being capable of handling an office /
2   say if I'm left on my own /
3   I feel I'm capable /

4 I had a situation where one of my employers that I've been /
5 ah previously worked for /
6 had to go on / a .. / a trip for say / ah three weeks and /
7 he was / . . . I was left alone to .. / handle the office and run it /
8 And at that time / ah I didn't really have what you would say /
   a lot of experience /
9 But I had enough experience to / .. deal with any situations that
   came up while he was gone /
10 and those that I couldn't / handle at the time /
11 if there was someone who had more experience than myself /
12 I asked questions / to find out / what procedure I would use /
13 If something came up / and if I didn't know / who to really go
    to /
14 I would jot it down / or write it down / on a piece of paper /
15 so that I wouldn't forget that .. /
16 if anyone that / was more qualified than myself /
17 I could ask them about it /
18 and how I would go about solving it /
19 So I feel I'm capable of handling just about any situation /
20 whether it's on my own / or under supervision

The first woman is simply using the "wrong" grammar (the wrong "dialect") for this type of middle-class interview. It's a perfectly good dialect (see discussion in Chapter 1 above and Labov 1972a; Rickford and Rickford 2000), but it is not the dialect normally used for job interviews, in part, of course, due to prejudice. In our society, you are expected to use "Standard" English for most job interviews, so this woman's grammar doesn't "fit" the context (Erickson and Schultz 1982; Gumperz et al. 1979; Roberts et al. 1992).

The second woman, the "success case," has not got a real problem with her grammar. (Remember this is speech, not writing.) Her grammar is, for the most part, perfectly normal "standard" English. Nor is there any real problem with the use to which she puts that grammar; all her sentences are formulated appropriately for the time, place, and occasion in which she is speaking (except the "say" in line 6, which sounds like she is "estimating" or "imagining," rather than "reporting").

However, she still is getting it "wrong" in a sense. This is so because she is, in the act of using the "right" grammar in the "right" way, nonetheless expressing the wrong values. She opens by saying that she is capable of handling an office on her own. In fact, she goes on to say that though she did not have a lot of experience, she had enough experience to deal with "any situations that came up" while her boss was away. But then she immediately (in line 10) brings up "those that I couldn't handle," which seems to contradict, and certainly mitigates, her claim that she could handle anything that came up. She proceeds (in lines 11 and 12) to elaborate on her inexperience and lack of knowledge by saying that she asked questions of those with more experience than herself. (We might begin to wonder why they weren't left in charge.)

Any chance we could construe this last point as, at least, "responsible humility" is destroyed as she goes on (in lines 13–18) to mention not just things she doesn't know how to handle, but things she doesn't even know who to ask about (and in line 16 once again mentions people more qualified than herself). The whole second part of her answer (after line 9) involves her search for people more knowledgeable than herself whose superior knowledge can supplement her lack of knowledge. In fact, for her, "responsibility," "initiative," and "independent judgment" amount to deferring to "other people's" knowledge.

Her response closes (in lines 19 and 20), as is fully appropriate to such interview talk, with a return to her original point: "So I feel I'm capable of handling just about any situation, whether it's on my own, or under supervision." But this is contradicted by the very attitudes and values she has just allowed us to infer that she holds. She seems to view being left in charge as just another form of supervision, namely, supervision by "other people's" knowledge and expertise. Though this woman starts and finishes in an appropriate fashion, she fails in the heart of the narrative to characterize her own expertise in the overly optimistic form called for by such interviews (Erickson and Schultz 1982). She is expressing herself, for this time and place, as the wrong sort of person for the job. Using this response as an example of "successful training" is possible only because the authors, well aware that language is more than grammar (namely, "use"), are unaware that communication is more than language use.

The moral of the above discussion is that what is important is language *plus* being the "right" *who* (sort of person) doing the "right" *what* (activity). What is important is not language, and surely not grammar, but saying(writing)–doing–being–valuing–believing combinations. These combinations I will refer to as Discourses, with a capital "D," a notion I want now to explicate (Gee 1992, 2005). Before I do that, let me point out that I will use "discourse" with a little "d" for language in use or connected stretches of language that make sense, like conversations, stories, reports, arguments, essays, and so forth. So, "discourse" is part of "Discourse"—"Discourse" with a big "D" is always more than just language.

Discourses

A Discourse with a capital "D" is composed of distinctive ways of speaking/listening and often, too, writing/reading *coupled* with distinctive ways of acting, interacting, valuing, feeling, dressing, thinking, believing, with other people and with various objects, tools, and technologies, so as to enact specific socially recognizable identities engaged in specific socially recognizable activities. These identities might be things like being–doing a Los Angeles Latino street-gang member, a Los Angeles policeman, a field biologist, a first-grade student in a specific classroom and school, a "SPED" student, a certain type of doctor, lawyer, teacher, African-American, worker in a "quality control" workplace, man, woman, boyfriend, girlfriend, or regular at the local bar, etc. and etc. through a nearly endless list. Discourses are all about how people "get their acts together" to get recognized as a given kind of person at a specific time and place.

The whole point of talking about Discourses is to focus on the fact that when people mean things to each other, there is always more than language at stake. To mean anything to someone else (or even to myself) I have to communicate who I am (in the sense of what socially situated identity am I taking on here and now) and what I am doing in terms of what socially situated activity I am carrying out (Wieder and Pratt, 1990). Language is, as we have seen, not enough for this. We have to get our minds and deeds "right," as well. We also have get ourselves appropriately in sync with various objects, tools, places, technologies, and other people. Being in a Discourse is being able to engage in a particular sort of "dance" with words, deeds, values, feelings, other people, objects, tools, technologies, places and times so as to get recognized as a distinctive sort of *who* doing a distinctive sort of *what*. Being able to understand a Discourse is being able to recognize such "dances."

Imagine what an identity kit to play the role of Sherlock Holmes would involve: certain clothes, certain ways of using language (oral language and print), certain attitudes and beliefs, allegiance to a certain lifestyle, and certain ways of interacting with others. We can call all these factors together, as they are integrated around the identity of "Sherlock Holmes, Master Detective" the "Sherlock Holmes Discourse." This example also makes clear that "Discourse," as I am using the term, does not involve just talk or just language.

The woman in the job interview was in danger of failing to be the "right kind of person" for entry into specific business and work-centered Discourses. She needed to signal that she was "responsible" even when the job she would be given would in all likelihood have given her little real responsibility. Her success at the social practice of job interviewing would simply have signaled that she had allegiance to certain middle-class values and was to be "trusted" not to disrupt the workings of power within the workplace and the wider society.

We are all multiple kinds of people. I use different combinations of words, deeds, attitudes, props (e.g., chalk, classrooms, sitting arrangements in office hours), and values to be a "professor" than I do to be a "bird watcher" or "(video) gamer," but I am all three and many other kinds as well, some of which are very hard to name (e.g., "first-generation middle-class baby boomer with class resentment"), but not all that hard to recognize. I once knew very well how, in words, deeds, attitudes, props (e.g., statues, pews, holy water, cassocks), and values, to "pull off" being a devout Catholic and knew well how to recognize (and police) others who attempted to "pull off" that identity. I don't any longer.

Discourses are not units or tight boxes with neat boundaries. Rather they are *ways of recognizing and getting recognized* as certain sorts of *whos* doing certain sorts of *whats*. One and the same "dance" can get recognized in multiple ways, in partial ways, in contradictory ways, in disputed ways, in negotiable ways, and so on and so forth through all the multiplicities and problematics that work on postmodernism has made so popular. Discourses are matters of enactment and recognition, then.

All recognition processes involve satisfying a variety of constraints in probabilistic and sometimes partial ways. For example, something recognized as a "weapon" (e.g., a baseball bat or a fireplace poker) may share some features with prototypical weapons (like a gun, sword, or club) and not share other features. And there may be debate about the matter. Furthermore, the very same thing might be recognized as a weapon in one context and not in another. So, too, with being in and out of Discourses, e.g., enacting and recognizing being–doing a certain type of street gang member, Special Ed student, or particle physicist.

While there are an endless array of Discourses in the world, nearly all human beings, except under extraordinary conditions, acquire an initial Discourse within whatever constitutes their primary socializing unit early in life. Early in life, we all learn a culturally distinctive way of being an "everyday person"—that is, a non-specialized, non-professional person. We can call this our "primary Discourse." Our primary Discourse gives us our initial and often enduring sense of self and sets the foundations of our culturally specific vernacular language (our "everyday language"), the language in which we speak and act as "everyday" (non-specialized) people, and our culturally specific vernacular identity.

As a person grows up, lots of interesting things can happen to his or her primary Discourse. Primary Discourses can change, hybridize with other Discourses, and they can even die. In any case, for the vast majority of us, our primary Discourse, through all its transformations, serves us throughout life as what I will call our "lifeworld Discourse" (Habermas 1984). Our lifeworld Discourse is the way that we use language, feel and think, act and interact, and so forth, in order to be an "everyday" (nonspecialized) person. In our plural world there is much adjustment and negotiation as people seek to meet in the terrain of the lifeworld, given that lifeworlds are culturally distinctive (that is, different groups of people have different ways of being–doing "everyday people").

All the Discourses we acquire later in life, beyond our primary Discourse, we acquire within a more "public sphere" than our initial socializing group. We can call these "secondary Discourses." They are acquired within institutions that are part and parcel of wider communities, whether these be religious groups, community organizations, schools, businesses, or governments.

As we are being socialized early in life, secondary Discourses very often play an interesting role. Primary Discourses work out, over time, alignments and allegiances with and against other Discourses, alignments and allegiances that shape them as they, in turn, shape these other Discourses. One way that many social groups achieve an alignment with secondary Discourses they value is by incorporating certain aspects of the practices of these secondary Discourses into the early (primary Discourse) socialization of their children. For example, some African-American families incorporate aspects of practices and values that are part of African-American churches into their primary Discourse (Rickford and Rickford 2000; Smitherman 1977), as my family incorporated aspects of practices and values of a very traditional Catholicism into our primary Discourse. This is an extremely important mechanism in terms of which bits and pieces of a valued "community" or "public" identity (to be more fully practiced later in the child's life) is incorporated as part and parcel of the child's "private," "home-based," lifeworld identity.

Social groups that are deeply affiliated with formal schooling often incorporate into the socialization of their children practices that resonate with later school-based secondary Discourses (e.g., see Rogoff and Toma 1997). For example, their children from an early age are encouraged (and coached) at dinner time to tell stories in quite expository ways that are rather like little essays, or parents interact with their children over books in ways that encourage a great deal of labeling and the answering of a variety of different types of questions, as well as the forming of inter-textual relationships between books and between books and the world. Of course, this fact has been a mainstay of the literature on school failure.

I refer to the process by which families incorporate aspects of valued secondary-Discourse practices into their primary Discourses as "early borrowing." Early borrowing is used as a way to facilitate children's later success in valued secondary Discourses. I want to stress the following point: *Early borrowing functions not primarily to give children certain skills, but, rather, to give them certain values, attitudes, motivations, ways of interacting, and perspectives, all of which are more important than mere skills for successful later entry into specific secondary Discourses "for real." (Skills follow from such matters.)*

There are, of course, complex relationships between people's primary Discourses and the secondary ones they are acquiring, as well as among their academic, institutional, and community-based secondary Discourses. These interactions crucially effect what happens to people when they are attempting to acquire new Discourses. Early borrowing is one of these relationships. Others involve forms of resistance, opposition, domination, on the one hand, or of alliance and complicity, on the other, among Discourses.

On being a "real Indian"

I am arguing, then, that we must always act, think, value, and interact in ways that together with language render *who* we are and *what* we are doing recognizable to others (and ourselves). As we have seen, to be a particular *who* and to pull off a particular *what* requires that we act, value, interact, and use language in sync with, in coordination with, others, as well as with various objects ("props") in appropriate locations and at appropriate times (Gee 1992–93; Knorr Cetina 1992; Latour 1987, 2005). All this is rather abstract, so let me turn to a specific example.

To see this wider notion of language as integrated with "other stuff" (other people, objects, values, times and places) in Discourses, I will briefly consider Wieder and Pratt's fascinating work on how American Indians (from a wide variety of different groups or "tribes") recognize each other as "really Indian" (Wieder and Pratt 1990a, b; Pratt 1985). Wieder and Pratt's work, of course, was done in 1990. Discourses change—as we will see later, they change in reaction to other Discourses—so the claims we discuss are not meant necessarily to apply to all Native Americans at all times. Nonetheless, Wieder and Pratt's work, based on close ethno-graphic observations, is a good example of how Discourses work.

Native Americans, at least of the sort Wieder and Pratt studied, "refer to persons who are 'really Indian' in just those words with regularity and standardization" (Wieder and Pratt, 1990a: 48). This example will also make yet clearer how the identities (the *whos*) we take on are not rigidly set by the states of our minds or bodies, but are, rather, flexibly negotiated in actual contexts of practice.

The problem of "recognition and being recognized" is very consequential and problematic for Indians. While one must be able to make some claims to kinship with others who are recognized as "real Indians," this by no means settles the matter. People with such (biological) ties can fail to get recognized as "really Indian," and people of mixed kinship (white and Indian) can be so recognized.

Being a real Indian is not something one can simply be. Rather, it is something that one becomes or is in the "doing" of it, that is, in the performance (for this general perspective, see Garfinkel 1967; Heritage 1984; Heritage and Maynard 2006). Though one must have certain kinship ties to get in the "game," beyond this entry criterion there is no being (once and for all) a real Indian, rather there is only doing being-or-becoming-a-real-Indian. If one does not continue to "practice" being a real Indian, one ceases to be a real Indian. Finally, "doing" being-and-becoming-a-real-Indian is not something that one can do all by oneself. It requires the participation of other Indians. One cannot be a real Indian unless one appropriately recognizes real Indians and gets recognized as a real Indian in the practices of doing being-and-becoming-a-real-Indian. Being a real Indian also requires appropriate accompanying objects (props), times, and places.

There are a multitude of ways one can do being-and-becoming-a-real-Indian. Some of these are (following Wieder and Pratt, see also Scollon and Scollon 1981): Real Indians prefer to avoid conversation with strangers, Indian or otherwise. They cannot be related to one another as "mere acquaintances," as some non-Indians might put it. So, for real Indians, any conversation they do have with a stranger who may turn out to be a real Indian will, in the discovery of the other's Indianness, establish substantial obligations between the conversational partners just through the mutual acknowledgment that they are Indians and that they are now no longer strangers to one another.

In their search for the other's real Indianness and in their display of their own Indianness, real Indians frequently proceed to engage in a distinctive form of verbal sparring. By correctly responding to and correctly engaging in this sparring, which Indians call "razzing," each participant further establishes cultural competency in the eyes of the other.

Real Indians manage face-to-face relations with others in such a way that they appear to be in agreement with them (or, at least, they do not overtly disagree); they are modest and "fit in." They show accord and harmony and are reserved about their own interests, skills, attainments, and positions. Real Indians understand that they should not elevate themselves over other real Indians. And they understand that the complex system of obligations they have to kin and other real Indians takes priority over those contractual obligations and pursuit of self-interest that some non-Indians prize so highly.

Real Indians must be competent in "doing their part" in participating in conversations that begin with the participants exchanging greetings and other amenities and then lapsing into extended periods of silence. They must know that neither they nor the others have an obligation to speak—that silence on the part of all conversants is permissible.

When they are among Indians, real Indians must also be able to perform in the roles of "student" and "teacher" and be able to recognize the behaviors appropriate to these roles. These roles are brought into play exclusively when the appropriate occasion arises for transmitting cultural knowledge (i.e., things pertinent to being a real Indian). Although many non-Indians find it proper to ask questions of someone who is instructing them, Indians regard questions in such a situation as being inattentive, rude, insolent, and so forth. The person who has taken the role of "student" shows attentiveness by avoiding eye contact and by being silent. The teaching situation, then, as a witnessed monologue, lacks the dialogical features that characterize much of Western instruction.

A very wide variety of gatherings provides the occasion for public speaking. Only elder males may speak for themselves as well as for others in the fashion of addressing the gathering. Younger males and all women must seek out an elder male who will "talk for" or "speak for them," if they have something they want to say.

While the above sort of information gives us something of the flavor of what sorts of things one must do and say to get recognized as a "real Indian," such information can lead to a bad mistake. It can sound as if the above features are necessary and sufficient criteria for doing being-and-becoming-a-real-Indian. But this is not true. The above features are not a test that can be or ever is administered all at once, and once and for all, to determine who is or is not a real Indian. Rather, the circumstances under which these features are employed by Indians emerge over the course of a developing history among groups of people. They are employed always in the context of actual situations, and at different times in the life history of groups of people. The ways in which the judgment

"He (or she) is (or is not) a real Indian" is embedded within situations that motivate it make such judgments intrinsically provisional. Those now recognized can spoil their acceptance or have it spoiled and those not now accepted can have another chance even when others do not want to extend it. The same thing applies, in fact, in regard to many other social identities, not just being "a real Indian" (e.g., McCall 1995). There are no all-at-once, once-and-for-all, tests for who is adept at physics or literature or being a member of a Los Angeles street gang, or a lawyer. These matters are settled provisionally as part and parcel of shared histories and on-going activities. It is the fact that school so often does not function in this way—for example, in school we very often act as if there are all-at-once, and once-and-for-all, tests of identity (e.g., "good reader," "SPED student," "gifted," "low achieving," etc.)—that helps to make school such a strange place for many children and adults.

Discourses again

To sum up, then, by "a Discourse" I will mean:

> A Discourse is a socially accepted association among ways of using language and other symbolic expressions, of thinking, feeling, believing, valuing, and acting, as well as using various tools, technologies, or props that can be used to identify oneself as a member of a socially meaningful group or "social network," to signal (that one is playing) a socially meaningful "role," or to signal that one is filling a social niche in a distinctively recognizable fashion.

There are number of important points that one can make about Discourses (Fairclough 1989, 1992, 2003; Gee 1992; Hodge and Kress 1988; Jameson 1981; Kress 1985; Lee 1992; Macdonell 1986; Thompson 1984):

1 Discourses are inherently "ideological" in the sense in which I have defined that term in the first chapter. They crucially involve a set of values and viewpoints about the relationships between people and the distribution of social goods, at the very least about who is an insider and who isn't, often who is "normal" and who isn't, and often, too, many other things as well.

2 Discourses are resistant to internal criticism and self-scrutiny, since uttering viewpoints that seriously undermine them defines one as

being outside them. The Discourse itself defines what counts as acceptable criticism.

3   Discourse-defined positions from which to speak and behave are not, however, just defined as internal to a Discourse, but also as standpoints taken up by the Discourse in its relation to other, ultimately opposing, Discourses. The Discourse we identify with being a feminist is radically changed if all male Discourses disappear. The Discourse of a regular drinking group at a bar is partly defined by its points of opposition to a variety of other viewpoints (non-drinkers, people who dislike bars as places of meeting people, "Yuppies," and so forth).

4   Any Discourse concerns itself with certain objects and puts forward certain concepts, viewpoints, and values at the expense of others. In doing so it will marginalize viewpoints and values central to other Discourses. In fact, a Discourse can call for one to accept values in conflict with other Discourses of which one is also a member (see below for more on this).

5   Finally, Discourses are intimately related to the distribution of social power and hierarchical structure in society, which is why they are always and everywhere ideological. Control over certain Discourses can lead to the acquisition of social goods (money, power, status) in a society. These Discourses empower those groups who have the least conflicts with their other Discourses when they use them. Let us call Discourses that lead to social goods in a society dominant Discourses and let us refer to those groups that have the fewest conflicts when using them as dominant groups. Obviously these are both matters of degree and change to a certain extent in different contexts.

All Discourses are the products of history (see Foucault 1966, 1969, 1973, 1977, 1978, 1980, 1985 and Fleck 1979). It is sometimes helpful to say that it is not individuals who speak and act, but rather that historically and socially defined Discourses speak to each other through individuals. The individual instantiates, gives body to a Discourse every time he or she acts or speaks, and thus carries it, and ultimately changes it, through time. Americans tend to be very focused on the individual, and thus often miss the fact that the individual is the meeting point of many, sometimes conflicting, socially and historically defined Discourses (see the next chapter for examples).

The discourse of law school

Once again we have gotten rather abstract, and I want therefore to develop a specific example—this time an example relevant to the conflicts between Discourses that can inhabit one and the same person. I will take as my example the Discourse of law school in the United States. This example will, in addition, show how literacy practices of quite specific sorts are embedded in Discourses. My discussion here is based on the work of Michele Minnis (1994; all page references below are to this article). Again, I caution that Discourses change—and, indeed, some law schools have sought to reform their pedagogies based on the sorts of things people like Minnis have discovered—but, again, too, Minnis's work was based on close ethnographic observations.

In the typical law school, instruction in the first year involves total immersion in the course material. Teachers do not lecture in class, rather they engage in adversarial interactions with students patterned after those of judge and lawyer in appellate courtrooms. The dominant instructional approach is the "case method." This method consists in discussing and comparing appellate opinions through a question-and-answer routine sometimes called "Socratic dialogue":

> Before every class meeting, students are expected to have read and briefed, or summarized in writing, several appellate opinions from a book containing pivotal case law on the course topic. When called on in class, students must be prepared to review and analyze specific opinions, compare the details of several opinions, and explain how the opinions might have been rendered differently.

The burden of divining pattern in the entire body of cases is on the students. Typically the professor's role is to expose, in the student's presentations, the hazards of ignoring alternative interpretations of the case material. Students are advised to be alert and ready to duck or strike lest their adversary, the professor, catch them off guard. In other words, law school classes, much like those in the martial arts, are run as a kind of contest between opponents. Always, discussion in such classes is exegetical; it is anchored in texts, in written accounts and judgments of past events (pp. 352–353).

To write a competent brief the student has to be able to read the text being briefed in much the same way as the professor does. Student readers must know how such texts are structured. They must know, for example, how sentence structure in such texts is used to signal emphasis, importance, and other communicative effects. They must also see "some statements as relatively general (or relatively specific) renderings of others, some ideas and discussions as subparts of others, and the whole of an exposition as integrated by an organizing idea" (p. 356). And they must do this is order ultimately to see and be able to summarize the argument the text propounds.

Students are not taught these reading skills—the ones necessary for them to be able to write briefs—directly. Briefs are not, for instance, turned in to the professor; they are written for the students' own use in class. "The feedback students receive on their briefs is provided indirectly and to everyone at once, through analysis of the briefed cases in class" (p. 357). This sort of indirect feedback is quite unlikely to involve overt attention to structural patterns and writing conventions, let alone reading conventions. Nonetheless, these must be "picked up," along with (and actually as part and parcel of) concepts, values, and ways of interacting that are specific to the legal domain.

In law school, then, the traditional instructional methods do not describe or explicate procedures (like writing briefs, engaging in legal argumentation, or reading legal texts). Rather they employ these procedures publicly. A key point here, then, is that instruction "occurs inside the procedure; it is not about the procedure, its rationale, its powers, or its limitations" (p. 361).

One of the basic assumptions of law school is that if students are not told overtly what to do and how to proceed, this will spur them on essentially to teach themselves. Minnis argues that this assumption does not, however, work equally well for everyone. Many students from minority or otherwise non-mainstream backgrounds fail in law school.

Minnis argues that this is so because these students have not, in their prior schooling and social experience, been exposed to and coached in the sorts of competitive academic behaviors and "other survival skills appropriate to the situation encountered in the law school classroom" (p. 362):

> Contemporary legal education is designed for the good students, those who can understand what the professors mean but never explicitly say in the classes. Not surprisingly, given that mutual unspoken understanding between teachers and students requires common prior experiences, most good law students are traditional law students. They are students whose economic, social, and educational backgrounds are much like those of traditional law professors. These students, that is, are members of middle- and upper-class

society, the dominant culture, the culture that shaped the law. Accordingly, they are inclined to accept without question beliefs that are characteristic of that culture and that give them an advantage in law school. In short, their personal histories have taught them to confront the world aggressively; they esteem reasoning over other ways of knowing, individual accomplishment over collective accomplishment, and competition over cooperation.

(380)

It should be stressed, however, that the problem is not just that non-mainstream student have not had the same sorts of educational preparations as those who take more "naturally" to law school instruction. Law school is a set of related social practices that constitute a "Discourse," which is, of course connected to the larger Discourse of law.

The social practices and positions of the Discourse of law school conflict, and conflict seriously, with the social practices and positions of the other Discourses to which many minorities and other non-mainstream students belong. They conflict much less—or not at all—with the social practices and positions of the other Discourses to which many mainstream students belong.

Let us put the matter somewhat differently: The Discourse of law school creates kinds of people who (overtly or tacitly) define themselves as different from—often "better" than—other kinds of people. For many minority and other non-mainstream students, the Discourse of law school makes them be both kinds of people. They get to define their kind (as law student) as different from—often "better" than—their own kind (as a member of one of their other Discourses). A paradox, indeed—unfortunately one they get to live and feel in their bodies and their minds.

Let us give a specific example of how these differences can work out in practice. The discussion in law school classrooms is intensely legal (Williams 1991). The professor is generally indifferent "to economic, social, or other contexts in which the events described in the judicial opinions might be viewed" (359). Minnis points out that several scholars (Gopen 1984; White 1984) see a close similarity between case analysis in the law classroom and the formalistic study of poetry. In the formal analysis of poetry, as well, large social, political, and cultural contexts are ignored in favor of an intense focus on language form, ambiguity, and possible meanings.

As we have seen in earlier chapters, and will see again in the next chapter, some people (in some of their social practices, connected often to their home and community-based Discourses) do not choose to isolate language from larger realms of experience. More generally, some families and social groups highly value cooperation, not competition, and some of these will not engage authority figures, like parents or teachers, including law school teachers, in adversarial dialogue. (Minnis discusses the case of a Chicana law student in some detail, based on her own account, pp. 382 ff.) For some, being inducted into law school social practices means learning behaviors at odds with their other social practices that are constitutive of their other social identities. People like us don't do things like that; we're not that kind of person. And yet law school summons us to do just that, to be just that kind of person.

The conflict, then, is not just that I am uncomfortable engaging in a new practice—much as a new physical activity may involve using new muscles. Rather, the conflict is between who I am summoned to be in this new Discourse (law school) and who I am in other Discourses that overtly conflict with—and sometimes have historically contested with—this Discourse. Since Discourses (e.g., law school student and Hispanic-American of a certain sort) always exist and mean in juxtaposition to each other, performances in one often have meaning in regard to—and repercussions for—others. I can be asked in mind and body to "mean against" some of my other social identities and their concomitant values. It is not for nothing that the ancient Romans asked the ancient Christians to spit on the cross as a sign of their loyalty.

Minnis recommends that, if they wish to treat their non-mainstream students fairly, law schools ought to "make their assumptions, their values, the culture of the legal community—everything that comprises "thinking like a lawyer"—concrete and accessible" (385). While I certainly agree with this advice, I would also caution that making things concrete and accessible—rendering overt the "rules of the game"—is not an educational panacea and involves complex problems.

First, this cannot really be done in any very exhaustive manner. All that goes into thinking, acting, believing, valuing, dressing, interacting, reading, and writing like a lawyer cannot be put overtly in words. Whatever we could say, however long we took to say it, would only be the fleeting tip of an iceberg. Further, as overt knowledge it would not ground fluent behaviors any more than overt knowledge of dance steps can ground fluid dancing. In the absence of the full immersion that mainstream students are getting in the law school classroom, all that would happen with overt information would be that non-mainstream students would engage in rather stilted performances that "hypercorrected" what "real" lawyers look, talk, and act like (Gee 1992; Perkins 1992, 1995).

This is certainly not to say that overt information could not help non-mainstream students know where to focus in the rich stream of texts and interactions that compose law school. It is certainly not to recommend "hiding" aspects of language and interaction that lead to success and which we can describe and explicate. However, we certainly cannot come close to describing and explicating even a small part of the "game" in any realistic detail. The game "works," in part, precisely because this cannot be done. Furthermore, no amount of description and explication will remove or necessarily mitigate very real conflicts between Discourses.

The practices of a Discourse—like those of law school—contain in their public interactional structures the "mentalities" learners are meant to "internalize." Immersion in such practices—learning inside the procedures, rather than overly about them—ensures that the learner takes on perspectives, adopts a world view, accepts a set of core values, and masters an identity often without a great deal of critical and reflective awareness about these matters, nor, indeed, about the Discourse itself.

In stating these problems, I am not offering a counsel of despair. My point is, rather, that literacy and the New Literacy Studies are deeply political matters. We must take overt value stances and engage in overt contest between Discourses, juxtaposing Discourses and using one to change another. Ultimately, for all the very real challenges they face, bi-Discoursal people (people who have or are mastering two contesting or conflicting Discourses) are the ultimate sources of change, just as bilinguals very often are in the history of language. The non-mainstream law student who manages to pull off recognizable and acceptable law school Discourse practices, but infuses them with aspects of her other Discourses, is a source of challenge and change. So, too, are more overt challenges by those who have gotten themselves—by hook or crook—inside the door. So, too, are challenges from other Discourses, even from people who have never gotten inside.

It is sometimes argued that a Discourse perspective is "deterministic," predestining people to success or failure in Discourses like law school based on conflicts or resonances of their other Discourses with the new Discourse (Delpit 1995). Nothing could be further from the truth. The history of Discourses is a history of struggle, contestation, and change. Far from always losing, "non-mainstream" people often win, and sometimes, for better or worse, they become a new "mainstream," a new center of social power.

A Discourse perspective simply argues that historic sociocultural struggles are enacted by and on people's bodies and minds, often with much pain and injustice. These struggles are always between "kinds" of people, but these "kinds" are enacted by specific people with their specific and idiosyncratic bodies, minds, and feelings. This battle of "kinds" acted out by specific individuals (who are actually many "kinds" of people at once) causes some of the deepest perplexities in human life (McCall 1995). The moral of a Discourse perspective is just this: no one, but no one, should feel like a "loser" when they have lost these Discourse wars (e.g., the non-mainstream law students Minnis discusses), given the subtle, complex, and often arbitrary ways in which Discourses connected to power "stack the decks" in the favor of certain "kinds of people."

Acquisition and learning

We can distinguish two broad sorts of Discourses in any society: The first sort is what I called "primary Discourses" above. The second sort I called "secondary Discourses." Primary Discourses are those to which people are apprenticed early in life during their primary socialization as members of particular families within their sociocultural settings. Primary Discourses constitute our first social identity, and something of a base within which we acquire or resist later Discourses. They form our initial taken-for-granted understandings of who we are and who people "like us" are, as well as what sorts of things we ("people like us") do, value, and believe when we are not "in public." Lots can happen to them as we go through life, and by the time we are no longer children our primary Discourse has transmuted into our lifeworld Discourse, our culturally distinctive way of being an "everyday" person, not a specialist of some sort.

Secondary Discourses are those to which people are apprenticed as part of their socializations within various local, state, and national groups and institutions outside early home and peer-group socialization—for example, churches, gangs, schools, offices. They constitute the recognizability and meaningfulness of our "public" (more formal) acts. A particular woman, for instance, might be recognized as a businesswoman, political activist, feminist, church member, National Organization of Women official, PTA member, and volunteer Planned Parenthood counselor, and many more, by carrying out performances that are recognizable within and by these Discourses.

This distinction between primary Discourses and secondary Discourses is not meant to be airtight and unproblematic. In fact, I draw the distinction precisely because the boundary between the two sorts of Discourses is constantly negotiated and contested in society and history. Many social groups borrow aspects of valued secondary Discourses into the socialization of their children in an attempt to advantage their children's acquisition of these secondary Discourses, whether they be school-based, community-based, or religion-based Discourses, for instance. For example, many middle-class homes use school-based language and practices with their small children at home long before they go to school, as we saw in Chapter 8 above, to advantage their children for school. Many African-Americans incorporate church-based language and practices into their early home-based interactions with their children, as, indeed, did my own family.

People also, later in life, strategically use aspects of their primary Discourses or community-based secondary Discourses in "pulling off" performances in some of their other secondary Discourses. For example, consider the ways in which Jesse Jackson combined a distinctive African-American church-based secondary Discourse with a mainstream political Discourse. Such a move is risky. If people had rejected Jackson as a national politician because they saw the African-American bits (e.g., his rhetorical devices) as "unacceptable" in mainstream political Discourse ("being/doing a national politician"), then he would have failed to get recognized as such. But the time and place was (eventually) right and lots of people—even political enemies—did recognize him as a national politician. Since his risk worked, he actually changed the political Discourse, allowing new types of performances to work. In turn, others followed him (to the point where even white Republican politicians use some of the same—admittedly attenuated—sorts of rhetorical devices in their speeches). This is one important way in which Discourses change—people mix them and their mixtures get recognized and accepted (but, of course, not always or even usually).

How do people come by the Discourses they are members of? Here it is necessary, before answering the question, to make an important distinction, a distinction that does not exist in non-technical parlance: a distinction between acquisition and learning (Krashen 1985a, b). This distinction is, like the one above between primary and secondary Discourses, not meant to be taken as airtight and unproblematic. What it really involves is a continuum whose two poles are "acquisition" and "learning," with mixed cases in between. (For a much more nuanced and detailed discussion about learning, see Gee 2003, 2004.)

We will distinguish acquisition and learning as follows:

Acquisition is a process of acquiring something (usually, subconsciously) by exposure to models, a process of trial and error, and practice within social groups, without formal teaching. It happens in natural settings which are meaningful and functional in the sense that acquirers know that they need to acquire the thing they are exposed to in order to function and they in fact want to so function. This is how people come to control their first language.

Learning is a process that involves conscious knowledge gained through teaching (though not necessarily from someone officially designated a teacher) or through certain life experiences that trigger conscious reflection. This teaching or reflection involves explanation and analysis, that is, breaking down the thing to be learned into its analytic parts. It inherently involves attaining, along with the matter being taught, some degree of meta-knowledge about the matter.

(Pinker 1989, 1994)

Much of what we come by in life, after our initial enculturation, involves a mixture of acquisition and learning. However, the balance between the two can be quite different in different cases and different at different stages in the developmental process. For instance, many of us initially learned to drive a car by instruction, but thereafter acquired, rather than learned, most of what we know.

Some cultures highly value acquisition and so tend simply to expose children to adults modeling some activity and eventually the child picks it up, picks it up as a gestalt, rather than as a series of analytic bits (Heath 1983; Scollon and Scollon 1981; Street 1984). Other cultural groups highly value teaching and thus break down what is to be mastered into sequential steps and analytic parts and engage in explicit explanation.

There is an up side and a down side to both acquisition and learning that can be expressed as follows: We are better at performing what we acquire, but we consciously know more about what we have learned. For most of us, playing a musical instrument, or dancing, or using a second language, are skills we attained by some mixture of acquisition and learning. But it is a safe bet that, over the same amount of time, people are better at (performing) these activities if acquisition predominated during that time.

What is undoubtedly true of first language development (Pinker 1994) and has been argued, controversially, to be true in the case of second language development (Krashen 1985a, b) is, I would argue, true of Discourses: Discourses are mastered through acquisition, not learning. That is, Discourses are not mastered by overt instruction, but by enculturation ("apprenticeship") into social practices through scaffolded and supported interaction with people who have already mastered the Discourse (Newman *et al.* 1989; Rogoff 1990, 2003; Tharp and

Gallimore 1988). This is how we all acquired our native language and our primary Discourses. It is how we acquire all later, more public-oriented Discourses. If you have no access to the social practice, you don't get in the Discourse, you don't have it.

As a Discourse is being mastered by acquisition, then, of course, learning can be used to facilitate "meta-knowledge." You cannot overtly teach anyone a Discourse, in a classroom or anywhere else. This is not to say that acquisition can't go on in a classroom, but only that if it does, this isn't because of overt "teaching," but because of a process of "apprenticeship" and social practice.

Acquisition must (at least, partially) precede learning; apprenticeship must precede overt teaching. Classrooms that do not properly balance acquisition and learning, and realize which is which, simply privilege those students who have already begun the acquisition process outside the school. Too little acquisition leads to too little mastery-in-practice; too little learning leads to too little analytic and reflective awareness and limits the capacity for certain sorts of critical reading and refection (though, of course, only certain sorts of learning lead beyond mere conscious awareness and reflectiveness to an actual "critical" capacity).

It is very important to realize that the English language often leads us to confuse terms for products/props/content and terms for Discourses. Thus, take an academic discipline like linguistics. You can overtly teach someone (the content knowledge of the discipline of) linguistics, which is a body of facts and theories; however, while knowledge of some significant part of these facts and theories is necessary to actually being a linguist, you cannot overtly teach anyone to do "being a linguist" (remember "doing being a real Indian" above), which is a Discourse.

A person could know a great deal about linguistics and still not be (accepted as) a linguist. "Autodidacts" are precisely people who, while often extremely knowledgeable, trained themselves and thus were trained outside of a process of group practice and socialization. They are almost never accepted as "insiders," "members of the club (profession, group)." Our Western focus on individualism makes us constantly forget the importance of having been "properly socialized."

Let us now turn to the *priviso* in the definition of learning above about "certain life experiences that trigger conscious reflection," causing the same effects as overt teaching. In our definition of learning we are concerned with what usually or prototypically counts as "teaching" in our culture. This involves breaking down what is to be taught into its analytic bits and getting learners to learn it in such a way that they can "talk about," "describe," "explain" it. That is, the learner is meant to have "meta-knowledge" about what is learned and to be able to engage in "meta-talk" about it. We often teach even things like driving this way. But not all cultures engage in this sort of teaching, and not all of them use the concept "teaching" in this way, nor, indeed, do all instances of what is sometimes called "teaching" in our own culture fit this characterization (Heath 1983; Scribner and Cole 1981; Scollon and Scollon 1981; Street 1984).

In many cultures where there is no such overt analytical teaching, some people still gain a good deal of "meta-knowledge" about what they know and do. This appears to come about by that fact they have had certain experiences which have caused them to think about a particular Discourse in a reflective and critical way (Goody 1977, 1986: 1–44). When we have really mastered anything (e.g., a Discourse), we have little or no conscious awareness of it. (Indeed, like dancing, Discourses wouldn't work if people were consciously aware of what they were doing while doing it.) However, when we come across a situation where we are unable to accommodate or adapt, we become consciously aware of what we are trying to do or are being called upon to do (Vygotsky 1987: 167–241). While such an experience can happen to anyone, they are common among people who are somewhat "marginal" to a Discourse or culture, and, thus, such people often have insights into the workings of these Discourses or cultures that more "mainstream" members do not. This is, in fact, the advantage to being "socially maladapted" (as long as the maladaptation is not too dysfunctional and, to be sure, this is not to say that there are not also disadvantages). And, of course, people in our culture can have such experiences apart from classrooms (and often have them in classrooms when it is the classroom, school, or teacher that is causing the maladaptation).

Ruth Finnegan (1967, 1988), in studies of the Limba, a nonliterate group in Sierra Leone, points out that the Limba have a great deal of meta-linguistic and reflective sophistication in their talk about language, sophistication of the sort that we normally think is the product of writing and formal schooling, both of which the Limba do not have. Finnegan attributes this sophistication to the Limba's multiple contacts with speakers of other languages and with those languages themselves. And here we have a clue, then. Good classroom instruction (in composition, study skills, writing, critical thinking, content-based literacy, or whatever) can and should lead to meta-knowledge, to seeing how the Discourses you have already got (not just the languages) relate to those you are attempting to acquire, and how the ones you are trying to acquire relate to self and society. But to do this, the classroom must juxtapose different

Discourses for comparison and contrast. Diversity, then, is not an "add on," but a cognitive necessity if we wish to develop meta-awareness and overt reflective insight on the part of learners.

Literacy and Discourses

All humans, barring serious disorder, become members of one Discourse free, so to speak—their primary Discourse. It is important to realize that even among speakers of English there are socioculturally different primary Discourses, and that these Discourses use language differently. For example, many lower socioeconomic African-American children use English within their primary Discourse to make sense of their experience differently than do middle class children (see Leona's stories in the last chapter and Heath 1982, 1983; Kochman 1972, 1981; Rickford and Rickford 2000; Smitherman 1977). And this is not due merely to the fact that they have a different dialect of English. So-called "African-American Vernacular English" is, on structural grounds, only trivially different from standard English by the norms of linguists accustomed to dialect differences around the world (see Chapter 1 above and Baugh 1983, 1999, 2000; Labov 1972a). Rather, these children use language, behavior, values, and beliefs to give a different shape to their experience.

A person's primary Discourse serves as a "framework" or "base" for their acquisition and learning of other Discourses later in life. It also shapes, in part, the form this acquisition and learning will take and the final result. Furthermore, Discourses acquired later in life can influence a person's primary Discourse, having various effects on it, (re-)shaping it in various ways. Adults can then pass on these reshaped primary Discourses to their children. These mutual influences among Discourses underlie the processes of historical change of Discourses.

Quite obviously in a society like the United States, where there is so much mobility, diffuse class and (sub-)cultural borders, class ambiguity, and so many attempts to deny, change, or otherwise hide one's initial socialization if it was not "mainstream" enough, there are many complexities around the notion of "primary Discourse" and many problems in tracing its fate through individual lives. Indeed, these problems are a difficulty not just for scholars studying these matters: the large amount of *anomie*, alienation, and worry about "self" and "identity" in the United States, and related societies, has its roots in these very problems. I want to embed the notion of "literacy" within the framework of Discourses precisely because I believe that issues like these, far from invalidating that framework, are just the ones that we need to study and relate to our educational practice.

Beyond the primary Discourse, there are other Discourses which crucially involve social institutions beyond the family (or the primary socialization group as defined by the culture), no matter how much they also involve the family. These institutions all share the factor that they require one to communicate with non-intimates (or to treat intimates as if they were not intimates). Let us refer to these institutions as secondary institutions (such as schools, workplaces, stores, government offices, businesses, churches, etc.). Discourses beyond the primary Discourse are developed in association with and by having access to and practice with (apprenticeships in) these secondary institutions. Thus, I refer to them as secondary Discourses.

These secondary Discourses all build on, and extend, the uses of language and the values, attitudes and beliefs we acquired as part of our primary Discourse, and they may be more or less compatible with the primary Discourses of different social groups. It is of course a great advantage when any particular secondary Discourse is compatible (in words, deeds, and values) with your primary one. But all these secondary Discourses involve uses of language, either written or oral, or both, as well as ways of thinking, valuing, and behaving, which go beyond the uses of language in our primary Discourse no matter what group we belong to.

Secondary Discourses can be local, community-based Discourses, or more globally oriented ("public sphere Discourses"). For example, many Americans have Discourses (of different sorts) connected to memberships in community-based churches. The role of certain types of "fundamentalist" Discourses in many lower and middle-class white communities and of "evangelical" church-based Discourses in many African-American communities has been well documented (e.g., Bellah *et al.* 1996; Kapitzke 1995; Rosenberg 1970; Smitherman 1977). These Discourses decidedly do not take place just in church buildings, but involve an intricate network of ways of talking, acting, and valuing that can be quite pervasive in the lives of these people. There are many other community-based Discourses, including, for instance, Discourses used for public contacts like shopping and interactions with authority figures (e.g., police) in various sorts of local communities. It can happen that some of these community-based secondary Discourses (as for example some church-based Discourses) "filter" into and influence the primary Discourse and the processes of family-based primary socialization, intimately influencing interaction in the home. Indeed, this is one way that Discourses interact and change historically.

In modern plural, urban societies, like ours, community-based Discourses often have links to and applications in spheres beyond the local community, and, thus, shade into more global, "public sphere" Discourses. Needless to say, there is a continuum, rather than a clear dichotomy between local community-based and more "public sphere" secondary Discourses. These more globally oriented, "public sphere" secondary Discourses include ones used in schools, national media, and in many social, financial, and government agencies, as well as many Discourses connected to various sorts of employment and professions. These "public sphere" secondary Discourses all involve interactions with people well beyond one's initial socializing group and local community. These, too, can "filter" into and influence certain groups' primary Discourses.

The key point about secondary Discourses, however, is that they involve by definition interaction with people with whom one is either not "intimate," with whom one cannot assume lots of shared knowledge and experience, or they involve interactions where one is being "formal," that is, taking on an identity that transcends the family or primary socializing group.

Discourses, primary and secondary, can be studied, in some ways, like languages. In fact, some of the literature on and approaches to second language acquisition (Bialystok and Hakuta 1994) are relevant to them (if only in a metaphorical way). Two Discourses can interfere with one another, like two languages; aspects of one Discourse can be transferred to another Discourse, as one can transfer a grammatical feature from one language to another. For instance, the primary Discourse of many middle-class homes has been influenced by secondary Discourses like those used in schools and business.

Furthermore, if one has not mastered a particular secondary Discourse which nonetheless one must try to use, several things can happen, things which resemble what can happen when one has failed to fluently master a second language. One can fall back on one's primary Discourse, adjusting it in various ways to try to fit it to the needed functions (very common, but almost always socially disastrous), or one can use another, perhaps related, secondary Discourse. Or one can use a simplified, or stereotyped version of the required secondary Discourse. These processes are similar to those linguists study under the rubrics of language contact, pidginization, and creolization (Romaine 1988).

I believe that any socially useful definition of "literacy" must be couched in terms of these notions of primary and secondary Discourse. Thus, I define "literacy" as:

Mastery of a secondary Discourse.

Therefore, literacy is always plural: literacies. (There are many of them, since there are many secondary Discourses, and we all have some and fail to have others.) If one wanted to be rather pedantic and literalistic, then we could define "literacy" as:

Mastery of a secondary Discourse involving print

(which is almost all of them in a modern society). And one can substitute for "print" various other sorts of texts and technologies: painting, literature, films, television, computers, telecommunications—"props" in the Discourse—to get definitions of various other sorts of "literacies" (e.g., "visual literacy," "computer literacy," "literary literacy," and so forth).

But I see no gain from the addition of the phrase "involving print," other than to assuage the feelings of people committed (as I am not) to reading and writing as decontextualized and isolable skills. In addition, it is clear that many so-called nonliterate cultures have secondary Discourses which, while they do not involve print, involve a great many of the same skills, behaviors, and ways of thinking that we associate with literacy—for example, the many and diverse practices that have gone under the label "oral literature."

While many families borrow aspects of secondary Discourses, and their concomitant literacy practices, into the home-based socialization of their children (a process I called early borrowing above), these practices have their true and final home in the secondary Discourse. These families are preparing their children for these secondary Discourses, most powerfully by embedding these practices into the child's development of his or her primary Discourse. Thereafter in life, the child feels an emotional bond between the primary Discourse and the secondary one, true mastery of which comes only later (and which is thereby greatly facilitated). I myself was facilitated in just such a way for entry into and mastery of a traditional "orthodox" Catholic Discourse, but not for mainstream school-based Discourses. (We had two books in the house, the Bible and *Mother Goose*—don't know why it was *Mother Goose*—and did not engage in any borrowing of school-based language or practices; my parents would not have known how to do so. But, then, luckily, perhaps, given my lack of an early head start and the sorting mania of public schools, I didn't go to public schools, but, rather, to Catholic ones.)

We can talk about community-based literacies or public sphere literacies in terms of whether they involve mastery of community-based or more public sphere secondary Discourses. We can talk about dominant literacies and non-dominant literacies in terms of whether they involve mastery of dominant or non-dominant secondary Discourses. We can also talk about a literacy being liberating ("powerful") if it can be used as a "meta-language" or a "meta-Discourse" (a set of meta-words, meta-values, meta-beliefs) for the critique of other literacies and the way they constitute us as persons and situate us in society. Note that what I have called a liberating literacy is a particular use of a Discourse (to critique other ones), not a particular Discourse.

Like the distinctions drawn above, this view of literacy is not meant to be unproblematic, but precisely to problematize key complexities. For instance, it is clear biologically and historically that, for all human beings, their primary Discourses are rooted in the oral, face–face word. But, as I have said above, some social groups siphon aspects of their valued secondary Discourses into their primary Discourses, including elements of print and "print-related talk." We will see a striking example of this in the next chapter. This does not, for me, constitute a literacy, because the true "home" (socially, culturally, and historically) of these elements is the secondary Discourse to which they are helping to "pre-tune" the child. If this were not true, such "pre-tuning" would not work. Since it is true, we can say that the child is getting early practice—often in a simulated fashion—in that secondary Discourse.

There are two principles which apply to Discourses and, thus, to literacies, as well, and which relate them to our previous distinction between acquisition and learning. These are as follows:

1   *The Acquisition Principle.* Any Discourse (primary or secondary) is for most people most of the time mastered only through acquisition, not learning. Thus, literacy (fluent control or mastery of a secondary Discourse) is a product of acquisition, not learning, that is, it requires exposure to models in natural, meaningful, and functional settings, and (overt) teaching is not liable to be very successful—it may even initially get in the way. Time spent on learning and not acquisition is time not well spent if the goal is mastery in performance.

2   *The Learning Principle.* One cannot critique one Discourse with another one (which is the only way to seriously criticize and thus change a Discourse) unless one has meta-level knowledge about both Discourses. And this meta-knowledge is best developed through learning, though often learning applied to a Discourse one has to a certain extent already acquired. Thus, liberating literacy, as defined above, almost always involves learning, and not just acquisition.

The point of these principles is that acquisition and learning are means to quite different goals, though in our culture we very often confuse these means and thus don't get what we thought and hoped we would. Note that it is a consequence of the second principle that the goal of learning is "liberation" in the sense of acquiring "liberating literacies."

Teaching that leads to acquisition means to apprentice students in a master–apprentice relationship in a Discourse wherein the teacher scaffolds the students' growing abilities to say, do, value, believe, and so forth, within that Discourse, through demonstrating her mastery and supporting theirs even when it barely exists (i.e., you make it look like they can do what they really can't do). Such teaching in regard to early literacy in school-based Discourses, for instance, amounts to doing much the same thing middle-class, "super-baby"-producing parents do when they "do books" with their children (we will see an example in the next chapter).

Teaching that leads to learning uses explanations and analyses that break down material into its analytic "bits" and juxtaposes diverse Discourses and their practices to each other. Such teaching develops "meta-knowledge." While many "liberal" approaches to education look down on this mode of teaching, I do not; I have already said that I believe that meta-knowledge can be a form of power and liberation. Teaching for acquisition alone leads to successful, but "colonized" students. Teaching for acquisition and teaching for learning are different practices, and good teachers do both.

Mushfake

Let me return to the notion of "tension" or "conflict" between Discourses and within individuals while they use certain Discourses. We can always ask about how much tension or conflict is present between any two of a person's Discourses. I have argued above that some degree of conflict and tension (if only given the discrete historical origins of particular Discourses) will almost always be present. However, for some people, there are more overt and direct conflicts between two or more of their Discourses than there are for others (e.g., many women academics feel conflict between certain feminist Discourses and certain standard academic Discourses, e.g., traditional literary criticism). I would argue that when such conflict or tension exists, it can deter acquisition of one or the other or both of the conflicting Discourses, or, at least, affect the fluency of a mastered Discourse on certain occasions of use, e.g., where other stressful factors also impinge on the occasion, as in interview (see McCall 1995: 328 for a compelling example of what I am talking about).

Very often dominant groups in a society apply rather constant "tests" of the fluency of the dominant Discourses in which their power is symbolized; these tests become both tests of "natives" or, at least, "fluent users" of the Discourse and gates to exclude "non-natives"—people whose very conflicts with dominant Discourses show they were not, in fact, "born" to them and who can often show this even when they have full mastery of a dominant Discourse on most occasions of use. The sorts of tension and conflict we have mentioned here are particularly acute when they involve tension and conflict between one's primary Discourse and a dominant secondary Discourse, since one's primary Discourse defines one's "home" identity and that of people with whom one is intimate and intimately connected.

"Non-mainstream" students and their teachers are in a bind. One is not in a Discourse unless one has mastered it, and mastery comes about through acquisition, not learning. The acquisition of many dominant school-based Discourses on the part of mainstream students is facilitated by the fact that their primary Discourses have adopted some of the features of these dominant Discourses, by their early practice in the home with these dominant Discourses (which their parents have usually mastered), and by the constant support in these Discourses their homes give to the schools. Their mastery is also facilitated by the lesser conflict they feel in acquiring and using these dominant Discourses.

All these facilitating factors do not exist for many non-mainstream students, who are further hampered by the fact that traditional classrooms and schools are poor at facilitating acquisition (Edelsky 1991; Erickson 1987; McDermott 1987; Treuba 1987, 1989; Varenne and McDermott 1998). These non-mainstream students often fail to fully master school-based dominant Discourses, especially the "superficialities of form and correctness" that serve as such good "gates" given their imperviousness to late acquisition in classrooms without community support (Shaughnessy 1977). In fact, they often gain just enough mastery to ensure that they continually mark themselves as "outsiders" while using them and are, at best, colonized by them.

So what can composition, ESL, and content teachers—teachers of Discourses—do? Well, as we said above, there happens to be an advantage to failing to master fully mainstream Discourses, that is, there is, in fact, an advantage to being socially "maladapted." When we come across a situation where we are unable to accommodate or adapt (as many minority students do on being faced, late in the game, with having to acquire mainstream Discourses), we become consciously aware of what we are trying to do or are being called upon to do, and often gain deep insight into the matter. This insight ("meta-knowledge") can actually make one better able to manipulate the society in which the Discourse is dominant, provided it is coupled with the right sort of liberating literacy (a theory of the society and one's position in it, that is, a base for resistance to oppression and inequality).

But, the big question: If one cannot acquire Discourses save through active social practice, and it is difficult to compete with the mastery of those admitted early to the game when one has entered it as late as high school or college, what can be done to see to it that meta-knowledge and resistance are coupled with Discourse development? The problem is deepened by the fact that true acquisition of many mainstream Discourses involves, at least while being in them, active complicity with values that conflict with one's home and community-based Discourses, especially for many women and minorities.

I certainly have no complete and final answer to what is a massive social question, but I have two views to push nonetheless. I will phrase my views largely as they are relevant to teachers in high school and college: First, for anything close to acquisition to occur, classrooms must constitute active apprenticeships in "academic" social practices, and, in most cases, must connect with these social practices as they are also carried on outside the "composition" or "language" class, elsewhere in the university and the world.

Second, though true acquisition leading to full fluency in a Discourse may not always or often be possible late in the game, what I will call "mushfake Discourse" is possible. "Mushfake" (Mack 1989) is a term from prison culture meaning to make do with something less when the real thing is not available. So when prison inmates make hats from underwear to protect their hair from lice, the hats are mushfake. Elaborate craft items made from used wooden matchsticks are another example of mushfake. By "mushfake Discourse" I mean partial acquisition coupled with meta-knowledge and strategies to "make do." I have in mind strategies ranging from always having a memo edited to ensure no plural, possessive, and third-person "s" agreement errors to active use of, for example, African-American cultural skills at "psyching out" interviewers, or strategies of "rising to the meta-level" in an interview so the interviewer is thrown off stride by having the rules of the game explicitly referred to in the act of attempting to carry them out in a taken-for-granted fashion.

For many of us not acculturated early in life to "mainstream" dominant Discourses, but who have lived large parts of our lives in them, we come to realize, I believe, that a significant part of our "success" in evading the gate-keeping efforts of elites in our society (a "success" which is rarely, in my experience, total) is due to "mushfake." This is by no means to demean our efforts at acquisition and learning within these Discourses. It is only, for me, to "name" the game for ourselves and not in the interests of those elites and the "token" representatives they have designated to represent them in placating non-mainstream people.

We cannot pretend mushfake will put an end to the effects of racism or classism, or that it will open all doors. We can hope it will open some doors, while helping to change the society in the process. It is, at least, something to do while "waiting for the revolution."

So I propose that we ought to produce "muskfaking," resisting students, full of meta-knowledge. But isn't that to politicize teaching? A Discourse is an integration of saying, doing, and valuing, and all socially based valuing is political. All successful teaching, that is, teaching that inculcates Discourse and not just content, is political.

Chapter 9

Language, individuals, and Discourses

Language in Discourses

The last chapter developed a view of literacies centered around Discourses. This chapter turns to the analysis of language within a Discourse framework, attempting to deepen and extend that framework. A text, or even a single sentence, is something like a playing card. A specific card has no value (meaning) apart from the patterns (hands) into which it can enter. And a specific hand of cards itself has no value (meaning) apart from the game it is part of. So, too, for language. A text is meaningful only within the pattern (or social configuration) it forms at a specific time and place with other pieces of language, as well as with specific thoughts, words, deeds, bodies, tools, and objects. And this pattern or configuration—this specific social action—is itself meaningful only within a specific Discourse or at the intersection of several Discourses. Pieces of language, as well as other symbols, bodies, deeds, and so forth, are cards; social practices are hands; and Discourses are games. None of these—cards, hands, and games—exists without the other (Giddens 1984, 1987).

Language is but a "piece of the action," and a social action is constituted as a social practice with value and meaning only in and through the Discourse of which it is a part—just as an assortment of cards constitutes a hand only in and through the card game of which it is a part. The card analogy breaks down in one respect, though: When we are playing cards, we usually know exactly what game we are playing. But when we play a piece of language within a specific social practice, what Discourse we are in is often a matter of negotiation, contestation, and "hybridity" (Bakhtin 1981, 1986). By "hybridity" I mean an integration or mixture—differently tight in different cases—of several historically distinct Discourses. Discourses "capture" people and use them to "speak" throughout history (Connerton 1989; Douglas 1986; Fleck 1979; Gee

1992); people "capture" Discourses and use them to strategize and survive (Bauman 1995; Giddens 1984; Goffman 1967, 1972; Shotter 1993). It is as if I could negotiate with you what card game we are playing as we play out our hands. My space for negotiation is, of course, limited by many factors, including what games are available to us historically, economically, socially, and culturally; your power and mine; our joint histories; the setting we are in; and the actual run of cards. Sometimes there is little negotiation and the game is obvious; sometimes there is lots of negotiation and matters are complex. And the negotiation is often not direct, conscious, and overt, though sometimes it is. Are you saying that as a colleague, a friend, a fellow male, or as an African-American? Should I respond to that as a citizen, a biologist, a woman, a feminist, or an upper middle-class professional?

This chapter will look at specific texts within their social contexts. We will start with texts relevant to schools and end with texts relevant to science and history. The whole point is to see the multiple ways in which language becomes meaningful only within Discourses and how language-within-Discourses is always and everywhere value-laden and "political" in the broad sense of "political" where it means "involving human relationships where power and 'social goods' are at stake" (see Chapter 1).

Language at home and at school

In order to see language-within-social-practices-within Discourses at work in the relationship between home and school, we will, in this section, focus on a story told by a five-year-old Anglo-American middle-class girl, whom we will call "Jennie." Jennie was holding a book and pretending to read it to her mother and older sister. I print the story below. Though it was spoken and not written, I have broken it into lines and stanzas, which makes it easier to understand in the absence of hearing it. Chapter 6 discusses the role of lines and stanzas in the production of speech.

I don't want to discuss Jennie's story in isolation. Rather, after analyzing it, I want to juxtapose it both to the sharing-time story the African-American girl "Leona" told at school about her family making cakes (Chapter 7) and to the sharing-time report that the Anglo-American girl "Mindy" gave at school on making candles (Chapter 7). Both these sharing-time turns are printed in Chapter 7 and were discussed there. The reader will, I hope, remember that sharing time in the classrooms these girls attended turned out to be "early literacy" training where the children were expected to speak in an "explicit" and linear way typical of essayist literacy. I ask the reader to look at the texts in Chapter 7 again and to keep them in mind as we discuss Jennie's story.

Text I Jennie's story

Stanza 1 (*Introduction*)

1   This is a story,
2   About some kids who were once friends,
3   But got into a big fight,
4   And were not.

Stanza 2 (*Frame: signaling of genre*)

5   You can read along in your story book.
6   I'm gonna read aloud.

[story-reading prosody from now on]

Stanza 3 (*Title*)

7   "How the Friends got Unfriend."

Stanza 4 (*Setting: introduction of characters*)

8   Once upon a time there was three boys 'n' three girls.
9   They were named Betty Lou, Pallis, and Parshin, were the girls,
10   And Michael, Jason, and Aaron were the boys.
11   They were friends.

Stanza 5 (*Problem: sex differences*)

12   The boys would play Transformers,
13   And the girls would play Cabbage Patches.

Stanza 6 (*Crisis: fight*)

14   But then one day they got into a fight on who would be which team.
15   It was a very bad fight.
16   They were punching,
17   And they were pulling,
18   And they were banging.

Stanza 7 (Resolution 1: storm)

19 Then all of a sudden the sky turned dark,
20 The rain began to fall,
21 There was lightning going on,
22 And they were not friends.

Stanza 8 (Resolution 2: mothers punish)

23 Then um the mothers came shooting out 'n' saying,
24 "What are you punching for?
25 You are going to be punished for a whole year."

Stanza 9 (Frame)

26 The end.
27 Wasn't it fun reading together?
28 Let's do it again,
29 Real soon!

Jennie is pretending to read a book (holding a book in front of her) and telling, in a "literary" way, a story about a real fight that had occurred at her birthday party. The episode in which her pretend reading took place was part of her primary socialization into her primary Discourse. Yet the story has obvious linguistic markers of the genre of "story book reading," a genre connected to both "children's literature" and "high literature," both of them forms of language central to important school-based secondary Discourses. So here we see resonance between a primary Discourse and later school-based secondary Discourses.

Let's consider the ways in which Jeanne's text can be construed as part of a "literary" Discourse. Within the genre of "high literature," certain literary devices are relevant. One of these, which this text draws on, is the "sympathetic fallacy" (Abrams 1953, 1971), a device in which nature, or the cosmos, is treated as if it is "in step with" ("in sync with," "coordinated with") human affairs (e.g., the beauty and peace of a sunset match the inner peace of the elderly poet resigned to the approach of the end of life).

In Jennie's story the sympathetic fallacy is a central organizing device. The fight between the girls and boys in stanza 6 is immediately followed in stanza 7 by the sky turning dark, with lightning flashing, and thence in line 22: "and they were not friends." Finally, in stanza 8, the mothers come on the scene to punish the children for their transgression. The sky is "in tune" or "in step" with human happenings.

The sympathetic fallacy functions in Jennie's story in much the same way as it does in "high literature." The story suggests that gender differences (stanza 4: boy versus girl) are associated with different interests (stanza 5: Transformers versus Cabbage Patches), and that these different interests inevitably lead to conflict when male and female try to be "equal" or sort themselves on other grounds than gender (stanza 6: "a fight on who would be which team"—the fight had been about mixing genders on the teams). The children are punished for transgressing gender lines (stanza 8), but only after the use of the sympathetic fallacy (the storm in stanza 7) has suggested that division by gender, and the conflicts which transgressing this division lead to, are sanctioned by nature, are "natural" and "inevitable," not merely conventional or constructed in the very act of play itself.

Once again, as we were in the case of Leona's story about cakes in Chapter 7, if we adopt a privatized view of meaning, we are tempted to ask: How can a five-year-old mean anything this sophisticated? How can it be that this little girl appears to mean beyond her own "private" resources? The answer, based on our earlier discussion is: If you place the sort of allusion to nature this little girl has used at just the sort of textual location she has, then you get these sorts of meanings "free," because to do this "resonates" with particular historically derived interpretive practices—i.e., Discourses—"owned and operated" by certain groups of people (Hodge 1990). You get it "free," of course, provided you and your text are at a site and within a social practice "owned and operated" at that time by a Discourse that can and will recruit you and your text.

Supported by her mother and sister, the five-year-old is apprenticing herself to a specific social practice, namely (mainstream, school-based) "story book reading." This social practice has an interesting feature in regard to the sociocultural group to which this child belongs: it is simultaneously an aspect of apprenticeship into her primary Discourse ("people like us do books this way") and a preparation for her later apprenticeship into several school-based secondary Discourses, including "('real' or 'high') literature." This child, when she goes to school to begin her more public apprenticeship into the social practice of literature, will look like a "quick study" indeed. But, importantly, she is coming to the see a deep compatibility between the who she is within her primary Discourse and the who she will be within several school-based secondary Discourses.

Thus home-based social practice, with its ways of interacting, talking, thinking, valuing, and reading, and its books and other physical props, enables this little girl to form a text of a certain type. And that form invites the operation of the interpretive practices that are part of literary (and school-based) Discourses.

Jennie's text also shows us something important about cultural models (see Chapter 5). Her text trades—partly through its use of the sympathetic fallacy—on a cultural model that is deeply embedded in many school-based and "high culture" secondary Discourses in Western society. This cultural model, through her text and the home-based practices within her primary Discourse that give rise to such texts, insinuates itself into her identity (sense of who she is, even within her primary Discourse). We can uncover this cultural model if we note that the sympathetic fallacy is a double-edged sword. On the one hand, it has been used, from time immemorial, to suggest a deep commonalty between human beings and Nature; on the other hand, it has also been used to suggest that "Nature" underwrites the hierarchies of power, status, and prestige—including gender—found at particular times and places within particular cultures.

The little girl's text resonates with a particular ideological message or theory (a cultural model) about the distribution of gender roles, a message that may well be against her own "self-interest" as she grows older and desires to see herself as a whole human, the equal of men. She is already becoming "at home" in certain social practices—in the way in which certain people are quite "at home" in a certain city—which will make her a bearer of meanings in conflict with her own interests within other social practices (e.g., women's groups). Just as she is open to attributions of intelligence based on what can be made of her performance by certain interpretive practices, so too she is open to attributions that she as female stands apart, "other," perhaps inferior to men, attributions that have come out of her own mouth.

The claim here is not that this little girl will necessarily end up a "dupe" of any particular cultural model or Discourse. People are used by Discourses and they, in turn, use Discourses as agents in their own right. The point is, rather, that being "at home" with and in these cultural models and Discourses, and "rewarded" by them, may make this little girl reluctant to reflect on and abandon them.

It is interesting to note that the sorts of "literary" or "poetic" devices that occur in Leona's story about cakes in Chapter 7, devices that stem from her culture's retaining rich ties to the values of "orality," show up in another form in Jennie's story. This is because Jennie is participating in an aspect of our print-based "high culture" literary tradition, a tradition that, of course, has its origins in oral-culture practices. (Think of the line running from Homer to Hesiod to Chaucer to Shakespeare, and beyond.)

188 Social Linguistics and Literacies

What is striking about the poor reception that Leona's stories received at school during sharing time is that her stories have deep meanings when she tells them in her own community or when we situate them within the interpretive setting of "poetics" and "linguistic stylistics," yet they have no very deep meaning when they are situated in school at sharing time of the sort Leona was engaged in (Cazden 1988, 2001; Michaels 1981). But the same thing is true of Jennie's story. It has a deep meaning at home and would have a deep meaning at school when "creative writing" or "literature" is being done. But Jennie would never have tried such a "literary" story during the type of sharing time Leona and Mindy were engaged in. Sharing time in these classrooms was early "essayist (reportative, linear, 'the facts') literacy" training. Neither Leona's nor Jennie's text resonates well with that practice, while other sorts of texts do.

In Chapter 7 we asked the question: While the sorts of "literary" stories that Leona told are not encouraged or recruited at her sharing time, why aren't they recruited within other school-based practices where "creativity" and "literariness" in language are being encouraged? The answer, we argued, has partly to do with the fact that Leona uses a different social language within which to engage in "poetic practices" than does "high literature." It has also to do with the fact that what counts is not simply linguistic features (after all, Leona's language has many features that could be easily recruited for an apprenticeship into poetry and other "high literature"), but who we are and what we are doing. And Leona's community-based *who* and *what* are, at best, not visible to the school, and, at worse, opposed by the school, which, in turn, fails to render visible and accessible to children like Leona the sorts of *whos* and *whats* that do count there.

Our three texts triangulate in an interesting way: Mindy's text is "prosaic," while Leona's and Jeanne's texts are "poetic." While neither of the "poetic" texts will "fly" at sharing time, nonetheless, Jeanne will, at school, "get" more for her "poetry" than will Leona. Mindy's text and Jeanne's could not look more different, yet they will both be recruited by school-based Discourses, when Leona's will not. Despite the fact that such matters are everyday occurrences in our urban schools, we should not lose a real sense of paradox here.

The answer here is not just that Leona needs to adapt to school-based Discourses, despite what clashes there may be between these Discourses and those of her home and community. It is also that schools need to adapt to Leona's Discourses, as well: to render them and her visible, valuable, and meaningful. Such an adaptation requires a genuine commitment on the part of the school and society at large to social justice—

to forgoing some of the automatic rewards of having excluded Leona's Discourses, and those of other sociocultural groups, from the school.

Borderland Discourses

The context of the second text I will discuss is as follows: It was written by a ninth-grade Puerto Rican inner-city junior high-school girl. The students at this girl's school (in the eastern United States) are drawn in roughly equal numbers from adjacent African-American, white, and Puerto Rican neighborhoods. The text is reprinted from Amy Shuman's study of the uses of oral and written texts by urban adolescents, *Storytelling Rights* (Shuman 1986: 9–11). The girl, whom Shuman calls pseudonymously "Wilma," offered an unsolicited account of her three years at the school Shuman was studying towards the end of Shuman's research.

This text represents a person communicating in the spaces between the Discourses of the school and her own home and community-based Discourses. Wilma goes to a school in which the students come from diverse local communities, communities that have certain tensions with each other. At the same time, many of the students from these communities are not fully trusting in and affiliated with school-based Discourses (for reasons not unlike those that emerge from considering Leona's case above). These students must, at times, interact with each other outside the influence of school-based Discourses "between" and outside their own home and community Discourses (since they come from different home- and community-based Discourses). That is, in a sense, they must communicate between home and school. To do this, they engage in what I will call a peer-based "borderland Discourse," a creation of their own.

Borderland Discourses—Discourses where people from diverse backgrounds, and, thus, with diverse primary and community-based Discourses, can interact outside the confines of public sphere and middle-class "elite" Discourses—are a common feature of life in contemporary society. We find them not only at school, but in many workplaces. Teenagers in many places tend to cross social, economic, and cultural boundaries more readily than do adults and, thus, often create their own borderland Discourses. Of course, these Discourses often draw on aspects of popular and "non-mainstream" culture. Like all Discourses, borderland Discourses carry social identities and values that render people, for that time and place, certain "kinds of people."

In the text below, Wilma describes her first day of school in each grade and compares her lack of familiarity with the system in the seventh grade with her mastery of it by the ninth grade. I first reproduce the first part of Wilma's text (devoted to seventh grade) as she wrote it, with no "corrections" (see Shuman 1986: 9). Below that I give a summary (with some direct quotes) of the parts of the text devoted to the eighth and ninth grades.

"The seventh grade"

When I first came to Paul Revere I was kind of scared but it was going to be my first year there but I was supposed too get used too going there. I started early in the Morning I was happy. Everybody talking about it sounded scarry, and nice. A couple of us caught the bus together. When we got there, since I was a seventh grader I was supposed to go to the auditorium—which I did. from there I appeared in the boy's gym. I didn't knew until they announced where we were at. From there I appeared somewhere else. That was my home room. Which they called advisory. I copy something from the board called a Roster. After that a Bell rang. We waited for another Bell and left. I met with my friends and cought the bus back home. They explained how to used the rosters. Which I learned very quickly.

The Classroom I was in like a regular elementary school which was only from one room to the other. I didn't understand that. Until our teacher explained that was called Mini School. Well we did a lot of things. Went on a lot of trips. And were treated fairly by both teachers.

I didn't hardly had any friends until I started meeting a lot of them. I had a friend by the name of Luisa and Alicia. Those were the only two friends I had at the beginning of the year. Almost at the middle I met one girl by the name of Barbara. We were starting to get real closed to each other and were starting to trust each other. As you know we still are very closed and trust each other.

Wilma

Summary of eighth and ninth grades

Eighth grade. On the first day, Wilma and Barbara are placed in the same class. They cut the first day of classes, and on the second day noticed that they didn't know very many people in their class. But then they met more and more people and it looked like it was going to be "a super year." Everybody was getting along and "[t]here were no argument between races or color." They cut school a great deal and "did not obey the teacher. Since that was our second year and we know the school by heart we didn't bother. We were really bad made almost all the teachers had a hard time with us." Wilma concludes: "I enjoy this year very much, had a nice time and enjoy every bit of it."

Ninth grade: Barbara and Wilma think they will be assigned to different classes, but are overjoyed when they are not. (Wilma writes: "I jump with such of joy that I thought that was going to be the end of us.") They are in a class with a strict teacher. Wilma likes it because the teacher reviews "what you had in the seventh and eighth grades." She concludes: "Like I say if you could hang until something thats very strict you do alright. But don't let her take over you at all. Stay quite when she talks to you in front of the class but when it by your self and her let everything out and you'll get everything your way."

It is very easy to misread Wilma's written text. We are tempted to read it as a failed attempt at a school-based dominant Discourse and the sort of "essayist" prose typical of many of these. But it is, in my view, no such thing. It is not written to be "recognized" and "valued" on the school's terms.

While traditional approaches to literacy assume that speaking is used for face-to-face communication and writing for more distanced communication, the students in Wilma's school often use oral stories to convey messages to absent third parties through "he said–she said" rumors that will be repeated back to them, and they often use writing as part of face-to-face exchanges in which documents are collaboratively produced and read aloud or as solitary communication with oneself in diaries. Shuman says that "The adolescents transformed the conventional uses of writing and speaking for their own purposes. They had their own understanding of what could be written but not said, and vice versa" (p. 3).

The fact is that Wilma and her peers have a secondary Discourse, what I have called a borderland Discourse, that uses speaking and writing (notes, diaries, letters) of various sorts to signal a particular social identity. This Discourse is used by adolescents from African-American, Puerto Rican and lower socioeconomic white groups—though somewhat differently by each group—each have their own versions which undoubtedly incorporate large parts of their own primary and other local community-based Discourses in their own ways. It is used in the school yard, on the way to and from school, in the community when adolescent peers come together, and at school for "off line" communication not under the school's control. It is a Discourse developed by these adolescents themselves. The Discourse conflicts with school-based Discourses at various points, and, indeed, partly defines itself by these conflicts and oppositions. Wilma's text must be read in terms of this Discourse.

But Wilma's text is not a "pure" instance of this secondary Discourse. In the real world of interaction in which Discourses are always jostling against each other, there are few "pure" instances. It was written for Shuman, who, though familiar with the girls and their social practices, was still a "mainstream" outsider (and, further, an academic and, thus, connected to school-based Discourses). Shuman points out that the text presents "one form of adolescent writing: in this case, a document intended for outside readers already familiar with the general situation but not with the details of personal experience" (p. 9), and "Wilma's description of her school years contained the same kinds of observations girls made in their diaries, but as a separate document it was the only account of its kind I saw in my three years of research at the school. In its attention to the unwritten rules of the adolescent's conventions for written texts, it is perhaps typical" (p. 11).

That is, Wilma is using her peer-based secondary Discourse, but adapting it to an aspect of a mainstream school-based Discourse, namely the "separate" document that is not in note, diary, or letter form. She is undoubtedly influenced in this adaptation by other aspects of school-based essayist Discourse as well, though without very careful study we can't know exactly at which points. Thus, too, we cannot say with any certainty what are "mistakes" in a Discourse she does not fully control and what just part of Wilma's practice.

Let's consider for a moment the reproduced part of Wilma's text above ("The seventh grade"). This story about the seventh grade is supposed to set the scene (by showing her initial incompetence) for her later discussion of the eighth and ninth grades, which stress her competence and control. Note how Wilma starts her story of the seventh grade, in her first paragraph, by going to school with her friends ("A couple of us caught the bus together"). Arriving at the school she is separated from her friends and has to confront the school alone. (She wanders from room to room not knowing where she is or what to do, and confronts a "strange" practice of the school's—the roster.) But eventually she is reunited with her friends for the return home and they explain to her how to use the rosters (which she learns quickly). Here we see Wilma confronting the new and foreign (and possibly hostile) Discourses of the school and classroom. She is initiated into these Discourses not by the school, but by her friends, whose Discourse is in conflict with the school (and vice versa), but which is used to initiate Wilma into school practices.

In her second paragraph, Wilma juxtaposes her friends' help with the teachers' help (they explain her classroom and treat her fairly). There is the hint here that Wilma can utilize the teachers' and the school's help only through the support given to her by her peers. As if to stress this, Wilma returns at the end of her story, in her third paragraph, to friends, closing on her new friendship with Barbara (who figures prominently in the next two stories). School is seen, not as a place just to learn, but as a place to forge more friendships within the peer-based Discourse that supports her presence at school and mediates her relationship with the school. Notice that Wilma's paragraphing makes perfect sense in terms of her own thematics.

If we look at her eighth and ninth grade stories we can see that conflict between her group's social practices and the school's, as well as her group's control over their experience, is an issue that runs throughout the whole bigger text. In the eighth grade her growing mastery of the school leads to her "not bothering" with the school's rules. She has a enjoyed this year greatly ("had a nice time and enjoy every bit of it"), expressing a value that is certainly not part of school-based Discourses. In the ninth grade she accepts, on her own terms, the school's rules, but also shows she understands ways of manipulating them (you deal with the teacher differently in front of the class and one on one). She concludes with "But don't let her take over you at all . . . ," a plea not to cede control to the teacher and the school even while living within the confines of that system.

Wilma enacts in thought, word, and values her own adolescent-based secondary Discourse, which is at various points in conflict with the school, but which has as one of its reasons for existing the function of mediating her own and her peers' interactions with the dominant, but often hostile, "public sphere" Discourses of the school. It is often said that the values embedded in a Discourse like Wilma's play a role in replicating her parents' place towards the bottom of the social hierarchy, since her resistance to the school will lead to lack of school success and thus a poor economic future (Willis 1977). While there is undoubtedly some truth in this, it misses the fact that adolescents like Wilma know that schools as currently constituted in the United States will never accept and value their community's social practices and never give that community, on a full and fair basis, access to dominant secondary Discourses and the "goods" that go with them. Her community-based Discourse is a form of self-defense against colonization, which like all organized resistance to power is not always successful, but does not always fail.

Wilma's text shows clearly the ways in which knowledge based in her peer-based Discourse mediates not only her transition into and movement through the "official" institution of the school, but also mediates her relationship to the "official" knowledge of the school. While these mediational processes may be extreme in Wilma's case, they are, in fact, typical of a great many students in our schools. The school's understanding of and adaptation to such knowledge ought to be part and parcel of the ways in which it socializes students into wider realms of public sphere knowledge. This does not mean colonizing popular and teenager cultural artifacts for academic literary and aesthetic analysis, but truly engaging with the full array of Discourses in which the school and all its members "swim." This issue is all the more acute today when modern digital technologies like the internet, instant messaging, digital video, etc., allow young people to collaboratively produce knowledge and share it with peers, creating and transforming popular Discourses in the act (Gee 2003, 2004).

There is the issue, as well, of what it means that young people like Wilma use literacy to encode their resistance to school and as an identity marker of their peer Discourses, while failing to accept and master school-based literacy practices. That schools simply go on with "business as usual" as this phenomenon becomes yet more common is one indication of how out of step many high schools are with the realities of the young people who attend them (Gee 2003).

The juxtaposition we see in Wilma's story of "local," "everyday" knowledge as against more "official" knowledge is a typical feature of our contemporary societies, with their high regard for science, technology, and "experts." We will take up this issue further below, when we look at the operation of Discourses in science.

Discourses, individuals, and performances

The behaviors of any individual person, at a specific time and place, are meaningful only against the Discourse or, more often, set of complementary or competing Discourses, that can "recognize" and give "meaning" and "value" to that behavior. It is much as if we are reciting lines on a stage, but where there are often several possible scripts or plays that could make sense of the lines—incorporate them into a plot. Humans spend a good deal of their time negotiating over which script or play (which Discourse) is operative in a given instance (Giddens 1984: 83–92; Goffman 1959, 1967, 1972, 1981). Of course, there are also times where clearly one Discourse applies, though in contemporary plural societies things are often more complex.

Furthermore, what a person says or does is always a product not just of the Discourse he or she is in at the time, but also of the other Discourses that person is a member of. What other Discourses I control can affect, in a variety of ways, what I think, do, and say in any given Discourse. One's primary Discourse always affects one's use of secondary Discourses to some degree—giving them a certain slant or style, while the secondary Discourses one masters can influence to some degree or other the ways in which one acts out one's primary Discourse (which, when people are adults, we can also call their Lifeworld Discourse, since by that time one's primary Discourse has undergone many influences) and one's other secondary Discourses.

Discourses can interact in yet other ways. My actions, words, or thoughts at certain times are very often a compromise or "balancing act" between several different Discourses. One Discourse is not just influencing another, I am actually trying to be in two or more Discourses at the same time, as if I tried to play a role in two different plays simultaneously. When my "significant other" (who, let us say, is herself an academic, perhaps even a linguist) asks me a linguistics question over a romantic dinner I have to simultaneously play a role in the Discourse of linguistics and one in the Discourse of romance and intimacy. We all pull off such matters quite deftly at times, and at other times we "blow it."

Things can get much more complicated: a religious-fundamentalist civic-minded biologist has to give a talk about recent developments in evolutionary theory to a civic group attended by his creationist minister, the mayor, and his department chairperson. Our belief that such people don't exist is just a product of our rationalizing belief in human unity and consistency: in one way or another we are all such people, though our conflicting Discourses may not be so easy to label.

Discourses allow ample room for individual style and human agency (Callinicos 1988). This is so because of the way they work: if you pull off a performance and it gets "recognized" as meaningful and appropriate in the Discourse, then it "counts." That performance carries, like a virus, aspects of your own individuality and, too, of your other Discourses. Thus, people and their Discourses infect each other all the time. In the United States, for instance, African-Americans have influenced a great many Discourses by getting their own variations accepted as valuable performances, and, thus, changing what "counts" in these Discourses. Of course, there is always a risk that your performance will not get "recognized," in which case, it does not "count" as in the Discourse or it "counts" as your being marginal to or altogether "foreign" to the Discourse.

Discourses are constituted by specific actions (performances) carried out by specific individuals, performances which are an amalgam of words, values, thoughts, attitudes, gestures, props. To make these matters more concrete, I will now analyze three such specific performances. In a given situation, we must act and then see how our performance is or is not "captured" by this or that Discourse. In turn, how people act tells us something about how they construe the Discourse and setting they take themselves to be in. So here we will take several performances, from three sociocultually diverse individuals, and ask how they must construe the situation they are in.

One of the performances we will study was carried out by a working-class African-American high-school student, one by a working-class white high-school student, and one by an upper-class white high-school student (whom I will refer to simply as "the upper-class student" to distinguish him from the other white student, whom I will refer to simply as "the white student"). Small groups of high-school students had been asked to discuss a (written) story called "The Alligator River story," and to come to a consensus about how the characters in the story (all of whom are "misbehaving" to a certain extent by someone's standards) should be ranked "from the most offensive to the least objectionable."

At the end of the task, each group chose one student, the ones I will deal with here, to orally give their group ranking to their teacher (who had given the students the task, but was not present for the discussion) and to say why the group had ranked the characters as they did. Each group was composed of six students from the same ethnic and social class, and each group contained three men and three women. The African-American group and the white group came from the same inner-city school, and the upper-class group came from a very elite school situated in a quite wealthy suburban community.

So all our students are in school doing a task that their teacher has set them and which she observes. At the same time, the task involves peer discussion on the sorts of issues not usually dealt with in school. Finally, the interaction is being recorded by an outsider. Thus, the setting is "odd." Nonetheless, as happens to us all, the participants must construe the situation somehow and act accordingly. How they do so tells us something about their tacit views of how language and Discourses work in (their) schools.

Below I reprint the story, and beneath that the responses of the three students chosen to represent their three respective groups. Each of the responses is divided into its stanzas.

The Alligator River story

Once upon a time there was a woman named Abigail who was in love with a man named Gregory. Gregory lived on the shore of a river. Abigail lived on the opposite shore of the river. The river which separated the two lovers was teeming with man-eating alligators. Abigail wanted to cross the river to be with Gregory. Unfortunately, the bridge had been washed out. So she went to ask Roger, a river boat captain, to take her across. He said he would be glad to if she would consent to go to bed with him preceding the voyage. She promptly refused and went to a friend named Ivan to explain her plight. Ivan did not want to be involved at all in the situation. Abigail felt her only alternative was to accept Roger's terms. Roger fulfilled his promise to Abigail and delivered her into the arms of Gregory.

When she told Gregory about her amorous escapade in order to cross the river, Gregory cast her aside with disdain. Heartsick and dejected, Abigail turned to Slug with her tale of woe. Slug, feeling compassion for Abigail, sought out Gregory and beat him brutally. Abigail was overjoyed at the sight of Gregory getting his due. As the sun sets on the horizon, we hear Abigail laughing at Gregory.

The African-American students' response

Stanza 1

All right
As a group
we decided Roger was the worse
because he should have never in the first place ask her to go to bed
    with him
just to get her across the water
to see her loved one

Stanza 2

Then we had Gregory
because when she arrived over there
he just totally disowned her you know
like I don't want you after what you did
which is wrong

Stanza 3

We got Slug for third
True Abigail told him to beat him up
but he didn't have to
He could have said no
and he just you know brutally beat him up

Stanza 4

Abigail is third
because she laughed and said
(Interruption: That's four) Yeah I mean fourth Yeah
she's fourth
because she never should have told Slug to beat him up
and then laughed you know

Stanza 5

Ivan we have last
because he did the right thing by saying
I don't want to be involved in the situation
He could be a friend and still not want to be involved
It's none of his business

The white students' response

Stanza 1

OK our findings were
that um the most offensive spot was Roger
mainly because for no other reason he just wanted to sleep with
     Abby
You know for his own benefit
you know kind of cheap

Stanza 2

OK Coming in second was Gregory
mainly because he didn't really listen to a reason from her
and he kinda . . . kinda . . . tossed her aside you know without thinking
you know he might have done the same if he was put in the same
     position you know
for love it was why she did it

Stanza 3

Then we put Abigail in the third spot
only because we took a vote (Laughter)
No, because we figured she didn't really do anything
She didn't I mean she didn't tell Slug to beat up Roger
She didn't tell Slug to beat up Gregory
so she really didn't have any bearing
She was just dejected, so

Stanza 4

Now Slug we figured was the fourth
because his only reason for beating up Gregory was through com-
     passion
so he wasn't really that offensive

Stanza 5

And Ivan came in fifth
because Ivan didn't do anything
He he just kind of sat out of the way
so he offended no one
And that's our ranking.

The upper-class students' response

Stanza 1

Okay see we can all sort of like come around seeing other people's
     point of view
but Roger seemed to have like a pretty pure motive
like we couldn't see any real good in what Roger was doing
it just seemed a pretty purely lecherous and sleazy thing to do

Stanza 2

And then Gregory seemed second
I think just because he hit a nerve
in that here was this girl
that had you know who had done such a desperate thing for him
and he had turned [against her] with disdain
and so I think he was just ranked as an emotional reaction to the
     [unclear]

Stanza 3

And Slug
we didn't like Slug's name
and to beat someone up brutally
I mean we could sort of see Gregory's point of view
and we could sort of see Slug's point of view
but they could have done something better
something to make the situation a little bit [better]

Stanza 4

And Abigail you know
we weren't really comfortable with Abigail at all
but yeah well we could see this you know desperate attempt at love
you know we had sort of empathy with that
and you know in the end she's just embittered you know
I mean you can sort of understand her being embittered
yeah she had died for love that day

Stanza 5

So another thing you know Ivan was just not really involved
so Ivan you know we figured
maybe Ivan was perceptive enough
to realize that these people were all really [sleazy?]

These students must "pull off" a performance in school. Thus, what they do tells us something about how they construe school-based Discourses, at least in this sort of setting. At the same time, talking to peers, they will be influenced by their primary, community-based, and peer-based Discourses to various degrees. Each student speaks, then, as a unique individual and yet speaks, too, out of a fully socialized identity. Indeed, we will see that the students speak from three different social positions, and display quite different value systems. (Of course, in a different setting, they might well have spoken differently.)

I will discuss differences among the responses of the three students in seven areas: (1) use of pronouns; (2) how inferences are drawn; (3) relationship to written text of the story; (4) the student's "moral theory"; (5) construal of social relations; (6) interactional style; and (7) the force or directness of the response. I want to bring out the ways in which language and non-language phenomena (e.g., values) interact in each performance. Of course, many more areas could be discussed, and I stress the ones that I as a linguist can most easily deal with.

I Use of pronouns

The African-American student, in his first stanza, uses the pronoun "her" to refer to Abigail, without having actually explicitly introduced her by name or through a description. This makes perfect sense, since he knows that the primary addressee (his teacher) has read the story and task instructions. Therefore, no one could fail to know who "her" refers to. In fact, the African-American student uses this strategy quite consistently throughout. He uses a pronoun for Abigail three times in the first stanza and twice in the second before mentioning her name in the third stanza. He uses "over there" in stanza 2 for the river bank, which is assumed to be mutually known, but is not explicitly introduced. He uses "him" for Gregory twice in stanza 3 and once in stanza 4, even though Slug has replaced Gregory as the topic in stanza 4. (He assumes that the listener knows from the story that it was Gregory who was beat up by Slug.) All of these devices signal that the speaker takes himself and the hearer (the teacher) to share certain knowledge (the story and the task), which they do in fact share.

The white student does not engage in the same strategy. For example, in his first stanza, he uses the name "Abby," rather than a pronoun, and in his fourth stanza he overtly mentions that it was Gregory who was beat up by Slug. The white student overtly states information that the hearer (the teacher) already knows and which he knows she knows. This may seem strange if one thinks about it, though, of course, it sounds normal to us who share this speaker's strategy for such tasks.

The African-American and the white student are signaling different contexts. Or, put another way, they are construing the context differently. The African-American student is treating the teacher as someone who shares knowledge with him and who is part of the overall task. He is also signaling that he takes the text he is orally constructing to be a continuous and integral part of the whole task, starting with the reading of the story and instructions, through the group discussion, and ending with his summary.

The white student is signaling that the teacher somehow stands outside the task. She is taken to be listening not in her role as a person who in fact shares knowledge of the story and task, but in some other role, perhaps an evaluative one. The white student also signals that the oral text he is constructing is autonomous (sealed off) from the rest of the overall task and the interaction it involves, and thus a pronoun cannot refer back out of this oral text to knowledge that is lodged outside his oral text in the mind of the teacher.

The upper-class student uses pronouns much as the white student does, in the sense that he does not rely on mutual knowledge outside the oral text he is constructing to give reference to any pronouns. However, he does differ from the white student in a significant way: He not only overtly introduces each character by name, but in each case, save one, he repeats the name two or more times before he will use a pronoun. In fact, throughout the text he avoids pronouns as much as possible. In stanza 1, Roger is mentioned twice by name and never pronominalized. In stanza 3, Slug is mentioned three times by name and never pronominalized. In stanza 4, Abigail is mentioned twice by name before she is pronominalized. And in the fourth line of that stanza (stanza 4) he says the group had empathy, not with "her" (Abigail), but with "that" (her desperate attempt at love). In the final stanza, Ivan is mentioned by name three times without ever being pronominalized. The upper-class student's failure to use pronouns creates distance between himself and the characters in the story. In this regard, the white student stands midway between the African-American student and the upper-class one.

2 How inferences are drawn

The differences in how the three speakers, through their use of pronouns, do or do not leave information to be inferred by the hearer are matched by differences in how the speakers themselves draw inferences from the story text. The African-American speaker says in stanza 3 that Abigail "told him [Slug] to beat him [Gregory] up"; the white student in his stanza 3 says Abigail "didn't tell Slug to beat up Gregory." The story text says, "Heartsick and dejected, Abigail turned to Slug with her tale of woe." Just as the African-American student is willing to see the oral text he is constructing as continuous with the earlier interaction, and to see the teacher as part of the social network involved in the task, so also he is willing to make inferences that go beyond and outside the written text. The white student, who treats his oral text as autonomous, sealed off from the earlier interaction and from the teacher's real knowledge, is unwilling also to go too far beyond the written story text, which he treats likewise as autonomous and sealed off.

The upper-class student avoids altogether mentioning whether he has inferred that Abigail did or did not tell Slug to beat up Gregory. This is because his focus is never on what the characters did or said, but on how they feel and how he feels about them. At a deeper level, as we will see below, characters in the story are never allowed to directly interact with each other in the upper-class student's stanzas. The characters are each treated as social isolates, sealed off and autonomous from each other. Thus, the question as to whether Abigail did or did not tell Slug to beat up Gregory cannot be "said" or dealt with in the language of the upper-class speaker's oral text, as it would require him to speak of the characters in direct interaction with each other.

3 Relationship to the written text of the story

The three groups had shown a quite different relationship with and attitude towards the written text of the Alligator River story. After reading it, the white students continually re-referred to it in their discussion when any points of disagreement could be settled by an "appeal" to the written text. White students would say things like "It [the text] says. . . ." The African-American students, having read the text, put it aside. If disagreements came up that were relevant to the text of the story, they settled them by appeal to the on-going discussion and their own social experience. African-American students in the discussion would not "quote" the text, but they would "mimic" its words, for example, picking up on the word "brutally." This difference between the white and African-American groups leads to the unwillingness on the part of the white student to draw inferences beyond the words of the text, and the willingness of the African-American student to do just that. It also, presumably, influences other aspects of each student's response as well.

The upper-class group shared with the white group allegiance to the written text. However, they did not consult the text as a group, the way the white group occasionally had. Rather, each student held the paper and, when delivering their individual contribution, would occasionally consult it. We will see below that this fits with the "private" and individualized style of this group. We can also note that the upper-class respondent is the only one to repeatedly use the names of the characters in his response and to comment on his reaction to these names as names (not just his reactions to the people so named). He is willing, even less than the white student, to see beyond the written words to a social world.

4 Tacit moral theories

The African-American student uses terminology that we traditionally associate with morality, terms such as "right" (stanza 5) and "wrong" (stanza 2), "should" (stanzas 1 and 4), "have to" (stanza 3), and "could" (stanzas 4 and 5). He appeals to moral principles ("which is wrong," stanza 2), though without stating the source or identity of these principles. He stresses social relationships. Roger was wrong to ask Abigail to sleep with him "just" to get her across the river when she wanted to see "her loved one." What seems to be wrong here is that the request violates the love relationship between Gregory and Abigail. Ivan did the right thing because his social relationship of friendship does not make the problem his business. Abigail is wrong because she laughed and thus didn't take the violence she was having Slug perpetrate seriously. For this speaker, morality seems to be a matter of following moral precepts, not violating social relationships, and taking social relationships seriously. .

The white speaker doesn't use traditional moral terminology. Instead he uses the language of "reasons" and "reason giving." Roger is offensive because he didn't have a good enough reason for what he did (stanza 1). Gregory was wrong not to listen to a reason from Abigail (stanza 2). Slug wasn't that offensive because his reason (compassion) is acceptable (stanza 4). In fact, psychological states are in general mitigating: witness Abigail's dejection in stanza 3 and Slug's compassion in stanza 4. The speaker states a version of the "golden rule" in stanza 2 (essentially a device for computing what is rational): "he might have done the same if he was put in the same position."

For this speaker, failing to act seems inherently exonerating (there appear to be only sins of commission, not of omission): Ivan is the least objectionable because he "didn't do anything" and so "offended no one," and Abigail didn't tell Slug to beat up Gregory so "she really didn't have any bearing." This speaker's "moral system" appears to be something like: an act (or an inaction) is right so long as it offends no one and the actor has a reason to do it, where psychological states (dejection, compassion) are mitigating factors. In computing reasons one should, beyond considering mitigating psychological states, consider what one would have done in the same circumstances. This is morality as rationality and psychology, not as social networks and responsibilities (it is, in fact, the moral system behind the U.S. constitution).

The upper-class speaker has a view of morality that is based not on a traditional moral vocabulary and a social network of mutual ties (as the African-American student does), nor on a process of rationality and decision based on reasons (as the white student does). Rather, he carries the white speaker's focus on psychological states to an extreme. Morality is a matter of two things: (1) the feelings and point of view (inner states) of the characters and (2) the feelings, sensitivities and point of view of the speaker (or his group). And it is really the latter that predominates.

The upper-class speaker starts his whole oral text by saying that "we can all sort of like come around [to] seeing other people's point of view," implying that the extent to which I can understand your point of view (thus the extent to which you are like me) determines the extent to which you are exonerated. Roger is ranked first (worst) because "we couldn't see any real good in what Roger was doing," where it is left entirely tacit what "good" means here. Gregory comes in second because "he hit a nerve" (of ours); "he was just ranked as an emotional reaction" (of ours). "We didn't like Slug's name." "We weren't really comfortable with Abigail at all." The focus is on how the speaker views (sees) the character or how the character affects the speaker. But the heart of the matter is really whether or not the character is "like us" (and ultimately none of them is).

We can see this even where the speaker at first seems to say he can understand the point of view of "the other" (a character in the story). In each case, he actually severely mitigates the claim that he can understand the other's point of view. In stanza 3, for example, he says "we can sort of" understand Gregory and Slug's points of view but Gregory and Slug could have done something better. (What they could have done we are not told, nor what constitutes "better".) The "but" right after saying that we can "sort of see" Slug and Gregory's points of view actually contradicts the claim that we can in fact see their points of view and stresses the force of "sort of" as a mitigator of the claim. What follows "but" seems, then, to imply that what is wrong is that Gregory and Slug aren't like us, don't affect us well, and we can't recognize their act as one we would have done, though we can't say in fact what we would have done.

As for Abigail, in stanza 4, the speaker says "we weren't really comfortable with Abigail at all," though "we could see this . . . desperate attempt at love," "we had sort of empathy," "you can sort of understand her being embittered." He thus, once again, mitigates the claim that he can see a character's point of view or empathize with one. Presumably it is the fact that he can "sort of" (almost) understand and empathize with Abigail's internal states (bitterness, desperation) that allows him to rank Abigail as relatively inoffensive, though he still has a good deal of disdain even for her.

Ivan gets closer to being accepted without disdain, because he was perceptive (could "see") enough to realize that the internal states of these other characters aren't acceptable to one's (our) sensitivities. Morality is then a type of seeing, seeing the internal states of others and judging how they affect one's own sensitivities, where the standard of judgment is oneself or people like us. The world is not just privatized and psychologized, it is solipsistic.

5 Construal of social relations

The African-American speaker frequently construes the relationships between the characters in terms of overt social interaction and dialogue, not internal states: "asked her" (stanza 1); direct quote in stanza 2; "told him" (stanza 3); "said" (stanza 3); "laughed and said" (stanza 4); "told" (stanza 4); "laughed" (stanza 4); "saying" (stanza 5); direct quote in stanza 5. He construes the story as a set of overt social encounters. The white speaker rarely uses this device, but rather stresses internal psychological states: in stanza 1, Roger is offensive not because he asked Abigail to sleep with him, but because he "wants" to sleep with her; in stanza 2, Gregory tosses Abigail aside without "thinking"; in stanza 3, Abigail is "dejected" and this explains her behavior; in stanza 4, Slug is compassionate; and in stanza 5, Ivan offends no one's sensibilities. The white speaker's world is more privatized than the African-American speaker's, with less stress on the social and more on the psychological.

For the upper-class speaker, the social-interaction aspects of the characters' relationships to each other are further attenuated beyond even what we find with the white speaker. The characters never directly confront each other in any stanza. For example, Abigail is never mentioned in stanza 1 where Roger is mentioned, and becomes "this girl" (not Abigail) in stanza 2 where Gregory is mentioned. In stanza 3 Gregory is at first just "someone" Slug beat up, and though both Gregory and Roger are mentioned in the stanza it is in relation to the speaker, not to each other. In stanza 4 no other character is mentioned in relation to Abigail; and in stanza 5 Ivan has an attitude to the characters as a whole, not a relationship to Abigail. The psychologized and privatized world of the previous white speaker is here carried to an absolute extreme.

6 Interactional style

Each group had its own style of interaction. The African-American group had engaged in excited conversation, with many interruptions and overlaps, none of which seemed to bother any speaker or throw off the speed and tempo of the interaction. The white group had a somewhat more "sedate" but still spirited discussion, with somewhat less interruption and overlap. The white and African-American groups both sat in a circle and addressed their contributions either to the group as a whole or to individuals when this was appropriate. The upper-class group sat in a curved line, not a circle. Each student first delivered a monologue response as to his or her opinion, addressing the monologue not to the group, but outward towards the camera. The group then engaged in discussion which almost always involved individuals addressing their comments to other individuals, or once again outward to the camera. One female student got upset at some of the "discussion" and, after arguing her case, pulled her chair away from the group and sat quietly, no longer interacting.

7 Force and directness of text

The African-American speaker expresses his oral text directly and with force. He uses very few hedges or mitigating devices. The white speaker, on the other hand, uses a great number of "hedges" or "mitigating devices," words and phrases like "mainly," "you know," "kind of," "really," which either mitigate the force of a claim made, lessen the force with which a property is attributed to a character, or worry about the extent to which the hearer may agree or disagree with a claim.

The African-American speaker uses only six such devices, and several of the few he uses do not in fact really function as a hedge, e.g., the "just" in stanza 1 (line 5) is stressed and the "just" in stanza 2 (line 3) is followed by "totally", which virtually removes any mitigating force it might have had. On the other hand, the white speaker uses twenty hedges and all of them function fully as mitigators. The upper-class speaker is more similar to the white speaker than to the African-American one, but once again takes what the white speaker does to an extreme. He uses thirty-nine hedges.

But, added to this already greater amount, the upper-class speaker does something neither the white nor the African-American speaker does: he repeatedly uses words or phrases that refer to acts of perception. (All of them refer to vision or are the word "seemed".) Perception is inherently relative to one's perspective/point of reference, and thus also functions as a mitigator of the force or universality of a claim. The more mitigating devices one uses, the less one appears to be concerned with the content of one's claim and the more with the fact that one is making it. The upper-class speaker appears to use these devices to modulate the relationship between him and the claim he is making, as well as the relationship between himself and the characters in the story. He is always aware of himself as the point from which the claim is made or the character is judged. Table 2 shows the number and type of mitigating devices used by each of the students and the perception terms used by the upper-class speaker:

Table 2 Hedges/mitigating devices and perception terms

African-American	White	Upper-class	
just (3)	just (2)	sort of (5)	see (5)
you know (2)	mainly (2)	like (3)	seeing
true (3)	you know (5)	come around	point of view
	kind of (2)	seemed (3)	seemed (3)
	really (4)	pretty (2)	perceptive
	only (2)	just (5)	
	we figured (2)	I think (2)	
	I mean	you know (8)	
		I mean (2)	
		really (3)	
		yeah (2)	
		well	
		we figured	
		maybe	
Total 6	20	39	13

Having looked at these seven features, it is clear that there are important differences among our three students. For example, the African-American speaker makes his claims from a universalist perspective, and he stresses social relationships in the way he treats the teacher as sharing knowledge with him, in the way in which he will not seal off the verbal interaction of the group from either his oral text or the written one, and in the way he stresses social relationships in discussing the characters in the story. The white speaker seals off the oral and written texts from each other and from the interaction that led up to the oral text, and he concentrates on the internal mental and psychological states of the characters in the story. The upper-class speaker sees the characters as aspects of his own sensitivities and is most impressed by himself (or his group, people like himself) as the focal point of judgment and perception. The social world collapses solipsistically into his mind.

If this were literature, we might say that the African-American student eclipses the voice of the narrator in favor of the outside social world; the white student keeps the narrator's voice clear and separate from the story line and enters into the mental life of his characters; and the upper-class student eclipses the social world in favor of the narrator's voice, the world becoming simply a reflection of the narrator's vision. We should keep in mind that powerful fiction has been written in all three of these modes.

Each of these students is giving a performance that they think appropriate for a school task—thus, appropriate to some school-based secondary Discourse. Each is also being influenced by their other Discourses—perhaps more so in a situation like this where peers are discussing out-of-school concerns.

Many African-American people are part of a primary Discourse that puts a high premium on mutual participation, cooperation, social networking, not overly intervening in others' affairs, and not privileging authoritarian texts, or outside (often white) institutions, or the written word, over people's voices. Such aspects of his primary Discourse, and undoubtedly other aspects as well, are helping to shape (influence) the African-American student's performance.

On the other hand, the "rationalistic," "individualistic," and "privatized" features of thought and interaction that we see in the case of the white student and his group have been associated with the growth of the Western middle class and modern capitalism and have been argued to have reshaped middle-class primary socialization, as well as to have set the foundation of modern formal schooling (Sennett 1974). Thus, it is not surprising that the school will reward the white student for his performance more highly than it will reward the African-American student, though they are in the same school. The white student's other Discourses have been historically complicit in a mutual shaping process with the very school-based Discourse he is acting out. The African-American student's primary and peer-based Discourses are not only not complicit with this process, they have actively opposed and resisted it at various points in space and time.

The different performances of the three students also make clear, however, the falsity of the often repeated claim that African-American students disproportionately fail in school just because their ways of engaging in discourse and interaction are different from those of the school. However much the African-American student's performance differs from that of the white student, it is surely the case that the white and African-American student behave more similarly to each other than either one does to the upper-class student and his group.

The upper-class student and his group, while they certainly do not match our standard characterizations of "school-based behavior" (the white student is, in fact, the closest to such characterizations), do succeed marvelously in school. Of course, they have a school that has been purposely set up both to meld its Discourse with the upper-class students' primary Discourse and to establish school-based secondary Discourses which fit with the sorts of elite jobs these students will have and the elite social worlds in which they will live out their public and private lives (e.g., making decisions about what's good for the rest of us). They have merely bought directly what the mainstream middle class has managed to get the state to provide for them at public expense: a school of their own.

Science and the lifeworld

When we discussed Wilma's text above, we dealt with the issue of how "everyday" knowledge comes into contact with "official" knowledge. In every culture there are sociohistorically determined, socioculturally variable, and multiple ways of being in the world that count as being an "ordinary" (non-specialized, non-professional) person. Such ways of being in the world constitute what I will call "the lifeworld" (borrowing, for my own purposes, from Habermas 1984). The lifeworld is that space where people can claim to know things without basing the claim on access to specialized or "professional" Discourses with their "special methods" for producing knowledge. Most of us are aware that in modern societies the lifeworld, under the colonizing pressures of specialized and professional Discourses, has been progressively shrinking for hundreds of years, and is shrinking ever faster as we speak.

Science plays a powerful and prestigious role in modern societies. As such, it is often thought that talk of multiple identities, values, and diverse social languages is applicable only to the non-specialized Discourses of the lifeworld. Many think that science transcends language and culture, achieving a sort of ethereal "objectivity." But science is carried out by humans and its greatest strengths and weaknesses are rooted, as are all human affairs, in social relationships. Science is a domain of complementary and competing Discourses, just as is school, society, and the lifeworld.

It is not just "ordinary" people doing "ordinary" things, then, who handle words differently on different occasions and who, thereby, take on different identities and enter into different relationships with their interlocutors. Everybody does, including scientists. Biologists, for example, write differently in professional journals than they do in popular science magazines and these two different ways of writing mean different things and display different identities. The popular science article is not merely a "translation" or "simplification" of the professional article.

To see this consider the two extracts below, the first from a professional journal, the second from a popular science magazine, both written by the same biologist on the same topic (example from Myers 1990: 150):

1   Experiments show that Heliconius butterflies are less likely to oviposit on host plants that possess eggs or egg-like structures. These egg-mimics are an unambiguous example of a plant trait evolved in response to a host-restricted group of insect herbivores.

(Professional journal)

2   Heliconius butterflies lay their eggs on Passiflora vines. In defense the vines seem to have evolved fake eggs that make it look to the butterflies as if eggs have already been laid on them.

(Popular science)

The first extract, from a professional scientific journal, is about the conceptual structure of a specific theory within the scientific discipline of biology. The subject of the initial sentence is "experiments," a methodological tool in natural science. The subject of the next sentence is "these egg mimics": Note how plant parts are named, not in terms of the plant itself, but in terms of the role they play in a particular theory of natural selection and evolution, namely "coevolution" of predator and prey (that is, the theory that predator and prey evolve together by shaping each other). Note also, in this regard, the earlier "host plants" in the preceding sentence, rather than the "vines" of the popular passage. Things are named, then, by the part they play in the scientist's theory, not as mere features of plants sitting out in nature.

In the second sentence, the butterflies are referred to as "a host-restricted group of insect herbivores," which, we will see, points simultaneously to an aspect of scientific methodology (like "experiments" did) and to the logic of a theory (like "egg mimics" did). Any scientist arguing for the theory of coevolution faces the difficulty of demonstrating a causal connection between a particular plant characteristic and a particular predator when most plants have so many different sorts of animals attacking them. A central methodological technique to overcome this problem is to study plant groups (like Passiflora vines) that are preyed on by only one or a few predators (in this case, Heliconius butterflies). "Host-restricted group of insect herbivores," then, refers to both the relationship between plant and insect that is at the heart of the theory of coevolution and to the methodological technique of picking plants and insects that are restricted to each other so as to "control" for other sorts of interactions. The first passage, then, is concerned with scientific methodology and a particular theoretical perspective on evolution.

The second extract, from a popular science magazine, is not about methodology and theory, but about animals in nature. The butterflies are the subject of the first sentence and the vine is the subject of the second. Further, the butterflies and the vine are labeled as such, not in terms of their role in a particular theory. The second passage is a story about the struggles of insects and plants that are transparently open to the trained gaze of the scientist. Further, the plant and insect become "intentional" actors in the drama: the plants act in their own "defense" and things "look" a certain way to the insects, they are "deceived" by appearances as humans sometimes are.

These two examples replicate in the present what, in fact, is an historical difference. In the history of biology, the scientist's relationship with nature gradually changed from telling stories about direct observations of nature to carrying out complex experiments to test complex theories (Bazerman 1989). I would argue that professional science is now concerned with the expert "management of uncertainty and complexity" and popular science with the general assurance that the world is knowable by and directly accessible to experts (Myers 1990). The need to "manage uncertainty" was created, in part, by the fact that mounting "observations" of nature led scientists, not to consensus, but to growing disagreement as to how to describe and explain such observations (Shapin and Schaffer 1985). This problem led, in turn, to the need to convince the public that such uncertainty did not damage the scientist's claim to professional expertise or the ultimate "knowability" of the world.

This example lets us see, then, not just that ways with words are connected to different identities (here the experimenter/theoretician versus the careful observer of nature), but that they are always acquired within and licensed by specific social and historically shaped practices representing the values and interests of distinct groups of people. They are always shaped by Discourses.

Knowing how to make sense by reading, writing, talking, or listening, is, we might say, a matter of "being in sync" with other people in the enacting of particular identities or "forms of life" (Discourses). However, it is not just a matter of being "in sync" with people. We live and move in a material world; the things in it—objects, visual representations, machines, and tools—take part in our dramas of meaning as well. Furthermore, we enter into social relations not just with the living and the present, but with the dead and the absent, thanks to the workings of history and institutions that tie us together (like clubs, academic disciplines, and countries). We need now to get things and history more deeply embedded into our account of making meaning.

When we handle words to make meaning we enter into coalitions (and "get in sync") with other people, things in the world, technologies, and various systems of representation. This is particularly clear in science (Latour 1987, 2005). Scientists' meaning making is rooted in their being able to coordinate and be coordinated by constellations of expressions, actions, objects, technologies, and other people (Knorr Cetina 1992). But, then, so, too, is the meaning making of teenage heavy-metal enthusiasts: they coordinate and are coordinated by symbols, concerts, posters, clothes, MTV, CDs, and other people, present and absent (for example, consider the new cyber-based "house" Discourse, where drugs, music, clothes, video, computers, virtual reality technology, and characteristic spaces and times are all coordinated by people—and, in turn, coordinate people—in the service of social identities).

To exemplify this point I will develop an example that concerns just one sentence uttered by an outstanding biologist in an undergraduate classroom presentation on the neuroanatomy of finches. We will see how even this single sentence aligns the scientist with a variety of objects, tools, and pieces of history.

In finches, only males sing, not females. The scientist was interested in the way in which the development, perception, and production of the male's song relates to the structure and functioning of its brain. In the course of her presentation, she drew a diagram of the male finch's brain on the blackboard. The diagram was a large circle, representing the bird's brain, with three smaller circles inside it, marked "A," "B," and "C," representing discrete localized regions of neurons that function as units in the learning and production of the male's song. When the young bird hears its song (in the wild or on tape), it tries to produce the various parts of the song (engages in something like "babbling"). As the young bird's own productions get better and better, the neurons in region A are "tuned" and eventually respond only to the song the young bird was exposed to and not to other songs. The regions marked "B" and "C" also play a role in the development of the song and in its production.

The scientist went on to discuss the relationship between the male's brain and the hormones produced in the bird's gonads. The A, B, and C regions each have many cells in them that respond to testosterone, a hormone plentifully produced by the testes of the male bird. If a male finch is deprived of testosterone, regions A, B, and C will not develop, and the bird will not sing. On the other hand, if a female bird is artificially treated with testosterone from birth, she develops areas A, B, and C, and eventually sings. The scientists also described the intricate methodological and experimental techniques that have been developed to isolate and describe discrete localized regions of the brain, like regions A, B, and C. These included intricate microscopic electrical probes that measure the activities of small groups of neurons.

In her presentation, the scientist uttered the following sentence: "If you look in the brain [of the finch] you see high sexual dimorphism—A/B/C regions are robust in males and atrophied or non-existent in females." The word "atrophied" here is a technical term—the correct term required by biology. Note that one could have viewed the male brain as containing "monstrous growths" and thus as having deviated from the "normal" female brain. Instead, however, the terminology requires us to see the male brain as having developed fully ("robust") and the female brain as having either "atrophied" or failed to develop ("non-existent").

It is clear that this sentence, as an act of sense making in science, does not belong just to the scientist who uttered it, even though she happens to be one of the researchers who has actively helped to produce this knowledge. The sentence is a tool allowing her to coordinate and be coordinated by the language of her discipline, diagrams, intricate electrical probes, neurons, hormones, and other objects, as well as the other scientists in her field. These things and people are also part of the "drama" of enacting meaning and identity. But I want to show you also that the scientist is also coordinating and being coordinated by history, even though she may not be consciously aware of it.

To show this, I will briefly discuss two important moments in the history of biology and its interactions with other sense-making traditions, two moments that have helped shape our scientist's sentence in the present. It turns out that it is not an historical accident that "atrophied" has ended up a technical term for the female finch brain (and other similar cases), though this brain is simply less "localized" in terms of discrete regions like A, B, and C. To see why, we need to talk both about females and brains.

First, females: in the West, for thousands of years, females have been viewed as either inferior to males or, at the least, deviant from the male as the "norm" or "fully developed" exemplar of the species (Fausto-Sterling 1985; Laqueur 1990). Rather than retrace this immense history, consider one very salient moment of it in regard to the sentence we have quoted above: Darwinian biology was based on the assumption that behavior and body shape go hand in hand. For example, the environment of a certain species of grain-eating birds changes—say, grain disappears—and they must crack nuts in order to eat; eventually the bodies of birds of this species become shaped to this task, because only birds with the thickest and hardest beaks survive and pass on their genes. Analogously, the argument goes (Degler 1991), throughout history, women's environment has been the home, while men's environment has been out in the world competing with other men and with animals (hunting). These different environments have differently shaped the bodies and minds (brains) of men and women. Hence, to quote Darwin himself:

It is generally admitted that with woman the powers of intuition, of rapid perception, and perhaps of imitation, are more strongly marked than in man; but some, at least, of these faculties are characteristic of the lower races, and therefore of a past and lower state of civilization. The chief distinction in the intellectual powers of the two sexes is shewn by man's attaining to a higher eminence, in whatever he takes up, than can woman—whether requiring deep thought, reason, or imagination, or merely the use of senses and hands.
(1859: 873)

Though Darwin usually did not himself interpret "evolution" as linear development upward to "better things," many of his followers did (Bowler 1990). The competition men have faced in their environments has caused their bodies and brains to "develop" further than those of woman, so that it is a commonplace by the nineteenth century and in the early decades of the twentieth that "anthropologists regard women intermediate in development between the child and the man" (Thomas 1897, cited in Degler 1991: 29). This logic, of course, leads us to see the whole woman, in body and brain, as an "atrophied" man (exactly as Aristotle and Galen had), less developed because less challenged by her environment.

The story we have just told about females is really a sub-part of a larger and equally long-running story in the history of bodies and biology. In the course of the development of Western culture and science, it has been standard to assume that all of life can be arranged on a single, linear, hierarchically organized developmental continuum, a "Great Chain of Being" (Lovejoy 1933; Schiebinger 1993), ranging from things like worms and fish at one end, through mammals and monkeys in the middle, and humans at the top. Not uncommonly, humanity itself was ranged into a hierarchy with children, women, and non-Westerners ranked below white males (who themselves might fall into an order like peasant, knight, priest, aristocrat and king). While modern biology (Gould 1993) is well aware that living creatures cannot be placed in a single linear hierarchy, but only in an ever-ramifying, branching bush, nonetheless, the assumption that things come in developmental grades, that they can be ranged from less developed to more developed on a single, linear scale, is a "master assumption" still prevalent in many non-scientific and scientific discussions (e.g., consider assumptions about intelligence in psychology).

Now, one may object at this point: "All right, it is no historical accident that "atrophied" has ended up getting attached as a technical term to the female finch's brain. Still the brain is localized into discrete regions, isn't it? And, thus, the male finch's brain just is the right thing to take as the 'norm' or 'standard' here." But, it turns out, that even the choice to see the male's brain as the obvious and worthy thing to study (and around which to develop intricate methodologies) was formed in and through history. Such a choice is not by any means "natural" or "obvious." Things could have turned out differently. This brings us to brains.

In the nineteenth century there was a raging debate over whether the brain is "localized" (that is, composed of distinct parts, such as the "speech area" or "motor area," each with its own unique function) or "diffuse," operating holistically, without "separation of parts or a pointilist division of labor" (Star 1989: 4). This debate was eventually settled in favor of the localized position, though not (initially, at least) on the basis of "objective" evidence (there was about equal evidence for both sides), but as part of the emergence of the modern medical profession in nineteenth-century England (Desmond 1989). Again, I want to point to but one moment in this history.

As modern "professional" medicine emerged out of an earlier system tied to aristocratic patronage and an education in the classics, there was significant "collusion" (coordination) between surgeons and those medical researchers who believed in the localized view of the brain. Based on the symptoms displayed by neurological patients (people suffering from aphasia or epilepsy, for example), these researchers claimed to be able to identify the location in the brain that was diseased (something the diffusionists denied could be done). Given this information, the surgeons claimed to be able to excise the offending tumor or abscess and cure the patient.

In actual fact, even after the development of relatively sophisticated surgical techniques for brain surgery, there was still no one-to-one correlation between symptoms thought to point to a tumor or abscess in a certain area ("localizing signs") and the actual location of such a tumor. Nonetheless, surgeons and researchers cited exemplary, but exceptional, cases in which the two matched as "proof" of localization of function. These claims benefited both surgery and those researchers devoted to the localizationist position, making the latter look like they had "special" knowledge which enabled them to find what the former, with their "special" skills, could cure. Evidence for localization was collected from both surgery and neurological research. Each field tended to attribute certainty to the other: Researchers pointed to medical evidence when their own results were anomalous or uncertain; doctors pointed to physiological research of the localizationist sort when they could not find clear post-mortem evidence for discrete functional regions.

The emerging professional medical schools demanded unambiguous pictures of typical brains to put in their textbooks. (What student wants to be told that things are complex and messy?) The researchers on the localizationist side offered unambiguous functional anatomical maps (for example, maps that could indicate the anatomical point in the brain that was the source of loss of speech), something the diffusionists could not do. These maps "hid" irregular or anomalous findings from theoretical sight. The demand for such maps in medical education, diagnosis, and texts "represented a market intolerant of ambiguity and of individual differences"; the localizationist theory became unambiguously packaged in the map of "the brain, not a brain" (Star 1989: 90). The localizationist view of the brain has, in important respects, won out in contemporary neurological studies. Far more research and effort has been devoted to it than to more holistic aspects of the brain's functioning, though this is now beginning to change with the development of new models of the mind/brain (Kosslyn and Koenig 1992). Localizationist views have, however, directed both the procedures and goals of research for some time now.

Thus, let us return to our scientist and her classroom presentation on finches and their brains. From the perspective of the history of views on females and brains, the male finch's brain, with its clear localized sites, in contrast to the female's, looks to be a particularly natural and obvious research site, reflecting not an anomaly, but a particular clear example of what is normal. Further, from this perspective, the female's brain does, indeed, look to be "undeveloped" and "abnormal," to deserve its classification as "atrophied."

Now, our point here is not that the science our scientist is doing is "wrong." Nor do we want to claim that she and her peers have not discovered important facts. Rather, imagine that the two moments we have described above had not occurred (the Darwinian "logic" on women, really part of the larger "developmental hierarchy" story, and the collusion between surgeons and researchers around localizationist theories of the brain). Imagine further that a different history had occurred, one in which women and holistic approaches to the brain had been advantaged. Then our scientist's presentation would have been different—her words and her science would have been shaped differently. And that science also might very well have not been "wrong" and might very well have discovered important facts too (there are plenty to be discovered or constructed), they simply would have been different facts.

In that science, the male finch's brain might have been seen as overly specialized and monstrous, and might, in fact, have not been a particularly worthy research site, at least for the purposes of developing initial theories in neurobiology. There might have been intricate techniques to measure diverse parts of the brain operating in tandem, and not tiny probes narrowing in on a small set of neurons (and such techniques, e.g., PET scans, are now being developed and are, indeed, starting up again and changing the character of the whole localizationist and diffusionist debate, see Rose 1992). The technical term "atrophied" would not have existed for the female finch's brain.

This extended example has been meant to make clear the ways in which any act of speaking or writing picks up its meaning from intricate coordinations of words (e.g., "atrophied," "female," etc.), representations (e.g., diagrams and maps), things (e.g., probes, birds, brains, neurons, and hormones), and people (alive and long dead) within an entire history of diverse and interacting discussions of different groups of people with different interests, sometimes conflicting and sometimes compatible. We humans are vastly radiating lines of meaning, lines radiating out into space and time.

One can see that alternatives would have been possible provided different Discourses had shaped modern biology if we consider that even today other Discourses by their own logic would view male and female finch brains differently than contemporary neurobiology does. Let us take linguistics as an example. Linguistics has as one of its major research strategies the identification of binary contrasts in which one member of a pair of linguistic items is seen as unmarked (more basic, more fundamental, the "norm") and the other is seen as marked (a special purpose deviation from the norm). This terminology is used because in many cases a language actually uses extra material (overtly has a mark) for the marked member of the pair. Thus, in pairs like "cat/kitty," "dog/doggie," "bird/birdie," the diminutive ("kitty," "doggie," "birdie") is marked in relation to the basic terms ("cat," "dog," and "bird") and shows an additional bit of material ("-y" or "-ie"). The analysis of all levels of language—from phonology to semantics—can be carried out on this basis.

Looked at in this way, in terms of "markedness theory," the female finch's brain is clearly the "unmarked" one (indeed, as the biologist said, it is the "default" value), and the male is the one with the extra "marks." This would have led linguists to concentrate research on the female's brain as the basic, "normal" case and to proceed only later to the male's brain as a special-purpose deviation from the female's brain. The linguist would have described the male's brain in terms of how it "deviated" from the female's as a norm. But our scientist's language had moved through a quite different region of sociohistorical space.

Let me end with a brief consideration of a current and future moment in biology that strongly resonates with the sentence we have analyzed (Longino 1990). I want to do this to show that the historical processes I have discussed above are never absent in the construction of knowledge. Many biologists are now studying the role of gonadal hormones—so-called "sex hormones"—in the sexual differentiation of the human brain. The idea is that, just as gonadal hormones induce differences in the reproductive tracts of males and females, they also induce differences in their brains, and, this, in turn, leads to differences in their behaviors. Gonadal hormones are seen as themselves somehow male or female, regardless of the many studies showing that their effects vary depending on other physiological factors. The current view is that testosterone—the so-called "male hormone"—is required for normal male sex organ development and that female differentiation is independent of fetal gonadal hormone secretion, that is, that "no particular hormonal secretion from the fetal gonad is required for female development" (see Longino 1990: 127). In fact, in many texts, the development of the male testes is simply identified with sexual development. Thus, males develop sexually and females, once again, are simply undeveloped—and this despite the fact that all sorts of complicated hormonal processes, including some involving testosterone, are going on in the development of females. Undoubtedly, as Longino points out (p. 127), if we knew more about female sexual development—our understanding of male sexual development, indeed, of development generally—would shift.

Indeed, here too, different disciplines would take a different view. Recent work in neurophysiology offers a different view of the brain than is presumed by the hormonal model, as Longino points out. This work views the brain not as a fixed device that transforms sensory input into behavior, but as an ever changing system that, in its operations, profoundly transforms sensory inputs and itself as well. There could be nothing so static as the male or the female brain, once and for all and for everybody.

Whenever we write or read, speak or listen, we always do so within a specific historically achieved and history-creating coordination, a coordination of an identity, a social language, things, tools, sites and institutions, as well as other minds and bodies. Our knowledge is not something sitting passively in our heads (though this is the common view of knowledge); rather, what is in our heads is just one aspect of larger, more public and historical coordinations that in reality constitute "our" knowledge. These coordinations are always dynamic (that is, adapting and changing) and always "interested," value-laden, and ideological. Our scientist represents one such coordination; so does a heavy-metal fan with her characteristic, but dynamic identity, language, things, tools, sites, and institutions. And, thus, we have arrived back at "Discourses."

Discourses "speak" to each other throughout history. (Think of how biology has spoken to religion, or Los Angeles street gangs to Los Angeles police, or women of various sorts to men of various sorts.) In Discourses, mind mixes with history and society; language mixes with bodies, things, and tools; and the borders that disciplinary experts have created, and which they police, dissolve as we humans go about making and being made by meaning.

Apart from Discourses language and literacy are meaningless. Thus, the study of literacy (or language, more generally) transcends any one discipline. Academics, in its drive for specialization, too often, encourages a narrow focus on bits and pieces of the sorts of coordinations I have named "Discourses." This is particularly disastrous when we want to study something like education, where people's "life chances" are at stake. Thus, those of us dedicated to the study of language, literacy, and education take on a particularly heavy, but important, burden. And, yet, what we study—or should study—namely, the workings of Discourses, is the foundation within which any other more narrow study relevant to human beings ultimately makes sense.

The end and the beginning

Schools—from the perspective of this book—ought to be about people reflecting on and critiquing the "Discourse maps" of their society, and, indeed, the wider world. Schools ought to allow students to juxtapose diverse Discourses to each other so that they can understand them at a meta-level through a more encompassing language of reflection. Schools ought to allow all students to acquire, not just learn about, Discourses that lead to effectiveness in their society, should they wish to do so. Schools ought to allow students to transform and vary their Discourses, based on larger cultural and historical understandings, to create new Discourses, and to imagine better and more socially just ways of being in the world. From this perspective, the exclusion of certain students' Discourses from the classroom seriously cheats and damages everyone. It lessens the map, loses chances for reflection and meta-level thought and language, and impoverishes the imagination of all.

Most of what a Discourse does with us and most of what we do with a Discourse is unconscious, unreflective, and uncritical. Each Discourse protects itself by demanding from its adherents performances which act as though its ways of being, thinking, acting, talking, writing, reading, and valuing are "right," "natural," "obvious," the way "good," and "intelligent" and "normal" people behave. In this regard, all Discourses are false—none of them is, in fact, the first or last word on truth.

This does not mean, however, that there are no values in terms of which we can praise or blame Discourses. When we unconsciously and uncritically act within our Discourses, we are complicit with their values and thus can, unwittingly, become party to very real damage done to others. In the first chapter of this book I argued that any Discourse is a theory about the world, the people in it, and the ways in which "goods" are or ought to be distributed among them. I also argued that each of us has a moral obligation to reflect consciously on these theories—to come to have meta-knowledge of them—when there is reason to believe that a Discourse of which we are a member advantages us or our group over other people or other groups. Such meta-knowledge is the core ability that schools ought to instill. This principle is not, for me, just a part of a Discourse, it is the condition under which I, at least (and I hope you), choose to be a Discoursing human at all. Should you choose not to adopt this moral stance, then I, and others, like the non-mainstream people we have studied in this book, reserve the right to actively resist you and the ways in which your unreflective performances limit our humanity.

Thus, if you, having read the book, agree with me, you have contracted a moral obligation to reflect on, gain meta-knowledge about your Discourses and Discourses in general. Such knowledge is power, because it can protect all of us from harming others and from being harmed, and because it is the very foundation of resistance and growth. Therefore, I believe you have contracted an obligation to continue to do linguistics as I have defined it in this book—it is a moral matter and can change the world. And in that regard, the book is by no means over. It is just a beginning.

References

Abrams, M. H. (1953). *The mirror and the lamp: Romantic theory and the critical tradition*. Oxford: Oxford University Press.

Abrams, M. H. (1971). *Natural supernaturalism: Tradition and revolution in Romantic literature*. New York: Norton.

Akinnaso, F. N. and Ajirotutu, C. S. (1982). Performance and ethnic style in job interviews. In John J. Gumperz, ed., *Language and social identity*. New York: Cambridge University Press, pp. 119–144.

American Educator (2003). The fourth-grade plunge: The cause. The cure. Special issue, spring.

Aronowitz, S. and Cutler, J., eds (1998). *Post-work: The wages of cybernation*. New York: Routledge.

Aronowitz, S. and DiFazio, W. (1994). *The jobless future: Sci-tech and the dogma of work*. Minneapolis, MN: University of Minnesota Press.

Austin, J. L. (1953). Other minds. In A. N. Flew, ed., *Logic and language*, Second Series. New York: Philosophical Library.

Bailey, G. and Maynor, N. (1987). Decreolization, *Language in Society*, 16: 449–473.

Bakhtin, M. (1981). *The dialogic imagination*. Austin, TX: University of Texas Press.

Bakhtin, M. (1986). *Speech genres and other late essays*. Austin, TX: University of Texas Press.

Ball, A. F. and Freedman, S. W., eds (2004). *Bakhtinian perspectives on language, literacy, and learning*. Cambridge: Cambridge University Press.

Barthes, R. (1972). *Mythologies*. New York: Hill and Wang.

Barton, D. (1994). *Literacy: An introduction to the ecology of written language*. Oxford: Blackwell.

Barton, D. and Hamilton, M. (1998). *Local literacies: Reading and writing in one community*. London: Routledge.

Barton, D., Hamilton, M. and Ivanic, R., eds (2000). *Situated literacies: Reading and writing in context*. London: Routledge.

Baugh, J. (1983). *Black street speech: Its history, structure and survival*. Austin, TX: University of Texas Press.

Baugh, J. (1999). *Out of the mouths of slaves: African-American language and educational malpractice*. Austin, TX: University of Texas Press.

Baugh, J. (2000). *Beyond Ebonics: Linguistic pride and racial prejudice*. Oxford: Oxford University Press.

Bauman, R. (1986). *Story, performance, and event: Contextual studies of oral narrative*. Cambridge: Cambridge University Press.

Bauman, R. and Sherzer, J., eds (1974). *Explorations in the ethnography of speaking*. Cambridge: Cambridge University Press.

Bauman, Z. (1995). *Life in fragments: Essays in postmodern morality*. Oxford: Blackwell.

Bazerman, C. (1989). *Shaping written knowledge*. Madison, WI: University of Wisconsin Press.

Bellah, R. N., Madsen, R., Sullivan, W. M., Swindler, A. and Tipton, S. M. (1996). *Habits of the heart: Individualism and commitment in American life*. Updated Edition. Berkeley, CA: University of California Press.

Benedict, R. (1959). *Patterns of culture*. Boston, MA: Houghton Mifflin (orig. 1934).

Berger, P., Berger, B. and Kellner, H. (1973). *The homeless mind: Modernization and consciousness*. New York: Random House.

Bernstein, B. (1971). *Class, codes, and control*, I. London: Routledge.

Bernstein, B. (1975). *Class, codes, and control*, II. London: Routledge.

Bex, T. (1999). *Standard English*. London: Routledge.

Bialystok, E. and Hakuta, K. (1994). *In other words: The science and psychology of second-language acquisition*. New York: Basic Books.

Billig, M. (1987). *Arguing and thinking: A rhetorical approach to social psychology*. Cambridge: Cambridge University Press.

Birch, D. (1989). *Language, literature and critical practice: Ways of analyzing texts*. London: Routledge.

Bolinger, D. (1986). *Intonation and its parts: Melody in spoken English*. Stanford, CA: Stanford University Press.

Bourdieu, P. (1991). *Language and symbolic power*. Cambridge, MA: Harvard University Press.

Bourdieu, P. (2002). *Distinction: A social critique of the judgement of taste*. Reprint Edition. Cambridge, MA: Harvard University Press.

Bowler, Peter J. (1990). *Charles Darwin: The man and his influence*. Oxford: Blackwell.

Brazil, D. (1997). *The communicative value of intonation in English*. Cambridge: Cambridge University Press.

Brown, G. and Yule, G. (1983). *Discourse analysis*. Cambridge: Cambridge University Press.

Bruner, J. (1987). *Actual minds, possible worlds*. Cambridge, MA: Harvard University Press.

Bruner, J. (2003). *Making stories: Law, literature, life*. Cambridge, MA: Harvard University Press.

Burger, R. (1980). *Plato's Phaedrus: A defense of a philosophical art of writing.* Tuscaloosa, AL: University of Alabama Press.

Cain, K. (1996). Story knowledge and comprehension skills. In C. Cornoldi and J. Oakhill, eds, *Reading comprehension difficulties: Processes and intervention.* Mahwah, NJ: Erlbaum, pp. 167–192.

Callinicos, A. (1988). *Making history: Agency, structure and change in social theory* Ithaca, NY: Cornell University Press.

Carnoy, M., Castells, M., Cohen, S. and Cardoso, F. M. (1993). *The new global economy in the information age: Reflections on our changing world.* University Park, PA: Pennsylvania State University Press.

Cazden, C. (1979). Peekaboo as an instructional model: Discourse development at home and at school, *Papers and Reports in Child Language Development,* 17: 1–29. Stanford, CA: Department of Linguistics, Stanford University.

Cazden, C. (1988). *Classroom discourse: The language of teaching and learning.* Portsmouth, NH: Heinemann.

Cazden, C. (1992). *Whole language plus: Essays on literacy in the United States and New Zealand.* New York: Teachers College Press.

Cazden, C. (2001). *Classroom discourse: The language of teaching and learning.* Second Edition. Portsmouth, NH: Heinemann.

Chafe, W. (1985). Linguistic differences produced by differences between speaking and writing. In D. R. Olson, N. Torrance and A. Hildyard, eds, *Literacy, language, and learning: The nature and consequences of reading and writing.* Cambridge: Cambridge University Press, pp. 105–123.

Chafe, W. L. (1980). The deployment of consciousness in the production of a narrative. In W. L. Chafe, ed., *The pear stories: Cognitive, cultural, and linguistic aspects of narrative production.* Norwood, NJ: Ablex, pp. 9–50.

Chafe, W. L. (1994). *Discourse, consciousness, and time: The flow and displacement of conscious experience in speaking and writing.* Chicago: University of Chicago Press.

Chall, J. S., Jacobs, V. and Baldwin, L. (1990). *The reading crisis: Why poor children fall behind.* Cambridge, MA: Harvard University Press.

Chambers, J. K. (1995). *Sociolinguistic theory.* Oxford: Blackwell.

Chambers, J. K., and Trudgill, P. J. (1980). *Dialectology.* Cambridge: Cambridge University Press.

Chomsky, N. (1986). *Knowledge of language: Its nature, origin, and use.* New York: Praeger.

Clark, A. (1989). *Microcognition: Philosophy, cognitive science, and parallel distributed processing.* Cambridge, MA: MIT Press.

Collins, J. and Bolt, R. (2003). *Literacy and literacies: Texts, power, and identity.* Cambridge: Cambridge University Press.

Comrie, B. (1976). *Aspect.* Cambridge: Cambridge University Press.

Connerton, P. (1989). *How societies think.* Cambridge: Cambridge University Press.

Cook-Gumperz, J., ed. (1986). *The social construction of literacy.* Cambridge: Cambridge University Press.

D'Andrade, R. (1984). Cultural meaning systems. In R. A. Shweder and R. A. LeVine, eds, *Culture theory: Essays on mind, self, and emotion.* Cambridge: Cambridge University Press, pp. 88–119.

D'Andrade, R. and Strauss, C., eds (1992). *Human motives and cultural models.* Cambridge: Cambridge University Press.

Darwin, C. (1859). *On the origin of species.* London: John Murray.

De Vries, G. J. (1969). *A commentary on the Phaedrus of Plato.* Amsterdam: Hakkert.

Degler, Carl N. (1991). *In search of human nature: The decline and revival of Darwinism in American social thought.* Stanford, CA: Stanford University Press.

Delpit, L. (1995). *Other people's children: Cultural conflict in the classroom.* New York: New Press.

Derrida, J. (1972). La Pharmacie de Platon, in *La dissemination.* Paris: Seuil, pp. 69–198.

Desmond, Adam (1989). *The politics of evolution: Morphology, medicine, and reform in radical London.* Chicago: University of Chicago Press.

Dickinson, D., ed. (1994). *Bridges to literacy.* Oxford: Blackwell.

Dickinson, D. K. and Neuman, S. B., eds (2006). *Handbook of early literacy research*, II. New York: Guilford Press.

diSessa, A. A. (2006). A history of conceptual change research: Threads and fault lines. In R. K. Sawyer, ed., *The Cambridge handbook of the learning sciences.* Cambridge: Cambridge University Press, pp. 265–281.

Donald, J. (1983). How illiteracy became a problem (and literacy stopped being one), *Journal of Education*, 165: 35–52.

Douglas, M. (1973). *Natural symbols.* Harmondsworth: Penguin Books.

Douglas, M. (1986). *How institutions think.* Syracuse, NY: Syracuse University Press.

Drucker, P. F. (1993). *Post-capitalist society.* New York: Harper.

D'Souza, D. (2001). *Virtue of prosperity: Finding values in an age of techno-affluence.* New York: Touchstone Books.

Duranti, A. (1997). *Linguistic anthropology.* Cambridge: Cambridge University Press.

Duranti, A. and Goodwin, C., eds (1992). *Rethinking context: Language as an interactive phenomenon.* Cambridge: Cambridge University Press.

Edelsky, C. (1991). *With literacy and justice for all: Rethinking the social in language and education.* London: Falmer.

Edwards, V. and Steinkewicz, T. J. (1990). *Oral cultures past and present.* Cambridge: Blackwell.

Elley, R. (1992). *How in the world do students read?* Hamburg: The Hague International Association for the Evaluation of Educational Achievement.

Erickson, F. (1987). Transformation and school success: The politics and culture of educational achievement, *Anthropology and Education Quarterly*, 18: 335–356.

Erickson , F. and Schultz, J. J. (1982). *The counselor as gatekeeper: Social inter-action in interviews*. New York: Academic Press.

Evans-Pritchard, E. E. (1937). *Witchcraft, oracles and magic amongst the Azande*. Oxford: Clarendon Press.

Evans-Pritchard, E. E. (1951). *Social anthropology*. London: Routledge.

Faigley, L. (1992). *Fragments of rationality: Postmodernity and the subject of composition*. Pittsburgh, PA: University of Pittsburgh Press.

Fairclough, N. (1989). *Discourse and social change*. Cambridge: Polity Press.

Fairclough, N. (1992). *Language and power*. London: Longman.

Fairclough, N. (2003). *Analysing discourse: Textual analysis for social research*. London: Routledge.

Fausto-Sterling, Anne (1985). *Myths of gender: Biological theories about women and men*. New York: Basic Books.

Ferguson, R. F. (1998). Teacher's perceptions and expectations and the Black–White test score gap. In C. Jencks and M. Phillips, eds, *The Black–White test score gap*. Washington, DC: Brookings Institution Press, pp. 273–317.

Fillmore, C. (1975). An alternative to checklist theories of meaning. In C. Cogen, H. Thompson, G. Thurgood, K. Whistler, and J. Wright, eds, *Proceedings of the first annual meeting of the Berkeley Linguistics Society*. Berkeley, CA: University of California at Berkeley, pp. 123–131.

Finegan, E. (1980). *Attitudes toward English usage: The history of a war of words*. New York: Teachers College Press.

Finegan, E. and Rickford, J. R. (2004). *Language in the USA: Themes for the twenty-first century*. Cambridge: Cambridge University Press.

Finnegan, R. (1967). *Limba stories and story-telling*. London: Oxford University Press.

Finnegan, R. (1977). *Oral poetry*. Cambridge: Cambridge University Press.

Finnegan, R. (1988). *Literacy and orality*. Oxford: Blackwell.

Fiske, J. (1993). *Power plays, power works*. London: Verso.

Fleck, L. (1979). *The genesis and development of a scientific fact*. Chicago: University of Chicago Press (orig. 1935).

Fletcher, P. and Garman, M., eds (1986). *Language acquisition: Studies in first language development*, Second Edition. Cambridge: Cambridge University Press.

Foley, J. M. (1988). *The theory of oral composition*. Bloomington, IN: University of Indiana Press.

Foucault, M. (1966). *The order of things*. New York: Random House.

Foucault, M. (1969). *The archeology of knowledge*. New York: Random House.

Foucault, M. (1973). *The birth of the clinic: An archaeology of medical percep-tion*. New York: Vintage Books.

Foucault, M. (1977). *Discipline and punish: The birth of the prison*. New York: Pantheon.

Foucault, M. (1978). *The history of sexuality*, 1. *An Introduction*. New York: Pantheon.

228   References

Foucault, M. (1980). *Power/knowledge: Selected interviews and other writings 1972–1977.* Ed. C. Gordon, L. Marshall, J. Meplam and K. Soper. Brighton: Harvester Press.

Foucault, M. (1985). *The Foucault reader.* Ed. Paul Rainbow. New York: Pantheon.

Frank, J. (1963). Spatial form in modern literature, in *The widening gyre: Crisis and mastery in modern literature.* Bloomington, IN: Indiana University Press, pp. 3–62.

Freire, P. (1970). *Pedagogy of the oppressed.* New York: Seabury Press.

Freire, P. (1973). *Education for critical consciousness.* New York: Seabury Press.

Freire, P. (1985). *The politics of education: Culture, power and liberation.* South Hadley, MA: Bergin and Garvey.

Freire P. and Macedo, D. (1987). *Literacy: Reading the word and the world.* Hadley, MA: Bergin and Garvey.

Gallas, K. (1994). *The languages of learning: How children talk, write, dance, draw, and sing their understanding of the world.* New York: Teachers College Press.

Garfinkel, H. (1967). *Studies in ethnomethodology.* Englewood Cliffs, NJ: Prentice Hall.

Garnham, A. (1985). *Psycholinguistics: Central topics.* London: Methuen.

Garton, A. and Pratt, C. (1989). *Learning to be literate: The development of spoken and written language.* Oxford: Blackwell.

Gee, J. P. (1985). The narrativization of experience in the oral style, *Journal of Education*, 167: 9–35.

Gee, J. P. (1986). Units in the production of discourse, *Discourse Processes*, 9: 391–422.

Gee, J. P. (1988). Legacies of literacy: From Plato to Freire through Harvey Graff, *Harvard Educational Review*, 58: 195–212.

Gee, J. P. (1989a). *Literacy, discourse, and linguistics: Essays by James Paul Gee*, special issue of the *Journal of Education*, 171 (edited by Candace Mitchell).

Gee, J. P. (1989b). Literacies and traditions, *Journal of Education*, 171: 26–38.

Gee, J. P. (1989c). Two styles of narrative construction and their linguistics and educational implications, *Discourse Processes*, 12: 287–307.

Gee, J. P. (1991). A linguistic approach to narrative, *Journal of Narrative and Life History*, 1.1: 15–39.

Gee, J. P. (1992). *The social mind: Language, ideology, and social practice.* New York: Bergin and Garvey.

Gee, J. P. (1992–93). Literacies: Tuning in to forms of life, *Education Australia*, 19–20: 13–14.

Gee, J. P. (1993a). *An introduction to human language: Fundamental concepts in linguistics.* Englewood Cliffs, NJ: Prentice Hall.

Gee, J. P. (1993b). Critical literacy/socially perceptive literacy: A study of language in action. *Australian Journal of Language and Literacy*, 16: 333–355.

Gee J. P. (2003). *What video games have to teach us about learning and literacy.* New York: Palgrave Macmillan.

Gee, J. P. (2004). *Situated language and learning: A critique of traditional schooling.* London: Routledge.

Gee, J. P. (2005). *An introduction to discourse analysis: Theory and method.* Second Edition. London: Routledge.

Gee, J. P. and Grosjean, F. (1983). Performance structures: A linguistic and psycholinguistic appraisal, *Cognitive Psychology*, 15: 411–458.

Gee, J. P., Hull, G. and Lankshear, C. (1996). *The new work order: Behind the language of the new capitalism.* Boulder, CO: Westview Press.

Gee, J. P., Michaels, S., and O'Connor, C. (1992). Discourse analysis. In M. D. LeCompte, W. Millroy and J. Preissle, eds, *Handbook of qualitative research in education.* New York: Academic Press, pp. 227–291.

Giddens, A. (1984). *The constitution of society: Outline of the theory of structuration.* Cambridge: Polity Press.

Giddens, A. (1987). *Social theory and modern sociology.* Stanford, CA: Stanford University Press.

Giroux, H. (1988). *Schooling and the struggle for public life.* Minneapolis, MN: University of Minnesota Press.

Goffman, I. (1959). *The presentation of self in everyday life.* Garden City, NY: Doubleday.

Goffman, I. (1967). *Interaction ritual: Essays on face-to-face behavior.* Garden City, NY: Anchor Books, Doubleday.

Goffman, I. (1972). *Interaction ritual.* London: Allen Lane.

Goffman, I. (1981). *Forms of talk.* Philadelphia, PA: University of Pennsylvania Press.

Goody, J., ed. (1968). *Literacy in traditional societies.* Cambridge: Cambridge University Press.

Goody, J. (1977). *The domestication of the savage mind.* Cambridge: Cambridge University Press.

Goody, J. (1986). *The logic of writing and the organization of society.* Cambridge: Cambridge University Press.

Goody, J. (1988). *The interface between the written and the oral.* Cambridge: Cambridge University Press.

Goody, J. and Watt, I. P. (1963). The consequences of literacy, *Comparative Studies in History and Society*, 5: 304–345.

Gonzalez, N., Moll, L. C. and Amanti, C. (2005). *Funds of knowledge: Theorizing practices in households and classrooms.* Mahwah, NJ: Erlbaum.

Gopen, G. D. (1984). Rhyme and reason: Why the study of poetry is the best preparation for the study of law, *College English*, 46: 333–347.

Gould, S. J. (1977). *Ontogeny and phylogeny.* Cambridge, MA: Harvard University Press.

Gould, S. J. (1993). *Eight little piggies: Reflections in natural history.* New York: Norton.

Graff, H. J. (1979). *The literacy myth: Literacy and social structure in the nineteenth century city*. New York: Academic Press.

Graff, H. J., ed. (1981a). *Literacy in history: An interdisciplinary research bibliography*. New York: Garland Press.

Graff, H. J. (1981b). *Literacy and social development in the West: A reader*. Cambridge: Cambridge University Press.

Graff, H. J. (1987a). *The labyrinths of literacy: Reflections on literacy past and present*. New York: Falmer Press.

Graff, H. J. (1987b). *The legacies of literacy: Continuities and contradictions in Western culture and society*. Bloomington, IN: Indiana University Press.

Graff, H. J. and Arnove, R., eds (1987). *National literacy campaigns in historical and comparative perspectives*. New York: Plenum.

Gramsci, A. (1971). *Selections from the Prison Notebooks*. Ed Q. Hoare and G. Nowell-Smith. London: Lawrence and Wishart.

Green, L. J. (2002). *African-American English: A linguistic introduction*. Cambridge: Cambridge University Press.

Grissmer, D., Flanagan, A. and Williamson, S. (1998). Why did the Black–White score gap narrow in the 1970s and 1980s? In C. Jencks and M. Phillips, eds, *The Black–White test score gap*. Washington, DC: Brookings Institution Press, pp. 182–226.

Griswold, C. L. (1986). *Self-knowledge in Plato's Phaedrus*. New Haven, CT: Yale University Press.

Gumperz, J. J. (1982a). *Discourse strategies*. Cambridge: Cambridge University Press.

Gumperz, J. J., ed. (1982b). *Language and social identity*. Cambridge: Cambridge University Press.

Gumperz, J. J., Jupp, T. C. and Roberts, C. (1979). *Crosstalk: A study of cross-cultural communication*. Southall: National Centre for Industrial Language Training and BBC Continuing Education Department.

Habermas, J. (1984). *Theory of communicative action*, I. Trans. T. McCarthy. London: Heinemann.

Halliday, M. A. K. (1976a). *Intonation and grammar in British English*. The Hague: Mouton.

Halliday, M. A. K. (1976b). The teacher taught the student English: An essay in applied linguistics. In P. A. Reich, ed., *The Second LACUS Forum*. Columbia: Hornbeam Press, pp. 344–349.

Halliday, M. A. K. (1978). *Language as a social semiotic*. London: Edward Arnold.

Halliday, M. A. K. and Hasan, R. (1976). *Cohesion in English*. London: Longman.

Halliday, M. A. K. and Hasan, R. (1989). *Language, context, text: Aspects of language in a social-semiotic perspective*. Oxford: Oxford University Press.

Halliday, M. A. K. and Martin, J. R. (1993). *Writing science: Literacy and discursive power*. Pittsburgh, PA: University of Pittsburgh Press.

Hanks, W. F. (1996). *Language and communicative practices*. Boulder, CO: Westview Press.

Harkness, S., Super, C., and Keefer, C. H. (1992). Learning to be an American parent: How cultural models gain directive force. In R. D'Andrade and C. Strauss, eds, *Human motives and cultural models*. Cambridge: Cambridge University Press, pp. 163–178.

Havelock, E. (1963). *Preface to Plato*. Cambridge, MA: Harvard University Press.

Havelock, E. (1976). *Origins of Western literacy*. Toronto: Ontario Institute for Studies in Education.

Havelock, E. A. (1982). *The literate revolution in Greece and its cultural consequences*. Princeton, NJ: Princeton University Press.

Havelock, E. A. (1986). *The muse learns to write: Reflections on orality and literacy from antiquity to the present*. New Haven, CT: Yale University Press.

Hayek, F. A. (1996). *Individualism and economic order*. Reissue Edition. Chicago: University of Chicago Press.

Heath, S. B. (1982). What no bedtime story means: Narrative skills at home and at school, *Language in Society*, 11: 49–76.

Heath, S. B. (1983). *Ways with words: Language, life, and work in communities and classrooms*. Cambridge: Cambridge University Press.

Heath, S. B., (1994). The children of Tracton's children: Spoken and written language in social change. In R. B. Ruddell, M. R. Ruddell and H. Singer, eds, *Theoretical models and processes of reading*. Fourth Edition. Newark, DE: International Reading Association, pp. 208–230.

Hecht, M. L., Collier, M. J., and Ribeau, S. A. (1993). *African-American communication*. Newbury Park, CA: Sage.

Hedges, L. V. and Nowell, A. (1998). Black–White test score convergence since 1965. In C. Jencks and M. Phillips, eds, *The Black–White test score gap*. Washington, DC: Brookings Institution Press, pp. 149–181.

Heritage, J. (1984). *Garfinkel and ethnomethodology*. Cambridge: Polity Press.

Heritage, J. and Maynard, D. W., eds (2006). *Communication in medical care: Interaction between primary care physicians and patients*. Cambridge: Cambridge University Press.

Hinds, J. (1979). Organizational patterns in discourse. In T. Givon, ed., *Syntax and semantics*. Hillsdale, NJ: Erlbaum, pp. 135–158.

Hirsch, E. D., Jr. (1987). *Cultural literacy: What every American needs to know*. Boston, MA: Houghton Mifflin.

Hodge, R. (1990). *Literature as discourse: Textual strategies in English and history*. Baltimore, MD: Johns Hopkins University Press.

Hodge, R. and Kress, G. (1988). *Social semiotics*. Ithaca, New York: Cornell University Press.

Hoff, E. (2004). *Language development*. Third Edition. Boston, MA: Wadsworth.

Hofstadter, D. and Fluid Analogies Research Group (1995). *Fluid concepts and creative analogies: Computer models of the fundamental mechanisms of thought*. New York: Basic Books.

Holland, D., Lachicotte, W., Skinner, D. and Cain, C. (1998). *Identity and agency in cultural worlds*. Cambridge, MA: Harvard University Press.

Holland, D. and Quinn, N., eds (1987). *Cultural models in language and thought*. Cambridge: Cambridge University Press.

Holland, J. H., Holyoak, K. J., Nisbett, R. E. and Thagard, P. R., eds (1986). *Induction: Processes of inference, learning, and discovery*. Cambridge, MA: MIT Press.

Holyoak, K. J. and Thagard, P. (1995). *Mental leaps: Analogy in creative thought*. Cambridge, MA: MIT Press.

Horton, R. (1967). African traditional thought and Western science, *Africa*, 37: 50–71, 155–187.

Huebner, T. (1983). *A longitudinal analysis: The acquisition of English*. Ann Arbor, MI: Karoma Press.

Hutchins, E. (1995). *Cognition in the wild*. Cambridge, MA: MIT Press.

Hymes, D. (1980). *Language in education: Ethnolinguistic essays*. Washington, DC: Center for Applied Linguistics.

Hymes, D. (1981). *"In vain I tried to tell you": Essays in native American ethnopoetics*. Philadelphia, PA: University of Pennsylvania Press.

Jakobson, R. (1980). *Selected writings*, III. *Poetry of grammar and grammar of poetry*. New York: Mouton.

Jameson, F. (1981). *The political unconscious: Narrative as a socially symbolic act*. Ithaca, NY: Cornell University Press.

Jencks, C. and Phillips, M., eds (1998). *The Black–White test score gap*. Washington, DC: Brookings Institution Press, pp. 401–427.

Johansson, E. (1977). *The history of literacy in Sweden*. Umea: Umea University Press.

John-Steiner, V., Panofsky, C. P. and Smith, L. W., eds (1994). *Sociocultural approaches to language and literacy*. Cambridge: Cambridge University Press.

Kapitzke, C. (1995). *Literacy and religion: The textual politics and practice of Seventh Day Adventism*. Amsterdam: Benjamins.

Kermode, F. (1979). *The genesis of secrecy: On the interpretation of narrative*. Cambridge, MA: Harvard University Press.

Kirsch, I. S., Jungeblut, A., with Johnson, E., King, B., Mead, N., Mislevy, R. and Rock, D. (1986). *Literacy: Profiles of America's young adults*, Final Report, National Assessment of Educational Progress. Report No. 16-PL-01, Princeton, NJ: Educational Testing Service.

Knorr Cetina, K. (1992). The couch, the cathedral, and the laboratory: On the relationship between experiment and laboratory, in science, in A. Pickering, ed., *Science as practice and culture*, Chicago: University of Chicago Press, pp. 113–137.

Kochman, T., ed. (1972). *Rappin' and stylin' out: Communication in urban black America*. Urbana, IL: University of Illinois Press.

Kochman, T. (1981). *Black and White styles in conflict*. Chicago: University of Chicago Press.

Kosslyn, S. M. and Koenig, O. (1992). *Wet mind: The new cognitive neuroscience*. New York: Free Press.

Kozol, J. (1985). *Illiterate America*. Garden City, NY: Anchor Press/Doubleday, 1985.

Krashen, S. (1985a). *Inquiries and insights*. Hayward, CA: Alemany Press.

Krashen, S. (1985b). *The input hypothesis: Issues and implications*. London: Longman.

Kreckel, M. (1981). Tone units as message blocks in natural discourse: Segmentation of face-to-face interaction by naive, native speakers, *Journal of Pragmatics*, 5: 459–76.

Kress, G. (1985). *Linguistic processes in sociocultural practice*. Oxford: Oxford University Press.

Labov, W. (1972a). *Language in the inner city: Studies in Black English vernacular*. Philadelphia, PA: University of Pennsylvania Press.

Labov, W. (1972b). *Sociolinguistic patterns*. Philadelphia, PA.: University of Pennsylvania Press.

Labov, W. (1980). *Locating language in time and space*. New York: Academic Press.

Labov, W. (2006). *Principles of linguistic change: Synthesis*. Oxford: Blackwell.

Ladd, R. D. (1980). *Intonational meaning*. Bloomington, IN: Indiana University Press.

Lakoff, G. (1987). *Women, fire, and dangerous things: What categories reveal about the mind*. Chicago: University of Chicago Press.

Lakoff, G. (2002). *Moral politics: How liberals and conservatives think*. Second Edition. Chicago: University of Chicago Press.

Lakoff, G. and Johnson, M. (2003). *Metaphors we live by*. Second Edition. Chicago: University of Chicago Press.

Lankshear, C. (1997). *Changing literacies*. Maidenhead: Open University Press.

Lankshear, C. with Lawler, M. (1987). *Literacy, schooling and revolution*. London: Falmer.

Lankshear, C. and Knobel, M. (2007). *New literacies*. Second Edition. Maidenhead: Open University Press.

Laqueur, Thomas (1990). *Making sex: Body and gender from the Greeks to Freud*. Cambridge, MA: Harvard University Press.

Larson, J. and Marsh, J. (2005). *Making literacy read: Theories for learning and teaching*. Thousand Oaks, CA: Sage.

Latour, B. (1987). *Science in Action*. Cambridge, MA: Harvard University Press.

Latour, B. (2005). *Reassembling the social: An introduction to actor-network-theory*. Oxford: Oxford University Press.

Lave, J. (1988). *Cognition in practice*. Cambridge: Cambridge University Press.

Lave, J. and Wenger, E. (1991). *Situated learning: Legitimate peripheral participation*. Cambridge: Cambridge University Press.

Lee, D. (1992). *Competing discourses: Perspective and ideology in language*. London: Longman.

Lemke, J. L. (1995). *Textual politics: Discourse and social dynamics*. London: Taylor & Francis.

Levi-Bruhl, L. (1910). *Les Fonctions mentales dans les sociétés inférieures*. Paris: Alcan.

Lévi-Strauss, C. (1963). *Structural anthropology*. New York: Basic Books.

Lévi-Strauss, C. (1966). *The savage mind*. Chicago: University of Chicago Press.

Lévi-Strauss, C. (1975). *Tristes tropiques*. New York: Athenaeum (orig. 1955).

Lévi-Strauss, C. (1979). *Myth and meaning*. New York: Schocken Books.

Levine, K. (1986). *The social context of literacy*. London: Routledge.

Longacre, R. E. (1979). The paragraph as a grammatical unit. In T. Givon, ed., *Syntax and semantics*. Hillsdale, NJ: Erlbaum, pp. 115–134.

Longacre, R. E. (1983). *The grammar of discourse*. New York and London: Plenum Press.

Longino, Helen E. (1990). *Science as social knowledge: Values and objectivity in scientific inquiry*. Princeton, NJ: Princeton University Press.

Lord, A. B. (1960). *The singer of tales*. Cambridge, MA: Harvard University Press.

Lovejoy, A. (1933). *The great chain of being: A study of the history of an idea*. Cambridge, MA: Harvard University Press.

Luke, A. (1988). *Literacy, textbooks and ideology*. London: Falmer.

Luria, A. R. (1976). *Cognitive development: Its cultural and social foundations*. Cambridge, MA: Harvard University Press.

Macdonell, D. (1986). *Theories of discourse: An introduction*. Oxford: Blackwell.

Macedo, D. (2006). *Literacies of power: What Americans are not allowed to know*. Expanded Edition. Cambridge, MA: Westview Press.

Mack, N. (1989). The social nature of words: Voices, dialogues, quarrels, *The Writing Instructor*, 8.4: 157–165.

Marx, K. (1967). *Capital: A critique of political economy*. Three Volumes. New York: International Publishers.

Marx, K. (1973). *Grundrisse: Foundations of the critique of political economy*. Harmondsworth: Penguin Books.

Marx, K. (1977). *Selected writings*. Ed. D. McLellan. Oxford: Oxford University Press.

Marx, K. and Engels, F. (1970). *The German ideology*. Ed. C. J. Arthur. New York: International Publishers.

McCall, N. (1995). *Makes me wanna holler: A young black man in America*. New York: Vintage Books.

McDermott, R. (1987). The explanation of minority school failure, again, *Anthropology and Education Quarterly*, 18: 361–364.

McLaren, P. (1989). *Life in schools: An introduction to critical pedagogy in the foundations of education*. New York: Longman.

Mead, M. (1928). *Coming of age in Samoa*. New York: Morrow.

Mehan, H. (1979). *Learning lessons*. Cambridge, MA: Harvard University Press.

Michaels, S. (1981). "Sharing time": Children's narrative styles and differential access to literacy, *Language in Society*, 10: 423–442.

Michaels, S. (1985). Hearing the connections in children's oral and written discourse. *Journal of Education*, 167: 36–56.

Milroy, L. (1987a). *Language and social networks*. Second Edition. Oxford: Blackwell.

Milroy, L. (1987b). *Observing and analysing natural language*. Oxford: Blackwell.

Milroy, L. and Gordon, M. (2003). *Sociolinguistics: Method and interpretation*. Oxford: Blackwell.

Milroy, J. and Milroy, L. (1985). *Authority in language: Investigating language prescription and standardisation*. London: Routledge.

Minnis, M. (1994). Toward a definition of law school readiness. In V. John-Steiner, C. P. Panofsky, and L. W. Smith, eds, *Sociocultural approaches to language and literacy: An interactionist perspective*. Cambridge: Cambridge University Press, pp. 347–390.

Mishel, L. and Teixeira, R. A. (1991). *The myth of the coming labor shortage: Jobs, skills, and incomes of America's workforce 2000*. Washington, DC: Economic Policy Institute.

Moll, L. C., ed. (1990). *Vygotsky and education: Instructional implications and applications of sociohistorical psychology*. Cambridge: Cambridge University Press.

Morson, G. S. (1986). Introduction, in G. S. Morson, ed., *Bakhtin: Essays and dialogues on his work*. Chicago: University of Chicago Press.

Mufwene, S. S., Rickford, J. R., Bailey, G. and Baugh, J., eds (1998). *African-American English: Structure, history, and use*. London: Routledge.

Musgrove, F. (1982). *Education and anthropology: Other cultures and the teacher*. New York: John Wiley.

Myers, G. (1990). *Writing biology: Texts in the social construction of scientific knowledge*. Madison, WI: University of Wisconsin Press.

NAEP [National Assessment of Educational Progress] (1997). *NAEP 1996 Trends in academic progress*. Washington, DC: U.S. Government Printing Office.

National Commission on Excellence in Education (1983). *A nation at risk: The imperative for educational reform*. Washington DC: Department of Education.

National Institute of Child Health and Human Development (2000). *Report of the National Reading Panel. Teaching children to read: An evidence-based assessment of the scientific research literature on reading and its implications for reading instruction*. NIH Publication No. 00-4769. Washington, DC: U.S. Government Printing Office.

Neisser, U., ed. (1998). *The rising curve: Long-term gains in IQ and related measures*. Washington, DC: American Psychological Association.

Newman, D., Griffin, P. and Cole, M. (1989). *The construction zone: Working for cognitive change in school*. Cambridge: Cambridge University Press.

Oakes, J. (1985). *Keeping track: How schools structure inequality*. New Haven, CT: Yale University Press.

Oakes, J. (2005). *Keeping track: How schools structure inequality.* Second Edition. New Haven, CT: Yale University Press.

Ochs, E. and Schieffelin, B. B. (1983). *Acquiring conversational competence.* London: Routledge.

Ogbu, J. (1978). *Minority education and caste: The American system in cross-cultural perspective.* New York: Academic Press.

Olson, D. R. (1977). From utterance to text: The bias of language in speech and writing, *Harvard Education Review,* 47: 257–281.

Ong, W. J. (1982). *Orality and literacy: The technologizing of the word.* London: Methuen.

Pahl, K. and Rowsell, J., eds (2005). *Literacy and education: Understanding the New Literacy Studies in the classroom.* Thousand Oaks, CA: Paul Chapman.

Pahl, K. and Rowsell, J., eds (2006). *Travel notes from the New Literacy Studies: Instances of practice.* Clevedon: Multilingual Mattters.

Parry, M. (1971). *The making of Homeric verse: The collected papers of Milman Parry.* Oxford: Clarendon Press.

Pattison, R. (1982). *On literacy: The politics of the word from Homer to the age of rock.* Oxford: Oxford University Press.

Perkins, D. (1992). *Smart schools: From training memories to educating minds.* New York: Free Press.

Perkins, D. (1995). *Outsmarting IQ: The emerging science of learnable intelligence.* New York: Free Press.

Philipsen, G. (1975). Speaking "like a man" in Teamsterville: Culture patterns of role enactment in an urban neighborhood, *Quarterly Journal of Speech,* 61: 26–39.

Philipsen, G. (1990). Reflections on speaking "like a man" in Teamsterville. In D. Carbaugh, ed., *Cultural communication.* Hillsdale, NJ: Erlbaum, pp. 21–25.

Pinker, S. (1989). *Learnability and cognition: The acquisition of argument structure.* Cambridge, MA: MIT Press.

Pinker, S. (1994). *The language instinct: How the mind creates language.* New York: William Morrow.

Pratt, S. (1985). Being an Indian among Indians. Unpublished doctoral dissertation, Norman, OK: University of Oklahoma.

Quinn, N. and Holland, D. (1987). Culture and cognition. In D. Holland and N. Quinn, eds, *Cultural models in language and thought.* Cambridge: Cambridge University Press, pp. 3–40.

Reddy, M. (1979). The conduit metaphor—a case of conflict in our language about language. In A. Ortony, ed., *Metaphor and thought.* Cambridge: Cambridge University Press, pp. 284–324.

Reich, R. B. (1992). *The work of nations.* New York: Vintage Books.

Reich, R. B. (2000). *The future of success: Working and living in the new economy.* New York: Knopf.

Richardson, R. R., Jr, Risk, E. C. and Okun, M. A. (1983). *Literacy in the open access college.* San Francisco: Jossey Bass.

Rickford, J. R. and Rickford, R. J. (2000). *Spoken soul: The story of Black English*. New York: John Wiley.

Roberts, C., Davies, E. and Jupp, T. (1992). *Language and discrimination: A study of communication in multi-ethnic workplaces*. London: Longman.

Rogers, R., cd. (2004). *An introduction to critical discourse analysis in education*. Mahwah, NJ: Erlbaum.

Rogoff, B. (1990). *Apprenticeship in thinking: Cognitive development in social context*. New York: Oxford University Press.

Rogoff, B. (2003). *The cultural nature of human development*. Oxford: Oxford University Press.

Rogoff, B. and Lave, J., eds (1984). *Everyday cognition: Its development in social context*. Cambridge, MA: Harvard University Press.

Rogoff, B. and Toma, C. (1997). Shared thinking: Cultural and institutional variations, *Discourse Processes*, 23: 471–497.

Romaine, S. (1988). *Pidgin and creole languages*. London: Longman.

Rose, M. (1989). *Lives on the boundary*. New York: Penguin Books.

Rose, S. (1992). *The making of memory: From molecules to mind*. New York: Doubleday.

Rosenberg, B. A. (1970). *The art of the American folk preacher*. New York: Oxford University Press.

Rowe, C. J. (1986). *Plato: Phaedrus*, translation and commentary. Warminster: Aris and Philips.

Sapir, E. (1921). *Language: An introduction to the study of speech*. San Diego, CA: Harcourt Brace.

Schiebinger, L. (1993). *Nature's body: Gender in the making of modern science*. Boston, MA: Beacon.

Schieffelin, B. B. and Gilmore, P., eds (1985). *The acquisition of literacy: Ethnographic perspectives*. Norwood, NJ: Ablex.

Schieffelin B. B. and Ochs, E., eds, (1986). *Language socialization across cultures*. Cambridge: Cambridge University Press.

Schiffrin, D. (1987). *Discourse markers*. Cambridge: Cambridge University Press, pp. 49–50.

Schiffrin, D. (1994). *Approaches to discourse: language as social interaction*. Oxford: Blackwell.

Schiffrin, D., Tannen, D. and Hamilton, H. E., eds (2003). *The handbook of discourse analysis*. Oxford: Blackwell.

Scollon, R. and Scollon, S. W. (1981). *Narrative, literacy, and face in interethnic communication*. Norwood, NJ: Ablex.

Scollon, R. and Scollon S. W. (1995). *Intercultural communication: A discourse approach*. Oxford: Blackwell.

Scribner, S. and Cole, M. (1973). Cognitive consequences of formal and informal education, *Science*, 182: 553–559.

Scribner, S. and Cole, M. (1981). *The psychology of literacy*. Cambridge, MA: Harvard University Press.

Sennett, R. (1974). *The fall of public man: On the social psychology of capitalism*. New York: Vintage Books.

Shapin, S. and Schaffer, S. (1985). *Leviathan and the air-pump*. Princeton, NJ: Princeton University Press.

Shaughnessy, M. P. (1977). *Errors and expectations: A guide for the teacher of basic writing*. New York: Oxford University Press.

Shotter, J. (1993). *Conversational realities: Constructing life through language*. London: Sage.

Shuman, A. (1986). *Storytelling rights: The uses of oral and written texts by urban adolescents*. Cambridge: Cambridge University Press.

Shuman (1992). Literacy: Local uses and global perspectives. Presentation to the Literacies Institute, Newton, Massachusetts, January.

Sikkink, K. (2004). *Mixed signals: U.S. human rights policy and Latin America*. Ithaca, NY: Cornell University Press.

Skehan, P. (1989). *Individual differences in second-language learning*. London: Edward Arnold.

Slobin, D. I., ed. (1985). *The crosslinguistic study of language acquisition*, I–II. Hillsdale, NJ: Erlbaum.

Smith, B. H. (1988). *Contingencies of value: Alternative perspectives for critical theory*. Cambridge, MA: Harvard University Press.

Smitherman, G. (1977). *Talkin and testifyin: The language of Black America*. Boston, MA: Houghton Mifflin.

Snow, C. (1986). Conversations with children. In P. Fletcher and M. Garman, eds, *Language Acquisition*. Second Edition. Cambridge: Cambridge University Press, pp. 69–89.

Snow, C. E., Burns, M. S. and Griffin, P., eds (1998). *Preventing reading difficulties in young children*. Washington, DC: National Academy Press.

Stahl, S. D. (1989). *Literary folkloristics and the personal narrative*. Bloomington, IN: Indiana University Press.

Star, Susan Leigh (1989). *Regions of the mind: Brain research and the quest for scientific certainty*. Stanford, CA: Stanford University Press.

Steele, C. M. (1992). Race and the schooling of Black America, *Atlantic Monthly* (April): 68–78.

Steele, C. M. and Aronson, J. (1995). A threat in the air: How stereotypes shape the intellectual identities and performance of women and African-Americans, *Journal of Personality and Social Psychology*, 69.5: 797–811.

Steele, C. M. and Aronson, J. (1998). Stereotype threat and the test performance of academically successful African-Americans. In C. Jencks and M. Phillips, eds, *The Black–White test score gap*. Washington, DC: Brookings Institution Press, pp. 401–427.

Strauss, C. (1988). Culture, discourse, and cognition: Forms of belief in some Rhode Island working men's talk about success. Unpublished PhD dissertation, Cambridge, MA: Harvard University.

Strauss, C. (1990). Who gets ahead? Cognitive responses to heteroglossia in American political culture, *American Ethnologist*, 17: 312–328.

Strauss, C. (1992). What makes Tony run? Schemas as motives reconsidered. In R. D'Andrade and C. Strauss, eds, *Human motives and cultural models*. Cambridge: Cambridge University Press, pp. 197–224.

Street, B. (1984). *Literacy in theory and practice*. Cambridge: Cambridge University Press.

Street, B., ed. (1993). *Cross-cultural approaches to literacy*. Cambridge: Cambridge University Press.

Stubbs, M. (1983). *Discourse analysis: The sociolinguistic analysis of natural language*. Oxford: Blackwell.

Stucky, S. (1987). *Slave culture: Nationalist theory and the foundations of Black America*. Oxford: Oxford University Press.

Tannen, D. (1985). Relative focus on involvement in oral and written discourse. In D. R. Olson, N. Torrance and A. Hildyard, eds, *Literacy, language, and learning: The nature and consequences of reading and writing*. Cambridge: Cambridge University Press, pp. 124–147.

Taussig, M. T. (1980). *The devil and commodity fetishism in South America*. Chapel Hill, NC: University of North Carolina Press.

Taussig, M. (1987). *Shamanism, colonialism, and the wild man: A study in terror and healing*. Chicago: University of Chicago Press.

Taylor, D. (1983). *Family literacy: Young children learning to read and write*. Portsmouth, NH: Heinemann.

Taylor, D. and Dorsey-Gaines, C. (1987). *Growing up literate: Learning from inner city families*. Portsmouth, NH: Heinemann.

Teale, W. H. and Sulzby, E., eds (1986). *Emergent literacy*. Norwood, NJ: Ablex.

Tedlock, D. (1983). *The spoken word and the work of interpretation*. Philadelphia, PA: University of Pennsylvania Press.

Tharp, R. and Gallimore, R. (1988). *Rousing minds to life: Teaching, learning, and schooling in social context*. Cambridge: Cambridge University Press.

Thomas, W. I. (1897). On a difference in the metabolism of the sexes, *American Journal of Sociology*, 3.1: 31–32, 39–40.

Thompson, J. B. (1984). *Studies in the theory of ideology*. Berkeley, CA: University of California Press.

Trueba, H. T., ed. (1987). *Success or failure? Learning and the language minority student*. New York: Newbury House.

Trueba, H. T. (1989). *Raising silent voices: Educating linguistic minorities for the twentieth Century*. New York: Newbury House.

U.S. Department of Education (1986). *What works: Research about teaching and learning*. Washington, DC: U.S. Government Printing Office.

van Dijk, T. A. (1980). *Macrostructures: An interdisciplinary study of global structures in discourse, interaction and cognition*. Hillsdale, NJ: Erlbaum.

Varenne, H. and McDermott, R. (1998). *Successful failure: The school America builds*. Boulder, CO: Westview Press.

Voloshinov, V. N. (1986). *Marxism and the philosophy of language*. Cambridge, MA: Harvard University Press (orig. 1929).

von Mises, L. (1997). *Human action: A treatise on economics*. Fourth Revised Edition. San Francisco: Fox and Wilkes.

Vygotsky, L. S. (1978). *Mind in society: The development of higher psychological processes*. Cambridge, MA: Harvard University Press.

Vygotsky, (1987). *The collected works of L. S. Vygotsky, I. Problems of general psychology. Including the volume Thinking and speech*. ed. R. W. Rieber and A. S. Carton. New York: Plenum.

Walberg, H. J. (1985). Improving the productivity of America's schools, *Educational Leadership*, 41: 19–27.

Wells, G. (1981). *Learning through interaction*. Cambridge: Cambridge University Press.

Wells, G. (1985). *Language development in the pre-school years*. Cambridge: Cambridge University Press.

Wells, G. (1986). *The meaning makers: Children learning language and using language to learn*. Portsmouth, NH: Heinemann.

Wenger, E. (1998). *Communities of practice: Learning, meaning, and identity*. Cambridge: Cambridge University Press.

Wertsch, J. V. (1985). *Vygotsky and the social formation of mind*. Cambridge, MA: Harvard University Press.

Wertsch, J. V. (1991). *Voices of the mind: A sociocultural approach to mediated action*. Cambridge, MA: Harvard University Press.

Wheatley, J. (1970). *Prolegomena to philosophy*. Belmont, CA: Wadsworth.

White, J. B. (1984). The judicial opinion and the poem: Ways of reading, ways of life. *Michigan Law Review*, 82: 1669–1699.

Wieder, D. L. and Pratt, S. (1990a). On being a recognizable Indian among Indians. In D. Carbaugh, ed., *Cultural communication and intercultural contact*. Hillsdale, NJ: Erlbaum, pp. 45–64.

Wieder, D. L. and Pratt, S. (1990b). On the occasioned and situated character of members' questions and answers: Reflections on the question "Is he or she a real Indian?" In D. Carbaugh, ed., *Cultural communication and intercultural contact*. Hillsdale, NJ: Erlbaum, pp. 65–75.

Williams, P. J. (1991). *The alchemy of race and rights: Diary of a law professor*. Cambridge, MA: Harvard University Press.

Williams, R. (1983). *The year 2000*. New York: Pantheon Books.

Williams, R. (1985). *Keywords: A vocabulary of culture and society*. Revised Edition. New York: Oxford University Press.

Willinsky, J. (1990). *The new literacy: Redefining reading and writing in the schools*. New York: Routledge.

Willis, P. (1977). *Learning to labour*. London: Saxon House.

Wittgenstein, L. (1958). *Philosophical investigations*. Trans. G. E. M. Anscombe. Oxford: Blackwell.

Wodak, R. and Myers, M., eds (2002). *Methods of critical discourse analysis*. Thousand Oaks, CA: Sage.

Wolfson, N. (1989). *Perspectives: Sociolinguistics and TESOL*. Cambridge, MA: Newbury House.

Index

Marxism 28–9; negotiation and
  meaning 12
practice account of literacy 78–9
Pratt, S. 82, 90, 151, 155, 158–61
prestige norm 117–18
*Preventing Reading Difficulties in
  Young Children* (National Academy
  of Sciences) 35–42
primary Discourses 156–7, 168–9,
  173–4, 175, 195; incorporation of
  secondary Discourses 157–8, 168–9,
  176, 177; individuals and
  performances 209–10; literacy and
  175–7
primary oral cultures 73–4
primary research 25
primary theories 25, 26–7
primitive-civilized dichotomy 50, 67–8;
  recoding 69–70
print 176, 177
professional journals 210–12
professional theories 6–7
pronouns, use of 201–2
prosody 119–20, 122–3
Protestant countries 57–8
psychological view of literacy 2
public sphere Discourses 174–5
Puppy story 132–3, 137, 139–41
pure totemic structure 69

Quinn, N. 39

racism 39
rationality 125
'razzing' (verbal sparring) 159
reading: aspirin bottle problem 45–9;
  literacy and social practices 42–5;
  National Academy of Sciences
  report 35–42; the word and the
  world 65–6
reading passage style 117–18
'real Indians' 158–61
recognition 155–6; 'real Indians'
  158–61
reflection 170, 171–3
Reformation 57
Reich, R.B. 41, 61
religion 56–8
Republic (Plato) 54–5
residual orality 74
resistance 27; to school 193–4
restricted literacy 72, 74
rhetoricians 52, 54–5
Rhode Island workers 109–11

Richardson, R.R. 75
riddles 84
Roadville 84–8
Romaine, S. 175

São Tomé and Principe 63
Sapir, E. 68
sausage case 10–12
scaffolding, verbal 144–8
Schaffer, S. 212
Schieffelin, B.B. 21, 85
Schiffrin, D. 121, 123
school-based literacy 62, 88
schools 49; borderland Discourses
  189–94; higher-order cognitive
  abilities and literacy 58–62, 76–80;
  and inclusive approach to
  Discourses 220–1; language at home
  and at school 183–9; secondary
  Discourses 157–8
Schultz, J.J. 154
science 101; abstract vs concrete
  thought 69–70; and the lifeworld
  210–20
Scollon, R. 82–4, 145
Scollon, S.W. 82–4, 145
Scribner, S. 58–9, 77–80
second language acquisition 175
secondary Discourses 157–8, 168–9,
  174–5, 195; borderland Discourses
  189–94; literacy and 175–7
sections 132–6, 138
self-judgments 109–11
Sennett, R. 49, 209
sense making 129, 130, 142, 186, 188;
  Leona's stories 142–4, 188; science
  212–18; *see also* meaning,
  interpretation
service workers 41, 59, 61
sexual development 219
Shapin, S. 212
sharing time 130–49, 183–4, 188; Cakes
  story 134–7, 138–9, 139–41, 142–4,
  144; discourse analysis of stories
  and their contexts 130–42; Puppy
  story 132–3, 137, 139–41; purpose
  of 145; reasons for failure in 144–9;
  sense making and stories 142–4
Shaughnessy, M.P. 179
Sherlock Holmes Discourse 155
Shuman, A. 12, 189–94
Sierra Leone 172
signs 143–4
Sikkink, K. 14